"Want to be a happier person? Give generously, especially to those in poverty. That is the astonishing argument Chris Marlin-Warfield makes in *Radical Charity*. Marlin-Warfield turns the whole concept of charity on its head. Instead of judging the poor or feeling superior to them, realize that through charity you are entering into a profound relationship with God, with the poor, and with your own soul. This book confronts our current culture of cruelty from the heart of Christianity, as well as from sound socio-economic research. It makes sense! And here's an amazing thing. You will feel a lot happier after you have read this book and started to practice radical charity. Get going!"

—Susan Brooks Thistlethwaite
Professor of Theology and Past President, Chicago Theological Seminary

"Justice versus charity. Loans versus giving. As one whose ministry includes shaping strategies and nurturing partnerships around the world with people working against poverty, these are debates I encounter daily. *Radical Charity* challenges the underlying assumptions of those common approaches. It offers a fresh perspective that roots charity in the generosity of God and offers a glimpse into a sharing economy that embodies abundance for all. I am inspired to see anew how 'charity works.'"

—Mary Schaller Blaufuss
Director, United Church of Christ Humanitarian & Development Ministries

Radical Charity

Radical Charity

How Generosity Can Save the World
(And the Church)

CHRISTOPHER MARLIN-WARFIELD

CASCADE *Books* · Eugene, Oregon

RADICAL CHARITY
How Generosity Can Save the World (And the Church)

Cascade Books
An Imprint of Wipf and Stock Publishers
199 W. 8th Ave., Suite 3
Eugene, OR 97401

www.wipfandstock.com

PAPERBACK ISBN: 978-1-5326-6584-4
HARDCOVER ISBN: 978-1-5326-6585-1
EBOOK ISBN: 978-1-5326-6586-8

Cataloguing-in-Publication data:

Names: Marlin-Warfield, Christopher, author.

Title: Radical charity : how generosity can save the world (and the church) / Christopher Marlin-Warfield.

Description: Eugene, OR: Cascade Books, 2019 | Includes bibliographical references and index.

Identifiers: ISBN 978-1-5326-6584-4 (paperback) | ISBN 978-1-5326-6585-1 (hardcover) | ISBN 978-1-5326-6586-8 (ebook)

Subjects: LCSH: Charity—Ethics—Religion. | Charity—Biblical teaching.

Classification: HV530 .M220 2019 (paperback) | CALL NUMBER (ebook)

Manufactured in the U.S.A.   05/31/19

Contents

Acknowledgements

The journey from an idea to a book is a long one. Along the way, I've racked up a lot of debts that I can only repay by saying "thank you":

To my parents, who were my first teachers and who instilled a love of learning in me and taught me to embrace questions. To the countless teachers, professors, pastors, and others who came after them, who encouraged me, and who taught me about life and faith. And to the wonderful faculty, administrators, and staff at Knox College and Chicago Theological Seminary.

To my colleagues in fundraising offices and in the church, especially the people at Chicago Theological Seminary, Northeast Ohio Medical University, Back Bay Mission, and First Congregational United Church of Christ (DeWitt, Iowa). I am good at a few things. I am also faking some things and hoping no one notices. All of you took a chance on me, and I am grateful.

They have no idea that they were instrumental in writing this book, but I returned again and again to the work of Gary A. Anderson, Abhijit Banerjee, Daryl Collins, Matthew Desmond, Esther Duflo, Jonathan Morduch, Sendhil Mullainathan, Helen Rhee, Stuart Rutherford, Orlanda Ruthven, Eldar Shafir, and Linda Tirado. Thank you for your insights into poverty, economics, history, and theology. I wouldn't have been able to write this without your research, scholarship, experience, and honesty.

To the team at Cascade Books, who took a collection of words and transformed it into a book. You answered questions, finessed language, and made something beautiful. My special thanks to Matt Wimer and Rodney Clapp for their invaluable work on this project.

Finally, to my wife, Mariah. You endured rants about charity skepticism, gave me time to write, read drafts, provided advice and encouragement, and believed in me. Thank you from the bottom of my heart.

I

The Scandal

Hamid and Khadeja are a married couple living in Dhaka, the capital city of Bangladesh. Hamid is uneducated and unskilled, with a history of being unemployed and occasionally working as a pedicab driver and a construction worker. More recently, he has taken a job as a reserve driver for a motorized rickshaw. However, as a reserve driver, he never knows for sure whether he will have work or how long he'll have work. Khadeja stays at home, raises their young son, and makes a small amount of money taking in sewing. Altogether, they live on the equivalent of about $70 a month, or about $0.78 per person per day.[1]

Martha lives in a town in the Mississippi Delta with her two daughters and her granddaughter. She has a small rented home that is paid for, in part, by the assistance she receives from Section 8. She receives $150 each month in child support from one of her daughters' fathers and, like Hamid and Khadeja, runs an informal shop out of her living room. A fair amount of her SNAP benefits goes to buy supplies for this shop, and she is able to sell the ingredients that she buys for roughly twice the price. The store usually nets about $400 each month. While she receives benefits like Section 8 and SNAP, her family probably doesn't live on much more than $7 per person per day.[2]

Jennifer works at a slightly-above-minimum-wage job cleaning condos, office suites, and foreclosed homes in Chicago. The work is difficult and

---

1. Collins et al., *Portfolios of the Poor*, Kindle locations 183–95.
2. Edin and Shaefer, *$2.00 a Day*, 129–31, 136–38.

occasionally dangerous, with long hours. It also pays $8.75 an hour (at the time of this writing, $0.50 more per hour than the Illinois minimum wage). When she works full time, she might make about $1,575 before taxes each month—about $1,290 after taxes—which she uses to support herself and her two school-age children. That's about $17.50 per person per day ($14.33 after taxes). She also receives SNAP benefits and a housing subsidy.[3]

Three families; three very different situations. Hamid's, Martha's, and Jennifer's families live in different places, have different histories, and face different financial circumstances. What they have in common, though, is that they live in poverty. Poverty may look different in Dhaka, Mississippi, and Chicago, but each of these families has the same basic problem: they don't have enough money to meet their basic needs. And they're not alone. According to the World Bank, in 2013—the last year when comprehensive data is available—an estimated 767 million people lived in poverty worldwide, meaning that they lived on $1.90 per day or less. That's a pretty arbitrary amount, and raising the threshold even a little bit would throw more people who already live in the social reality of poverty into official poverty. Closer to home, the United States Census Bureau estimates that about forty-three million Americans lived in poverty in 2016. For a family of four with two children under eighteen, that means they live on a maximum of $24,000 per year or about $16 per person per day. Again, that's an arbitrary amount. When she was working full time for the cleaning company, Jennifer made more than that. But looking at her life, no one would doubt that she was experiencing poverty. Raising the poverty line just slightly would push many more people into official poverty.[4]

Poverty—and related social issues like inadequate housing, food insecurity, lack of access to clean water, and lack of healthcare—is a huge problem. It often looks like an unsolvable one. The Comparative Research Program on Poverty (CROP), for example, describes poverty as a "wicked issue." A wicked issue is an issue that is "complex, multidimensional, unclear and changeable." Describing poverty this way makes it sound like there isn't a single, clear-cut solution. Instead, it implies that addressing poverty and related problems means coming at them from a variety of angles. That's fine as far as it goes, but it's also possible to think of poverty as a very simple problem: not having enough money. From that perspective, it also has a

---

3. Edin and Shaefer, *$2.00 a Day*, 35–37.

4. World Bank Group, *Poverty and Shared Prosperity 2016*, 3; Center for Poverty Research, "What Is the Current Poverty Rate in the United States?," lines 2–3; Center for Poverty Research, "What Are the Poverty Thresholds Today?," line 14.

simple solution: instead of trying to address a long list of causes, we could just give people enough money.[5]

Either way, the fact is that the world doesn't have to be this way. Poverty is intertwined with many other social issues, and one of the biggest—one that is almost synonymous with poverty—is wealth inequality. According to Oxfam, the eight wealthiest men in the world control roughly as much wealth as the poorest 3.5 billion people. As of this writing, that means that Bill Gates, Warren Buffett, Carlos Slim, Jeff Bezos, Mark Zuckerberg, Amancio Ortega, Larry Ellison, and Michael Bloomberg control as much wealth as the poorest half of the global population. And, according to the Credit Suisse Research Institute, if all of that wealth—all of the wealth in the world—were equally distributed to every adult in the world, then every adult would have about $53,000. Obviously, no one wants to liquidate and redistribute all of the world's wealth, and no one is seriously demanding absolute economic equality. But these figures point to a simple reality: poverty is not inevitable. It is the result of the systems that we have created to produce and distribute wealth.[6]

There are many stories about poverty and how we can address it. Is inequality a problem, or is it healthy? How much of it is healthy? Is poverty a wicked issue or a simple one? Do people living in poverty just need more money or do they need to have broader social issues addressed? In this chapter, I'm going to give you a bird's eye view of two stories about poverty; stories that I'll be looking at in more detail throughout this book. The first story is a popular one with a long pedigree. According to this story, poverty is a wicked issue that can't be solved by giving people money. It tells us that instead of giving our money, we should address deeper problems and help people adjust to the modern economy. It also tells us that we might need to make big changes to the nonprofit sector in order to do that. The second story is based on emerging research but is rooted in the ancient wisdom of Judaism and Christianity. According to this story, poverty is a simple problem and has a simple solution: giving people money. It tells us that charity is good for the people who receive it and good for the people to give it, and that we can create a more just and merciful world by sharing freely with each other.

5. Spicker, "Poverty as Wicked Problem," 1.

6. Hardoon, "An Economy for the 99%," 2; Kottasova, "These 8 Men Are Richer Than 3.6 Billion People Combined," lines 1–3; Kersley and Koutsoukis, "The Global Wealth Report 2016," lines 5–6.

The First Story: Addressing Poverty through Compassionate Capitalism

On Christmas Eve in 1981, Robert Lupton sat in an urban apartment, sipping coffee with his new neighbors. The room had that smell that tells you it's been cleaned recently, and the children were giddy with anticipation. Eventually, the knock came, and the door opened to reveal a well-dressed family with young children. The mother in Lupton's neighbor-family invited them in and accepted armfuls of gifts, which were distributed to the children. No one noticed that the father in the neighbor-family had quietly gone out through the back door. And when one of the children did notice, no one questioned the mother's insistence that he had run to the store. Except for Lupton. He saw a man emasculated and embarrassed by his inability to provide for his own family. He saw a woman forced to shield her children from that side of their father. He saw children who were learning that good things come, for free, from rich people out there. He saw that charity was toxic and vowed that it had to stop.[7]

A few years later, in his 1986 State of the Union Speech, Ronald Reagan echoed Franklin Roosevelt by calling welfare "a narcotic, a subtle destroyer of the human spirit" and insisting that welfare should be judged by how many of its recipients become independent of it. That theme would be a staple of State of the Union Speeches until, ten years later, Bill Clinton would sign the Personal Responsibility and Work Opportunity Act. Welfare reform did many things. Most importantly, it ended cash welfare and replaced it with a new program that required work, imposed lifetime limits, and gave states more latitude in how they used money. The Act was deeply divisive within the Clinton administration, and a handful of advisors resigned, but it was also nationally popular. Welfare was dead, and people were okay with that.[8]

Much later, in 2012 or so, my parents sent me a copy of Lupton's book, which they were reading in their book group at church. It was my introduction to a movement—let's call them "charity skeptics"—that wants to do for private charity what Bill Clinton did for government welfare. As Lupton describes it, when welfare reform passed, America rejected the idea of doing for others what they can (or should be able to) do for themselves; but, through private charity, we continue to perpetuate a welfare system that creates dependency, erodes the work ethic, and cannot alleviate poverty. According to charity skeptics, to solve the problem of poverty, we should dramatically

---

7. Lupton, *Toxic Charity*, 32–35.

8. Reagan, "Address Before a Joint Session of Congress on the State of the Union"; Edin and Shaefer, *$2.00 a Day*, 27–29.

reduce charity in favor of a different approach: one that favors employment, lending, and investing. And, of course, Lupton is not alone in this. Thought leaders like Steve Corbett, Brian Fikkert, Ruby Payne, Steve Rothschild, and Dan Pallotta all make similar or complementary arguments.[9]

The arguments made by this movement have tapped into something deeply ingrained in the American psyche. The movement's books, articles, videos, workshops, seminars, and other media are incredibly popular. And they echo ideas about poverty that we've seen before. As we've already seen, Lupton's refrain that charity erodes the recipients' work ethic, deepens their dependency on the giver, and fosters a sense of entitlement echoes statements made by President Reagan. Similarly, Payne's argument that multigenerational poverty has its own culture, and that this poverty culture explains why those families find it so difficult to move into the middle class, is based on the work that anthropologist Oscar Lewis carried out in the 1950s and '60s. And arguments for job training, lending programs, entrepreneurship, and consumerism speak to the capitalist heart of modern America. It is, perhaps, the American story about poverty.[10]

In this section, I'm going to look at a few facets of this story. First, I'll look at how charity skeptics think about poverty and how that influences the solutions they suggest. I'll examine those ideas more in chapter two. Second, I'll look at skeptics' claims that charity is toxic and that helping hurts. These ideas will come up repeatedly throughout this book, but I'll look at them in more detail in chapters five and six. Third, I'll look at the ideas for alleviating poverty that skeptics champion. Again, this topic will come up several times in this book, but I'll focus on it especially in chapter five. Finally, I'll look at the skeptics' suggestions for reforming the nonprofit sector. I'll cover those suggestions in more detail in chapter seven. Together, all of these ideas make up the skeptical case against charity that I'll be arguing against in the rest of this book.

In *Bridges Out of Poverty*, Ruby Payne tells a story about some teachers who went in together to buy a refrigerator for a family that didn't have one. A short time after they did that, the children in that family disappeared from school for a week. When they returned, the teachers asked where they had been. Through their questions, they learned that the family had sold the refrigerator and gone camping to relieve stress. Poverty, according to Payne, isn't simply a matter of not having enough money (or not having a

---

9. Lupton, *Toxic Charity*, 22, 128

10. Lewis, "The Culture of Poverty," 19–25; Payne et al., *Bridges Out of Poverty,* Kindle locations 137–38.

refrigerator); that idea is a myth. Finances don't explain why people leave or stay in poverty. In fact, "the ability to leave poverty is more dependent upon other resources [e.g., emotional and mental resources, relationships, knowledge about the hidden rules of different classes] than it is on financial resources." Giving that family a refrigerator wasn't going to help them out of poverty. That family needed someone to help them with those other resources . . . someone to help them overcome the mind-set of poverty.[11]

In line with this, Payne draws a distinction between two kinds of poverty: situational poverty and generational poverty. Situational poverty is the kind of poverty that someone experiences when she is poor because of a particular event, like a medical problem, a divorce, or a natural disaster. Generational poverty is the kind of poverty that someone experiences when they and their parents have grown up in poverty. According to Payne, generational poverty has its own culture, passed on from parents to children, characterized by housing instability, violence, exposure to addiction, periodic homelessness, incarceration, and undereducated adults, among other things. And people who grow up in that "poverty culture" carry that culture with them regardless of how much money they have.[12]

Steve Rothschild, who cites Payne approvingly, takes a similar approach. According to Rothschild, people who live in poverty—again, especially people who have lived in generational poverty—often feel "victimized, powerless, and entitled," and have usually learned a set of "beliefs, thoughts, feelings, and behaviors" that may help them in poverty, but that can keep them from rising out of poverty. When someone who grew up in poverty gets a job with a living wage, she carries her more fundamental beliefs—rooted in her poverty—with her. Even if she learns the rules of the workplace, a single incident can trigger those beliefs and set her back. Again, not having enough money is a symptom of a mind-set or culture that someone carries with them.[13]

This way of imagining poverty creates a bit of a challenge for Payne and Rothschild. On the one hand, poverty still means something like not having enough money. On the other hand, it clearly refers to something deeper: poverty means having a certain culture, beliefs, thoughts, and behaviors that include a sense of victimhood, powerlessness, and entitlement. This double nature of poverty can be confusing.

---

11. Payne, *A Framework for Understanding Poverty,* Kindle locations 144–57, 218–19; Payne et al., *Bridges Out of Poverty,* Kindle locations 635–38, 193–236.

12. Payne, *A Framework for Understanding Poverty,* Kindle locations 1112–45; Payne et al., *Bridges Out of Poverty,* Kindle locations 695–848.

13. Rothschild, *The Non Nonprofit,* 16, 102.

Steve Corbett and Brian Fikkert manage to avoid this ambiguity by taking a different, but similar, approach. According to Corbett and Fikkert, all of us suffer from broken relationships with God, with ourselves, with our communities, and with the rest of creation. Different kinds of poverty—material poverty, poverty of spiritual intimacy, poverty of being, poverty of community, and poverty of stewardship—express different kinds of broken relationships. This way of imagining poverty lets Corbett and Fikkert do two things. First, it lets them recognize that there is a kind of generic poverty that everyone suffers from and a more specific poverty as not having enough money. That means that everyone is poor in some way—putting the materially poor and the materially wealthy on the same footing—and that the materially poor are a special case. Second, it lets them root material poverty (and generic poverty) in a deeper problem, leaving room for Corbett and Fikkert to insist that truly addressing material poverty means focusing on other problems (or even other forms of poverty).[14]

When I talk more about what poverty is and how people experience it in the next chapter, I'll talk about the poverty mind-set and about broken relationships and systems. Those are real things. But it's important to be clear that charity skeptics aren't saying that there's a mind-set that goes along with not having enough money. They aren't saying that not having enough money causes people to have a certain way of looking at the world. Instead, they're arguing that poverty *is* the mind-set, and that not having enough money is a result of that mind-set. They are making an argument about the direction of causality . . . and it's an argument that is almost certainly wrong.

The biggest consequence of that argument is that it means that simply giving money to someone who is poor will not make her not-poor. According to charity skeptics, someone who moves from (material) poverty into the middle or upper class will still carry her poverty mind-set and still have those broken relationships. To some degree, she'll still think and act according to the dictates of her deeper poverty. Solving the financial problem might take care of a symptom of the underlying condition, but it does not cure it. By defining poverty as a deeper problem, the charity skeptics begin an argument against charity by asserting that charity is useless.

Of course, charity skeptics aren't arguing that charity is useless, they're arguing that charity is dangerous. They're arguing that the wrong kind of helping hurts both the giver and the receiver. And this isn't just true of charity in the sense of giving people money. As Lupton puts it, any time we do

---

14. Corbett and Fikkert, *When Helping Hurts*, 41–43, 58–59, 67.

for someone else what they can (or should be able to) do for themselves, we are contributing to both their material poverty and their deeper issues.[15]

We already saw Lupton's Christmas story and how it showed him what he believes is the true nature of charity: that it erodes the recipients' work ethic, deepens their dependency on the people who give them things, and fosters a sense of entitlement. In *When Helping Hurts*, Corbett and Fikkert tell a story about poor families and Christmas presents that is essentially the same. While they draw the same lesson—that gift-giving by wealthier families only contributes to the deep sense of shame that the fathers of poor families feel—they also use the story to illustrate how charity hurts the donors. Remember that Corbett and Fikkert believe that there are many different kinds of poverty all springing from the same source. In Corbett and Fikkert's version of the Christmas story, when the donor families saw that recipient families weren't improving their situations, they went from feeling pride in their generosity to disdain for the people they were helping. The donor families suffered more from poverty of being as their resentment of the recipient families grew.[16]

As I mentioned above, according to charity skeptics, this harm isn't done only by giving money, Christmas presents, or other goods. It's done any time we do for someone else what they can (or should be able to) do for themselves. For example, short-term mission trips are a staple of white American Protestantism. Every year, countless youth and adults travel to inner cities, Appalachia, the Mississippi Gulf Coast, Native American reservations, Central America, Africa, and other places to serve others. And, according to the skeptics, these volunteers are hurting the individuals and communities that they believe they're helping. On the one hand, according to Lupton, they are not only hurting people in all of the ways that he listed above, but taking work away from locals. On the other hand, according to Corbett and Fikkert, they are harming themselves by contributing to their own poverty of being. And all of this is happening without providing these volunteers with the meaningful and transformative experiences they crave.[17]

All of these criticisms, and others, come together in the image that Lupton uses for his book title: charity as toxic. As we've already seen, the idea that giving to others is poisonous is hardly new. For example, the conversation around welfare reform in America started with President Franklin D.

---

15. Lupton, *Toxic Charity*, 129.

16. The Christmas story is found in Lupton, *Toxic Charity*, 31–33. Lupton's characterization of charity is a virtual refrain in Lupton, *Toxic Charity*, 16, 22, 34, 38, 41, 130, 132, and so on; Corbett and Fikkert, *When Helping Hurts*, 62–64.

17. Lupton, *Toxic Charity*, 11–18; Corbett and Fikkert, *When Helping Hurts*, 64, 106–13, 155–58.

Roosevelt's characterization of welfare as a narcotic and "a subtle destroyer of the human spirit." Charity skeptics are applying that same reasoning to private charity, and at the core of this is the idea that charity is poisonous to its recipients, its donors, and society as a whole.[18]

In *Toxic Charity*, Lupton tells the story of a village in Nicaragua. Farmers in this village grew yucca as a staple crop. A community developer from Minnesota saw potential here. If the farmers could grow higher quality yucca and preserve it for export, the village could enter the global economy, make money, and lift itself out of poverty. Twelve farmers took the gamble: they spent their savings and took out loans to buy new yucca plants (though it had to be rushed to a wholesaler since they couldn't afford the equipment to preserve it). A few months later, the farmers stood in a waist-high field of yucca, joined by more farmers who wanted in on the next round. If all continued to go well, Lupton writes, the crop would be successful, they would be able to start preserving it, their market streams could go as far as Miami, and their children would go to college and come home to a growing agricultural economy![19]

If charity skeptics are certain that giving time, talent, and treasure to people in need hurts both the donor and the recipient, they are doubly certain that people in poverty can make their way out of poverty through hard work, entrepreneurship, and consumerism. For example, Lupton tells a story about hiring day laborers in a Home Depot parking lot to help him clear an empty lot. He can imagine any number of reasons that they might be willing to get up early and wait in a parking lot, hoping for a day's work: overdue rent, child support, alcohol, families in Mexico. To Lupton, however, the underlying reason is simple: meaning. "Life," he writes, "offers no fulfillment without work."[20]

Good work isn't always available, of course, and in the absence of employment, charity skeptics advocate for entrepreneurship. Microloans, like the one the yucca farmers took out, are one way for people in low-income communities to get the capital they need to start and expand their own businesses. Corbett and Fikkert, for example, write about a "microfinance

18. Lupton praises welfare reform in Lupton, *Toxic Charity*, 22; Payne praises it in Payne et al., *Bridges Out of Poverty*, Kindle locations 89–93.

19. Lupton, *Toxic Charity*, 109–12.

20. Lupton, *Toxic Charity*, 152–54. Lupton writes that he negotiated a $10 wage with these workers, and I think that he meant "for the day." Assuming that's true, and it was even just a six-hour day, that's a mere $1.60 per hour. Of course, one of the advantages of day labor, though not an advantage for the workers, is that it allows "employers" to pay extremely low—some might even say feloniously low—wages.

revolution," although it's telling that what they highlight is the repayment rate—that is, the profitability of the bank for lenders—and not the success stories of loan recipients. Similarly, Lupton champions micro-lending—again highlighting the high repayment rates—and points to reasons why micro-lending isn't common in the United States: his refrain that a welfare-fostered culture of dependency has eroded the work ethic, that complex regulations stifle entrepreneurship, and that family structures among the urban poor are broken. Where employment is difficult or impossible, entrepreneurship—even if it means going into debt—is the pathway out of poverty.[21]

Employment and entrepreneurship, of course, help us avoid situations like the one Lupton observed that fateful Christmas Eve. If that father had been able to get and keep a decent-paying job, he might have been able to provide gifts to his children and been spared the embarrassment of charity. After that Christmas Eve, Lupton ended his nonprofit's gift-giving program and replaced it with a family store. People could donate gifts to the store, and others could purchase them at bargain prices. The idea of replacing charitable giving with opportunities to buy things—gift-giving programs with bargain toy stores, food pantries with co-ops—is a theme in *Toxic Charity*.[22]

The point of all of this is to avoid the problems that charity skeptics believe that charity creates or fosters. According to the charity skeptics, the global economy—employment, entrepreneurship, and consumption—is the real pathway out of poverty for individuals, families, and communities in the United States and around the world.

When Ruby Payne and Steve Rothschild describe poverty, they're describing a wicked issue: complex, multidimensional, unclear, and constantly changing. Similarly, in his TED talk, Dan Pallotta describes social problems like breast cancer, homelessness, and poverty as "massive in scale" and the organizations that are trying to address them as "tiny up against them." He's not entirely wrong. Looking at the scope of many social issues and the size of most nonprofits, it's difficult to imagine how the nonprofit sector could ever hope to end poverty or homelessness or any other issue.[23]

Charity skeptics like Pallotta and Rothschild have a solution: reforming the nonprofit sector. In this case, reforming the nonprofit sector means making it look more like the for-profit one. Rothschild, for example, suggests being market-driven. For his organization, which provides job training

---

21. Corbett and Fikkert, *When Helping Hurts*, 189; Lupton, *Toxic Charity*, 120–23.

22. Lupton, *Toxic Charity*, 38–39, 51–54.

23. Pallotta, "The Way We Think About Charity is Dead Wrong," 2:34.

for low-income people and places them in jobs with a wage that lifts them out of poverty, that means focusing on the needs of the employers who hire his clients. When asked why he centers his focus on employers instead of participants, he responds with an apocryphal quote from the bank robber Willie Sutton, "Because that's where the money is." Pallotta emphasizes paying nonprofit executives considerably more than they usually make and spending more money on advertising and marketing. He even goes so far as to suggest that nonprofits should be able to spend years building their fundraising capacity without actually serving the people who need their help.[24]

The most profit-friendly recommendation made by Pallotta and Rothschild is allowing people to invest in nonprofit organizations and make a return on those investments. Pallotta doesn't spend much time on this, simply suggesting that it's unfair that nonprofit organizations can't use the lure of profits—and what's known in the nonprofit sector as private inurement—to open large capital markets. Rothschild takes a deeper look at this option. He recommends supplementing no-return investments (philanthropy, government appropriations, and grant-making) with investments that provide returns to investors. Some investment vehicles might provide returns that are below the market rate, others might produce market-rate returns. Effectively, they are both saying that we should make the nonprofit sector something more like a socially conscious version of the for-profit sector.[25]

This mirrors what we saw above with employment, entrepreneurship, and consumerism for low-income individuals, families, and communities. The way for people to move out of poverty is to become better participants in the global economy. The way for organizations to get the money they need to help people do that is to become members—or, at least, associate members—of the for-profit economy.

---

24. Rothschild, *The Non Nonprofit*, 65. It's important that this quote is apocryphal. Willie Sutton denied having given the quote, and in fact wrote that he robbed banks because it made him feel alive. It wasn't a practical decision. He robbed banks because it brought him joy. Pallotta, "The Way We Think About Charity is Dead Wrong," 8:23. Pallotta misunderstands the point he's making here. He says that Amazon was allowed to spend six years building scale without turning a profit, while a nonprofit wouldn't be allowed to spend six years developing scale while no money went to the needy. Of course, it wasn't that Amazon was doing nothing but building that scale during that time. Amazon wasn't returning a profit to investors, but it was selling books. A similar situation for a nonprofit would be spending six years without returning a profit to investors while serving people in need.

25. Pallotta, "The Way We Think About Charity is Dead Wrong," 8:50; Rothschild, *The Non Nonprofit*, 155–56.

This is the first story about poverty and how we address it. In this story, poverty and related issues are complex and multifaceted issues that have systemic aspects, but whose more important roots are found in the cultures, mind-sets, and behaviors of people who are poor. That means that the most powerful way to address poverty is to help people overcome the mind-sets that keep them in poverty, help them join the economy, and let them work their way into the middle class. It's a popular story. It resonates with the rags to riches, pull yourself up by your own bootstraps mythology of America. It is also almost certainly wrong, and I'll spend much of the rest of this book arguing against it. Fortunately, there is an alternative.

The Second Story: Generosity Saves the World

Most of us have a pretty intuitive definition of poverty: it means something like not having enough money. We might make it a little more technical by saying that it means not having enough wealth or not having sufficient financial resources. We might create subcategories between people who don't have enough to meet their basic needs and people who don't have enough to participate in their communities. We might differentiate between people who don't have enough income, people who don't have enough assets, and people who don't have enough savings. We might contrast people who don't have enough because of a specific event with people who don't have enough because of systematic injustices. But in all of these cases, the basic idea of poverty is the same: it means not having enough money. And if poverty is not having enough money, then it makes sense that the solution to poverty would be giving money to people.

In this section, I'm going to outline the second story about poverty and charity. First, I'll look at modern capitalism and how it affects people who are living in poverty, a subject that I'll spend more time with in chapter seven. Second, I'll look at some studies on how people living in poverty use money that is given to them and how those studies mesh with research on the psychology of poverty. I'll look at these topics in depth in chapters two and five. Third, I'll look at how giving affects the people who give, an area that I focus on in chapter six. Finally, I'll talk about the deep connection between charity and Judaism and Christianity. That topic will appear repeatedly throughout this book, but will get special attention in chapters four and seven. Together, these ideas make up a case for charity that I'll be expanding on, and defending, for the rest of this book.

In 2013, the Rana Plaza textile factory in Savar, Bangladesh, collapsed, killing more than 1,100 workers and injuring another 2,500. Twenty-seven multinational companies contracted with the factory, including Benetton, Joe Fresh, and Primark. While building codes should have protected the workers, and while those workers were already concerned about cracks they had seen, powerful apparel manufacturers prevented the codes from being enforced, and workers did not want to lose their pay (or their jobs) by not coming to work. None of the apparel companies directly employed the workers, of course. None of them had even directly contracted with the factory that did employ the workers. Thanks to the magic of the global supply chain, they had effectively outsourced the human costs of profitable production to the developing world. Some people, like me, enjoy the benefits of this supply chain: I can buy cheap, but fashionable, clothing. Other people, like Bangladeshi textile workers, bear the cost.[26]

One of those textile workers is Rehana Khatun. She was twenty in 2013, working six days a week at Rana Plaza for slightly less than $0.30 an hour. When the building began to collapse, she ran down the stairs, but fell in the crowd. A wall collapsed on her and she was trapped in the rubble. She was rescued twenty hours later. Both her legs had to be amputated. In 2016, she was living with her husband and baby in a rehabilitation center in Savar. She suffered from depression and anxiety, had already had additional surgery, and was unable to work. She was part of a Canadian class action lawsuit against Loblaws (a supermarket chain and parent company of Joe Fresh). A similar suit in the United States was dismissed for a simple reason: the Western companies being sued didn't directly employ the textile workers or own the factory. They didn't have a "duty to care." The Canadian suit failed in 2017.[27]

As I wrote at the beginning of this chapter, it doesn't have to be this way. People don't have to live in poverty while others live in opulent wealth. Rana Plaza didn't have to collapse, Rehana Khatun didn't have to lose her legs, workers didn't have to die. All of these things happen because of choices we've made about how we produce and distribute wealth. Choices, in other words, about the economy.

We often treat the economy as though it's a kind of natural force "out there," like the weather or the laws of physics. Sure, we can analyze it, learn to predict it (more or less), and respond to it. If we're very smart—or very lucky—we might even be able to anticipate it and respond in ways that help

---

26. Loomis, *Out of Sight*, 9–11.

27. Beaumont, "Three Years After a Factory Collapse Killed 1,130 Workers"; Kaye, "U.S. Court Dismisses Rana Plaza Lawsuit"; Shaw, "Judge Rejects Joe Fresh Class Action Related to Bangladesh Factory Disaster."

us. And if we're very powerful, we might be able to shift it a little bit. But we tend to live like the economy is mostly its own thing, and the most we can do is hope that our home value increases, that our retirement portfolio performs well, and that there isn't another recession. But the fact is that the economy is made up of the choices made by people just like you and me. As much as we want to treat the economy as rational, objective, and natural, it is nothing more than the aggregate choices of often irrational people in response to scarcity and abundance.

That means that the modern economy is, at the least, the result of the ways that a lot of systems have interacted over centuries, including sexism, racism, colonialism, capitalism, industrialism, urbanization, and globalization. As uncomfortable as it might make us, the Rana Plaza collapse might not have happened if not for the long chain of events, and network of social attitudes, that made it possible for Western retailers to turn a blind eye to their supply chains and for companies closer to the textile factory to treat Bangladeshi workers as essentially expendable, all in the name of profits. That doesn't mean that the modern economy is all bad, of course. There's no doubt that the actual standard of living has increased for many people around the world. And it's wonderful that, even in my own small metropolitan area, I can enjoy the food, entertainment, and arts of countless other countries and cultures. But there's also no doubt that the modern economy exploits some communities for the benefit of others.

It also means that we can choose another way of organizing the economy. Those of us who live in relative wealth could choose to share our abundance with others by, for example, providing unconditional cash grants to people living in poverty or volunteering to build homes for people without adequate shelter. We could, in short, choose to organize our economy on the basis of generosity. We could be charitable.

In 2008, a program in northern Uganda gave unconditional cash grants of about $763 (roughly a year's wages) to young adults between eighteen and thirty-four. The recipients applied in small groups and were asked to provide a statement about how they would invest the money in a trade. But there was no monitoring; people were free to spend the money however they wanted. About 12,000 people received the grants and went about their business. Later, a group of economists selected some people who had received the grants and some people who were denied them. They surveyed the groups two years after they received the money and again two years after that. And what they found was amazing: the people who received the grants had in fact invested them in developing skills and businesses. They were 65 percent more likely to practice a skilled trade, experienced a 49 percent boost in earnings (41 percent after four years), and worked 17 percent more hours than the people who didn't receive the grants![28]

Between 2011 and 2013, the nonprofit organization GiveDirectly gave unconditional cash grants of at least $404 (about twice the amount that the average household spent in a month) to 503 households in Kenya who lived in homes with thatched roofs. The recipients of the money used a mobile money service on their phone. This let GiveDirectly track spending closely. Again, the results were amazing. Households who received the grants increased their spending on things like food and education, without increasing spending on things like alcohol and tobacco; made investments in assets like livestock and metal roofs; and saw measurable improvements in psychological health. The roofs are an interesting piece because thatched roofs need to be repaired or replaced almost every year. By using the grants to buy metal roofs, households were saving money in the long run.[29]

These two studies mesh well with other research into the psychology of poverty. Imagine, for a moment, that your mind is like a computer. Specifically, imagine that it has a certain amount of processing power. Scarcity in general, and poverty specifically, takes up a good chunk of that processing power. When you have a looming deadline for a project at work and not enough time to finish that project, it's hard to think about other things. Similarly, when you don't have enough money and a pile of bills that need to be paid, it's hard to think about anything but the fact that you don't have enough money. The pull of the problem—the fact that you don't have enough money—is so strong that it can effectively lower your IQ score by thirteen or fourteen points, enough to move someone from average to borderline deficient. Similarly, it makes it harder to resist temptation, decide on a course of action, and pay attention to things. Being poor makes it harder to make the best decisions.[30]

What's important here is the direction of causality. Sure, bad financial decisions can cause poverty. But it looks like causality flows at least as strongly in the other direction: poverty causes the mind-set that leads to making bad choices. That theory has a lot of experimental support. And studies like the ones in Uganda and Kenya—and a lot of others—only make

28. The $763 is in terms of purchasing power parity; it was about $382 at 2008 exchange rates. Yglesias, "The Best and Simplest Way to Fight Global Poverty"; Blattman et al., "The Economic and Social Returns to Cash Transfers."

29. Again, the $404 is in terms of purchasing power parity; some of the households received an additional $1,112 as part of the experiment. Haushofer and Shapiro, "Household Response to Income Changes"; Innovations for Poverty Action, "The Impact of Unconditional Cash Transfers in Kenya."

30. Mullainathan and Shafir, *Scarcity*, 39–56.

it stronger. It isn't just possible, but highly likely, that people who don't have enough money will make good decisions if they have enough money. That doesn't mean that everyone will make the right call every time. But, overall, it looks like people in poverty know what they need to do to improve their lives and will do those things if they're given the opportunity.

And that leads us back to our intuitive definition of poverty. If poverty means something like not having enough money, then it seems like the simplest solution to the problem of poverty is giving people money. The research into both the practice of giving people money and the psychology of poverty suggests that simply giving money to people living in poverty may be one of the most powerful tools we have for addressing poverty.

How often has this happened to you? You're flipping through your mail, sorting the bills and catalogs and bank statements into the right piles, when you see an envelope with a nonprofit's logo on it. You drop the rest of your mail and open that envelope. Inside is a letter with a story about something that the nonprofit has done (or is doing, or wants to do). Maybe it's about building a house. Maybe it's about finding a job for a veteran. Maybe it's about finding a forever home for a puppy. You read the story with rapt attention, laughing and tearing up at all the right moments. Then you come to a simple request: please give $25 right now. You run to your computer and go to the organization's website to make your gift. You not only give that $25 gift, you decide to make it a monthly gift. You enter your information, hit the donate button, and see the page that thanks you. Endorphins flood your body and you feel amazing.

Okay, that's never happened to you. But here's a fact: it feels good to give. Every fundraiser knows about the warm fuzzies and post gift glow that people who give to their cause feel. And generous people don't just feel good right after they give. Giving is good for you over the long run, too.

Over several years, sociologists Christian Smith and Hilary Davidson conducted surveys and interviews with thousands of Americans. What they found was as amazing as the results we saw for people living in poverty in Uganda and Kenya. People who gave (especially 10 percent of their income or more), volunteered, engaged in relational or neighborly generosity (things like paying attention to other people's problems or watching other people's children), thought of themselves as generous, or thought that generosity was important were more likely than people who were less generous to report that they were very happy, were in very good or excellent physical health, had a purpose in life, and were interested in personal growth. On the flip side, they were less likely to report that they were very or somewhat unhappy, were in poor or fair health, didn't have a good sense of what they were trying to accomplish in life, had symptoms of depression, or had low interest in personal growth. That's a lot to take in, but the short version is simple: people who give and volunteer are happier, healthier, and more certain of their purpose than people who do not give.[31]

Again, the important thing here is the direction of causality. It's probably true that people who are happier, healthier, more certain of their purpose, and so on are more likely to be generous. But, according to Smith and Davidson, that can't completely explain the relationship between those attributes and generosity. Generosity improves well-being. It fosters and reinforces positive emotions, causes the brain to release happy chemicals (the post gift glow I mentioned above), increases personal agency, creates positive social roles, reduces self-absorption, reinforces the idea that we live in a world of abundance, expands social networks, promotes learning about the world, and increases physical activity. All of these factors improve people's lives. Not in every case, of course, but often enough that generous people—and especially people who practice generosity as a habit—lead happier, healthier, more abundant lives.[32]

In the fourth century, Julian became the emperor of the Roman Empire. Christianity had been legal for almost half a century, and had probably been the religion of the majority—however nominally—for about a decade. One of his biggest projects was restoring Roman paganism, and he had an interesting strategy. Julian thought that it was disgraceful that no Jewish person ever had to beg, that Christians took care of poor Roman pagans as well as poor Christians, and that everyone knew that Roman pagans didn't take care of their poor neighbors. He allocated supplies to the province of Galatia and ordered a (pagan) high priest there to give a fifth of them to the poor who served the priests and the rest to strangers and beggars. Julian thought there should be a pagan religious obligation to provide for people living in poverty.[33]

To people living today, that makes sense. We're used to religious institutions and their food pantries, homeless shelters, clinics, hospitals, retirement homes, after-school programs, soup kitchens, and dozens of other ministries designed specifically for people in poverty. But this made no sense to the pagan priests in Galatia. Roman religion was concerned with many things: sacrifices to the gods, for example, or maintaining purity. But it wasn't concerned with helping the poor. Julian wasn't trying to do

---

31. Smith and Davidson, *The Paradox of Generosity*, 11–45.

32. Smith and Davidson, *The Paradox of Generosity*, 46–98.

33. Stark, *The Triumph of Christianity*, 157; Anderson, *Charity*, 16–17.

something obvious; he was trying to import a Jewish and Christian practice to Roman religion. And it failed.[34]

And while charity—the religious obligation to help the poor—was ignored in ancient Roman religion, it's almost impossible to overemphasize its importance in Judaism and Christianity. In those religions, the responsibility to care for the poor and marginalized is often connected directly to a responsibility towards God. And a charitable gift to a person in poverty is no different from a gift given directly to God.

In Deuteronomy, the Israelites are commanded to pay a tithe from the first crops of their harvest each year on a seven-year cycle. In the first, second, fourth, and fifth years, they were to bring that tithe to the temple in Jerusalem, donate some of it to the Levites (a priestly group who didn't own any land), and eat it during the festivals. In the third and sixth years, they were to keep it locally and share it with Levites, resident foreigners, widows, and orphans. In other words, with groups who were traditionally marginalized in ancient Near Eastern societies. After paying the tithe to the poor, the Israelites were to "say before the Lord" that they hadn't eaten any of it while mourning, moved any of it while unclean, or offered any of it to the dead. Basically, they had to treat it as though it was an offering being made at the altar in the temple. In the seventh year, they were to leave their fields alone, so there was no harvest and therefore no tithe. Providing to the poor was so central to Jewish law that it was directly connected to the tithe paid at the temple![35]

The commands around the tithe are an example of *mitzvoth*. A *mitzvah* (plural *mitzvoth*) is a commandment, whether that's the commandment not to worship other gods, the commandment not to eat pork, or the commandment to take a tithe for the poor. All of the commandments of the Torah are *mitzvoth*. Several centuries after Deuteronomy was written, however, the word *mitzvah* took on an additional meaning: a charitable act. Similarly, *bar mitzvah* had always meant a person who was subject to the law. It took on the additional meaning of a generous person. As biblical scholar Gary Anderson writes, "charity toward the poor had become the commandment that towered above all others."[36]

Moving to the New Testament, in the Gospel of Matthew, Jesus tells a parable about the Son of Man coming to judge the nations. He divides the nations into sheep, who he puts at his right hand, and goats, who he puts at his left. He tells the sheep that they are entering the kingdom of

34. Anderson, *Charity*, 16–18.

35. Anderson, *Charity*, 26–28; Deut 14:22–29, 26:1–15.

36. Anderson, *Charity*, 16–17.

God because they had fed him when he was hungry, given him something to drink when he was thirsty, welcomed him when he was a stranger, and so on. Likewise, he tells the goats that they are being sent into eternal fire because they failed to do those things. Both groups are confused by this, and the Son of Man tells them that whatever they have done (or failed to do) to "the least of these," they have done (or failed to do) for him. Christians, of course, recognize the Son of Man as Christ. As in the Torah, then, giving to the poor is treated as the same as giving to God.[37]

The same attitude can be found in the story of St. Martin of Tours. A catechumen (someone who was studying for his baptism) and a soldier, Martin was approaching the city of Amiens in France when he saw a beggar wearing hardly anything. Martin took his military cloak, cut it in half, and gave half of it to the beggar. That night, Martin dreamt that he saw Jesus bragging about him to the angels, "Martin, who is still but a catechumen, clothed me with this robe." Several centuries later, Martin's cloak became a relic. The priest who cared for the relic was called a *cappellanu*, and the small temporary churches that it was kept in while traveling were called *capella*. Both of these come from the world for cloak. St. Martin's act of charity with his cloak ultimately led to our modern words chaplain and chapel. Most importantly, of course, when Martin gave part of this cloak to that beggar, he was giving it to Christ.[38]

What's important in all of these stories is that giving to the poor is the same as giving to God. For Christians, it is even an imitation of Christ. The word *charity* comes from one of the two Latin words used to translate the Greek word *agape*. And *agape* is the word used to describe Christ's sacrificial love for the world. Giving charity is, in a sense, a way doing the same thing: just as Christ gave his life for the world, we are called to give what we have to the poor in whom we encounter Christ. Charitable giving is an act of worship. More than that, it is the heart of the Christian faith.

This is the second story about poverty and how to address it. In this story, poverty is a simple problem in the sense that we can describe it easily: it's not having enough money. It also has a simple solution, which is giving money to people who don't have enough of it. This doesn't resonate as well with our modern American sensibilities, but it is central to how Christianity thinks about poverty. It is the story of Christian charity.

---

37. Matt 25:31–46.

38. Anderson, *Charity*, 6–7; Severus, "On the Life of Saint Martin," chapter 3. It's worth pointing out that Severus implies that the reason that Martin used his cloak for this purpose was that he had already given away much of the rest of his clothing.

The Great Scandal

Not long after I first read *Toxic Charity*, I was filling out an application for a grant from a church. I don't remember what church it was, but what I do remember is that it included Lupton's Oath for Compassionate Service as grant criteria. The Oath includes points like "never do for the poor what they have (or could have) the capacity to do for themselves," "limit one-way giving to emergency situations," "strive to empower the poor through employment, lending, and investing," and "listen closely to those you seek to help, especially to what is not being said." Clearly, this church had taken the lessons of *Toxic Charity* to heart. Charity skepticism was a condition of receiving their support! And they aren't the only ones. Churches and Christian nonprofits across the United States are adopting Lupton's Oath, implementing Payne's curricula, and imagining how they can be more business-like.[39]

Christian organizations, in other words, have adopted a kind of compassionate capitalism. They've taken on the belief that the same principles that led to Rana Plaza could, if they were more socially conscious, end problems like poverty, hunger, and homelessness. They're doing this for a good reason: the first story about poverty and how we should address it seems intuitive, caring, and effective. The Christian organizations who are adopting that story believe that they are doing the right thing for people living in poverty and for the people who want to help them.

The problem is that there's an alternative story: a story about how generosity—and, specifically, charity—can help people living in poverty and the people who want to help them. This is a story that sits at the intersection of Christianity and emerging social scientific and economic research. On the one hand, charity is rooted in the Jewish and Christian traditions. In fact, it is at the center of the Christian gospel; human charity is a reflection of God's love for the world and an expression of the fundamental nature of God's creation. On the other hand, as economists, psychologists, sociologists, and others delve deeper into poverty and related social problems, they are discovering that generosity works. Charity has the potential to change the world into a place of greater justice and mercy.

More than that, it has the power to transform and reinvigorate the church. By returning to its ancient story—with help from this new research—the church can present a compelling alternative vision for society and the world. It can help people imagine a world that isn't governed by the inflexible law of the markets, where everyone but the lucky few must bury their passions in the name of buying and selling. It can help people imagine

39. Lupton, *Toxic Charity*, 8–9, 128–32.

a world where people are free to live in *agape*, the kind of reckless love that saves the sinner and embraces the outcast. In other words, it can invite people to live in charity. And if that way of living is more than an assertion—if that way of living really does fill the hungry, welcome the stranger, and heal the sick—then the church will be a vibrant and revolutionary force in the world. And it is nothing short of a scandal that so many churches and organizations are willing to abandon that tradition in favor of an ideology that is indistinguishable from what secular capitalism has to offer.

In this book, I'm going to advocate for the second story. As we move through the chapters, I'll look at poverty and giving through several lenses, ranging from theories of behavioral economics to practical applications like the studies in Uganda and Kenya we saw earlier. Just as importantly—perhaps more importantly—I'll look at them through the lens of Christian theology and practice, with a particular eye on how they fit into the Christian narrative of creation, sin, and redemption. Charity, both as a generous act and as a cultivated virtue, has a central place in the story that Christians tell about the world. As I do all of this, I'll return occasionally to the ideas of the charity skeptics, both to point to things they get right and to note some mistakes I believe they make.

But before I move on to that, there's one final introductory point I need to make. The two stories that I outlined above are not the only two stories about poverty and how to address it. And neither of them is completely right or completely wrong. There is, for example, a place for ideas like job training programs, personal empowerment, microfinance, and entrepreneurship. In fact, when it comes to helping people living in poverty, we need all of the tools we can get our hands on. The problem with charity skepticism is that it leans too heavily on one set of tools (a set that happens to be very amenable to an unjust global economic system) while throwing out another tool that may prove to be one of the most powerful ones we have at our disposal. I am not advocating that we throw out every tool except charity. Instead, I'm offering a corrective to the idea that we can somehow solve problems like poverty and inequality while leaving the systems that maintain those problems in place.

2

Poverty

Like Hamid and Khadeja, Subir and Mumtaz live in Dhaka, Bangladesh, along with their five sons. The family pieces their income together from a variety of sources. Depending on the day, they are rickshaw drivers, garment factory workers, scrap metal scavengers, rag pickers, maids, and even landlords. The diverse nature of their work, and uncertainty of work when they have it, means that their income varies wildly. During the year that they kept financial diaries for researchers, their family income ranged from $1.90 a day (about $0.27 per person) to $3.15 ($0.45 per person).[1]

Jennifer, who we met in chapter one, lives almost literally half a world away in Chicago with her two children. We met her when she had a job for a cleaning company, but that was unusual. For ten months before she got that job, she had no cash income at all. She relied on the Supplemental Nutrition Assistance Program (SNAP, the successor to food stamps), homeless shelters, and her ability to find free stuff. Just because she didn't have a job doesn't mean she wasn't looking for one. Every day, she would spend time filling out online applications before hitting the streets to hand out dozens of resumes. At various times in her life, she's been a cashier, sandwich maker, and custodian.[2]

Adam is a professor of economics at a small, private, liberal arts college. He makes about the average salary for that position: $93,500 a year. His paycheck is deposited directly into his bank account twice a month. And

1. Collins et al., *Portfolios of the Poor*, Kindle locations 507–49.
2. Edin and Shaefer, *$2.00 a Day*, 35–38, 44–45.

while things are never certain, he has no reason to doubt that he'll still be teaching and researching next month, next semester, and next year. He also suffers from workaholic tendencies. These tendencies have put strain on his relationships with family and friends, and taken their toll on his spiritual life.[3]

All of us should intuitively recognize Subir and Jennifer's families as poor. Most of us would also intuitively recognize Adam's family as not-poor (if not outright wealthy); though it's worth noting that some charity skeptics—notably Corbett and Fikkert—would say that he is poor, just not materially poor. But what do we mean when we say that Subir and Jennifer and their families live in poverty? Is it just a matter of money? Is there something deeper going on? How do they experience poverty? Why do they live in poverty in the first place? And why don't they just work their way out of it?

In this chapter, I'm going to look at poverty from a few different angles. First, I'll talk about what poverty is and how we might divide it up in different ways. Then, I'll look at the mind-set or psychology of poverty and how living in poverty affects the way that people think. After that, I'll look at how people living in poverty manage money. Finally, I'll look at the moral dimension of poverty in our society. Through all of this, I'm going to be working off of a very simple definition of poverty: that "being poor" means something like "not having enough money." And that one of the biggest things that changes when someone is poor is how the rest of us treat them.

Defining Poverty

As I said in the last chapter, most of us have a pretty intuitive definition of poverty: poverty means something like "not having enough money." Since *money* can be a pretty slippery word, let's refine that a bit and say that poverty is the condition of not having enough wealth. Wealth includes a lot of different kinds of financial resources. It includes income, liquid assets like savings accounts, financial instruments and holdings like stocks and bonds, and non-liquid assets like houses and cars. In general, when we talk about poverty like that experienced by Subir or Jennifer's families, we mean that they don't have enough wealth, period. They have little income, no savings, no assets, and so on. But we also understand the risk involved in having non-liquid assets but not enough income (like being "house poor") or having a good income but nothing to draw on if that income disappears (living paycheck to paycheck).

---

3. Ley, "Salary for a Professor of Economics," line 14.

While all people living in poverty share something in common—not having enough wealth—different people experience poverty differently. That's why we can differentiate between being poor, being house poor, and living paycheck to paycheck. Subdivisions like this might be useful as we think about how to address poverty. After all, it's possible that someone living paycheck to paycheck has different needs than someone who is house poor. Accepting the intuitive definition of poverty lets us see what they have in common. Identifying different varieties of poverty helps us understand how poverty affects different people.

In this section, I'm going to look at three different ways that we can subdivide poverty. Each of these ways reflects a different question that we can ask about our basic definition of poverty. First, there's the difference between absolute and relative poverty, which answers the question, "enough wealth to do what?" Second, there's the difference between income, asset, and liquid asset poverty, which answers the question, "what kind of wealth?" Third, and finally, there's the difference between circumstantial and systemic poverty, which answers the question, "why doesn't this person have enough wealth?"

Subir and Jennifer's families are both poor. Subir's family consistently lives on less than $0.50 per person per day. When Jennifer is doing well, her family might live on about $17.50 per person per day. Obviously, there's a big difference between what Subir can do with his resources and what Jennifer can do with hers. There's also a big difference between what Subir can do with his resources and what a beggar on the streets of Dhaka, with even less money than Subir, can do. There's a difference between someone who is poor and someone who is destitute.

Something that can help us think about this difference is the distinction between absolute poverty and relative poverty. Absolute poverty means not having enough wealth to meet basic needs for things like food, shelter, and clothing. For people living in absolute poverty, that poverty means hunger or malnutrition, homelessness or the threat of homelessness, and other life-threatening problems. Relative poverty means not having enough wealth to participate fully and meaningfully in the life of the community. This is necessarily more vague than absolute poverty, and varies from society to society. People in absolute poverty don't have enough wealth to meet their basic needs; people in relative poverty are noticeably poor compared to other people in their community. So, for example, Subir's family, living on less than $1 per person per day, lives in absolute poverty. Jennifer's family, when she's working for the cleaning company, is much wealthier than

Subir's family, but is still poor compared to most other Americans. She and her family live in relative poverty.

Absolute poverty is a major global and, for Americans, national concern. People living on less than two dollars a day are in fragile, potentially life-threatening situations. But we shouldn't dismiss the reality of relative poverty. While no one should be so poor that they can't meet their basic needs, neither should anyone be so poor that they are excluded from the ordinary life of their broader community. Both forms of poverty matter to the people who live in them. And any fair, equitable, and just society will work to address both of these kinds of poverty.

Subir and Jennifer's families' incomes are so low that they live in constant poverty. Whether they have problems meeting their basic needs or not, none of them have enough income to be not-poor. Adam's family, on the other hand, does not live in poverty. But, like many Americans, his family might fall into poverty if they have an unexpected medical problem, lose a job, or encounter another substantial financial obstacle. Maybe he has plenty of savings and would be able to draw on that. More likely, he would use his savings very quickly and have to start selling assets like his house or car. There is a difference between never having enough, living paycheck to paycheck, and not being able to weather a disaster.

Something that can help us think about this difference is the distinction between income poverty, asset poverty, and liquid asset (or savings) poverty. Income is how we normally measure poverty: a household income below a certain threshold means that a family is poor. Asset poverty expands on that idea to include the household's potential financial cushion. Prosperity Now (formerly the Corporation for Economic Development, or CFED) defines asset poverty as not having a big enough net worth to stay above the poverty line for three months without income. Liquid asset poverty expands this further to include savings. Prosperity Now defines liquid asset poverty as not having enough savings to remain above the poverty line for three months without income and without losing important assets like a home or business.

Since each of these distinctions builds on the previous one, we can expect more people to qualify as poor as we move from income poverty to asset poverty to liquid asset poverty. Prosperity Now identifies 13.4% of Americans as living in income poverty (what we normally think of as poor), 25.5% of Americans as living in asset poverty (what we might think of as paycheck to paycheck), and 36.8% of Americans as living in liquid asset poverty. It also identifies 17% of Americans as living in extreme asset poverty, a situation where the household has no or negative net worth even if they have major assets (think of the family who owns a nice home, but whose mortgage is a major drain on their resources).[4]

Like absolute poverty, income poverty is obviously a major global and national concern. Again, however, we shouldn't overlook asset and liquid asset poverty. A quarter of Americans may be able to survive day-to-day and paycheck to paycheck, but are unable to withstand a major financial shock. And an even larger number of Americans cannot weather that shock without losing important assets. This means that a large number of people are one or two emergencies away from poverty. And that is a problem that needs to be addressed.

Charity skeptics don't spend much time talking about different kinds of poverty, with one exception: situational and generational poverty. Situational poverty is usually defined as poverty that is caused by a particular event like a death, chronic illness, or divorce. Generational poverty is defined as ongoing familial poverty for at least two generations.[5]

These categories may be useful, but they're problematic for a few reasons, the biggest of which is the amount of heavy lifting that generational poverty is forced to do. Payne, for example, asserts that generational poverty "has its own culture, hidden rules, and belief systems." Those hidden rules include knowing things like which churches have the best rummage sales, how to get someone out of jail, how to get a gun (legally or illegally), and how to move house quickly. More importantly, according to Payne people living in generational poverty tend to have an attitude that "society owes one a living." For charity skeptics, the underlying culture of generational poverty explains a lot about why these families remain in poverty, and changing that underlying culture—or, at least, the underlying mind-set in individuals—is the key to helping people escape poverty. The culture of generational poverty becomes *the* explanatory tool, all but erasing the distinctions between, for example, families who have lived in poverty for two generations due to shifting economies and families who have lived in poverty for a dozen generations due to things like racism and colonialism.[6]

The distinction between situational and generational poverty may be problematic, but it does open up another possibility: the difference between circumstantial and systemic poverty. Circumstantial poverty, like

4. Prosperity Now, "Income Poverty Rate," "Asset Poverty Rate," "Liquid Asset Poverty Rate," and "Extreme Asset Poverty Rate." The income, asset, and liquid asset poverty figures are based on data from 2013. Extreme asset poverty rate is based on data from 2011.

5. Payne et al., *Bridges Out of Poverty*, Kindle locations 695–98.

6. Payne et al., *Bridges Out of Poverty*, Kindle locations 567–88, 698.

situational poverty, is poverty that can be traced to a discrete cause. For example, someone who is thrust into poverty because of a house fire is living in circumstantial poverty. Systemic poverty is poverty that is caused and maintained by larger social forces like racism, colonialism, globalization, or environmental exploitation. If Adam falls into poverty because of an unforeseen medical emergency, he will live in circumstantial poverty. Subir and Jennifer's families, on the other hand, live in systemic poverty.

The line between circumstantial and systemic poverty is blurry, and there is certainly substantial overlap. For example, if someone is pushed into poverty because of a medical emergency and the bills that come with it, they are in poverty both because of their particular circumstances (the medical emergency) and a broader system (the way that the American healthcare system works). Similarly, there is variation within each category. The systemic poverty of Bangladesh is different from the systemic poverty of Chicago. Even as we see those differences, however, we can see the similarities.

Remember our basic definition of poverty: poverty is the condition of not having enough wealth. Each of the distinctions I looked at above adds a dimension to that definition based on three questions that follow from this definition: "The wealth to do what?," "What kinds of wealth?," and "Why doesn't this family have wealth?" These differences might affect how we understand specific cases of poverty, what strategies we use to address poverty, and how we prioritize different kinds of poverty. So, for example, we might address systemic absolute income poverty through something like universal basic income. And we might help people with systemic relative asset poverty through strategic investments in historically disadvantaged communities. Adding these dimensions, though, doesn't change the basic definition of poverty. Poverty, regardless of how we want to treat specifics, is the condition of not having enough wealth. Poverty is not having enough money.

The Poverty Mind-Set

Remember the story that Payne tells about the family who received a refrigerator? A group of teachers bought a refrigerator for a family that didn't have one, and learned later that the family sold the fridge in order to go on a stress-reducing camping trip. To many people, selling a fridge in order to take a camping trip is nonsensical. It would be in that family's economic self-interest to keep the fridge, save money, and build their way out of poverty. Payne finds the explanation for selling the fridge and taking the vacation in the culture of generational poverty: while middle class people make decisions against a background of work and achievement; and wealthy people make decisions against a background of financial, social, and political relationships; people in generational poverty make decisions against a background of entertainment and personal relationships. A camping trip strengthens family bonds and is more fun than owning a refrigerator.[7]

While a "culture of poverty"—generational or otherwise—is a somewhat outmoded idea, Payne and other charity skeptics aren't wrong when they note a correlation between poverty and a certain mind-set. Where they are wrong is in imagining that the arrow of causality points in only one direction. While charity skeptics believe that an ill-defined poverty mind-set keeps people in poverty, and that the key to helping someone out of poverty is changing their mind-set, emerging research is showing that poverty itself causes the poverty mind-set and that people change their mind-set when they come out of poverty. Sure, the poverty mind-set can keep people from changing their financial circumstances, but it isn't the cause of poverty.

In this section, I'm going to look at a few components of the poverty mind-set as understood by emerging research. Specifically, I'm going to look at the effects of poverty—of not having enough money—on fluid intelligence and executive control, as well as the mental process of tunneling. In all of this, I'm indebted to the excellent research of Sendhil Mullainathan and Eldar Shafir.

Imagine taking a simple test on problem solving. In this test, you're shown a series of shapes and patterns. Then you're shown another series, but one of the elements is missing. Your task is to figure out what the missing piece should be. Maybe you're good at this kind of thing. Maybe you're not. But no matter how good you are at this kind of test when things are quiet and you have plenty of time, you would do significantly worse if you were pressed for time or had someone yelling at you the entire time. It turns out that scarcity of any kind—like scarcity of time or room for concentration—but especially poverty, affects a part of our mental toolkit called fluid intelligence.[8]

Fluid intelligence is the ability to do things like think about abstract concepts and solve problems that aren't dependent on specific knowledge. That's why the test I described above is about finding the missing part of a pattern. If doesn't matter if you're a physician practicing in Manhattan or a farmer in India; you can perform on this test without having to know

---

7. Payne et al., *Bridges Out of* Poverty, Kindle locations 635–38.

8. Mullainathan and Shafir, *Scarcity*, 47–49.

Fluid Intelligence

anything specific. This test, called Raven's Progressive Matrices, lets us measure fluid intelligence by measuring the closely related concept of IQ. In the research performed by Mullainathan and Shafir, the link between poverty and IQ is undeniable: poverty lowers IQ by thirteen to fourteen points. That's enough to move someone from superior to average or from average to borderline deficient. Or, to use another analogy, living in poverty is the mental equivalent of always having just pulled an all-nighter.[9]

Ad See why we stay

That doesn't mean that people who are living in poverty are less intelligent than people who aren't. Mullainathan and Shafir's research showed that the same person had fewer IQ points when she was thinking about scarcity than when she was not. People living in poverty face the constant stress of trying to manage tightly limited resources, leaving them with fewer cognitive resources to use for complex reasoning and problem solving. What's particularly important here is the direction of causation. It is not that low fluid intelligence causes poverty (although it certainly may). It's that poverty causes a drop in fluid intelligence.

Imagine a different test. In this test, you're taken into a room where there is a table with a single marshmallow. Your host tells you that you can eat that marshmallow now or, if you wait while he goes to get another marshmallow, you can have two. Maybe you have the self-control to resist the single marshmallow. Maybe you don't. But, again, no matter how good your self-control, you would have a significantly harder time resisting that marshmallow if you haven't eaten in a few days (or, for some of us, a few hours). Scarcity, and especially poverty, affects another part of our mental toolkit: executive control.

Executive control includes our abilities to plan, pay attention, take action, and refrain from taking action. Mullainathan and Shafir's research has shown that executive control, and especially self-control, is a limited resource. In their experiments, subjects' minds were unloaded or loaded: some were asked to memorize a two-digit number (their minds were unloaded), others were asked to memorize an eight-digit number (their minds were loaded). Those who were asked to memorize the eight-digit number had more difficulty controlling their impulses and self-control. Living in poverty means making more difficult decisions, resisting more temptations, and so on, meaning that the limited supply of executive control gets exhausted more quickly. Scarcity of any kind, but especially poverty, decreases executive control.[10]

9. Mullainathan and Shafir, *Scarcity*, 47–49, 51–52.
10. Mullainathan and Shafir, *Scarcity*, 47, 52–56.

As with fluid intelligence, this doesn't mean that people living in poverty inherently have less executive control than people who are not living in poverty. Mullainathan and Shafir's research showed that the same person had less executive control when she was thinking about scarcity than when she was not. Again, the important point is the direction of causation. It is not that low executive control causes poverty (although it certainly may). It's that poverty causes a loss of executive control.

Challenges to fluid intelligence and executive control come together in a concept that Mullainathan and Shafir call the bandwidth tax. Imagine that your brain is a computer with only so much processing power. Scarcity of any kind is like having too many applications open and running, eating up processing power, and leaving people with less power to use for fluid intelligence and executive control. Poverty, though, has a compounding effect. As bandwidth gets used on dealing with not having enough money, it becomes harder to control impulses, plan ahead, and think abstractly. That means it becomes harder to resist foolish purchases, remember to pay bills, and budget for the future. And each of those challenges comes with a financial cost that maintains poverty.

This is easily seen in two cognitive behaviors that Mullainathan and Shafir call focusing and tunneling. We've all experienced these two sides of the same coin. For example, we experience focusing when we have a project that's up against a deadline. I can easily think of a dozen or so times when I've struggled to write a sermon until Friday or Saturday, when everything became clear. I might attribute that the movement of the Holy Spirit, but it's also the result of how our brains work. When we have plenty of time, it's easy to get distracted by social media or decide to binge watch a TV show. When time is short, it becomes much easier to focus on the project that absolutely positively must be done right now.[11]

Tunneling is the other side of that. As I focus on the project that absolutely positively must be done right now, it also becomes easy to forget about the project that I need to prepare to start next. The project that needs to be done now captures my attention and distracts me from the other things I need to be doing. I forget to do laundry or start dinner or outline the next sermon. I get tunnel vision as I focus on the things inside the tunnel and forget about things outside it. The cost of my focus is that I'm already behind when I start the next project. When scarcity captures our attention, we neglect things that we need to be dealing with.[12]

11. Mullainathan and Shafir, *Scarcity*, 24–27.
12. Mullainathan and Shafir, *Scarcity*, 27–29.

Focusing and tunneling are caused by any kind of scarcity, like the hunger we feel when we're on a diet or the busyness we feel when we're overworked. Poverty is a particular kind of scarcity, but one with some special features. The most important special feature is its consistency. If you're on a diet, you can choose to eat something. If you're overworked, you can choose to take a vacation. If you're too busy at home, you can hire help. But you can't just choose not to live in poverty. And the bandwidth tax that people living in poverty pay shows up in a variety of ways: difficulty remembering things, reduced productivity, less self-control, more trouble sleeping. Poverty means not having enough money, but it also means not having enough bandwidth.[13]

Again, a critical point here is the direction of causation. It's easy to imagine that poverty is the result of some personal or cultural failure like a lack of tenacity or a social idea that the world owes one a living. And there might be some truth to that. But it is certainly the case that the arrow of causation also points in the other direction. Not having enough money causes us to think and feel differently; that, in turn, causes us to behave differently. This is especially true for people who have spent a long time—perhaps, even, their entire lives—in poverty. These people have been paying the bandwidth tax throughout their lives, affecting their performance in school and at work. For them, it isn't as simple as saying that their mind-set causes their poverty; poverty caused the mind-set in the first place.

Does this help us explain the story of the family with the refrigerator? Without more details about that family, it's impossible to say for certain. But this cognitive approach to poverty does provide a theory. Obviously, that family was living in poverty and under stress. To draw on an analogy that I've already used, it was always like they had just pulled an all-nighter. Imagine the last time you had to function on no sleep and add to that the idea that you had to make it through every day in that condition. That will give you some idea of what it's like to live in poverty.

Stress was in this family's tunnel. It was a problem that was in their immediate line of sight. The potential economic benefits of the refrigerator were outside the tunnel. They existed in an uncertain and unpredictable future. We can add to that the idea that the refrigerator may not have been what that family needed. Could they afford the additional electricity? Did they have access to fresh food or other food that needs refrigeration? And so on. Given what we learned above about fluid intelligence, executive control,

13. Mullainathan and Shafir, *Scarcity*, 147–64.

focusing, and tunneling, it makes sense that they would give up an uncertain future benefit for the solution to an immediate problem.

For Payne and other charity skeptics, the family's behavior is best explained by a poverty culture that prizes entertainment and relationships over work, achievement, and wealth. For behavioral economists like Mullainathan and Shafir, it's best explained by the cognitive reality of scarcity in general and poverty in particular. And this suggests an alternative solution. Where charity skeptics suggest that people living in poverty need to change their culture or mind-set in order to work their way out of poverty (effectively, learn to function better on no sleep), what we've learned in this section suggests that giving people money would help them change their mind-sets (effectively, getting some sleep would help them function better). As we'll see later, this method—giving people money—seems to work. And it works better if we give people cash that they can use to meet their needs as they understand them than if we give people things like refrigerators that may not meet those needs.

Complex Financial Instruments

Like many professionals, my financial life is a tangle of different accounts: checking and savings accounts, credit cards, retirement portfolios, student loans, a mortgage, and so on. Much of that financial life happens online and automatically. My paychecks are—well, used to be—deposited directly into my bank account, my bills are scheduled to come out of that same account, I make purchases with my credit or debit card, I almost never carry cash or write a paper check. In fact, a while ago I was registering for a meeting, and because the organization didn't have an online registration page, I had to write and mail in a check. Despite the fact that my checking account was four years old at the time, I registered using the first check on that account. And when I make a payment or receive a paycheck, that information goes into a piece of budgeting software on my computer. I can know at a glance where my money comes from and where it goes.

That life is made possible by several things. There are the devices and connections that let me access my accounts online and tie them together in a way that makes sense. There's the fact that my previous employer required direct deposit and that the companies and creditors I deal with let me schedule payments from my bank account. I have a steady income that's large enough that I don't have to worry about whether I'll have enough money for those scheduled payments. I have an excellent credit score. As much as

I might like to think that I'm good at managing money, the fact is that I rely on having money and being part of systems that help me with that.

Things are different for people who live in poverty. Not only do they not have enough money, their incomes and expenses are often unreliable, making money management more difficult. They're also usually unbanked or underbanked, meaning they don't have reliable access to tools like checking accounts, savings accounts, and credit lines. People living in poverty face a different financial reality and have a different set of tools to use. Despite these challenges—perhaps even because of them—low-income families are often financially savvy and low-income communities have developed innovative financial instruments to help themselves survive in poverty.

In this section, I'm going to look at three important parts of the financial reality of poverty. First, the absence of what Mullainathan and Shafir call slack. Slack is, more or less, the feeling of being able to absorb additional expenses. Second, and related, the need for flexibility. Because low-income families have little or no financial slack, every new expense must be paid for using money that's already been earmarked for something else. This means that people living in poverty need the ability to move money from one expense to another as seamlessly as possible. Third, the lack of formal financial tools to help people living in poverty do what they need to do. Most financial institutions are focused on helping their middle-class and wealthy clientele, so low-income families have had to create their own financial instruments. Finally, I'm going to look at a story that Payne tells and interprets through her lens of poverty culture and explore how we can understand it in terms of rational financial thinking.

One of the biggest challenges that people living in poverty face is that, when you don't have enough money, there's no room for a change in circumstances or a mistake. Changes in circumstances are common. Subir and Mumtaz's family income, over the course of a single year, ranged from $1.90 to $3.15 per day. Closer to home, over the course of a few months, Jennifer's family made anywhere from less than $2 to about $52 per day. If household income could fluctuate that much over such a short period of time, you can just imagine how much other circumstances could change. Similarly, because of the challenges with the poverty mind-set we saw above, mistakes are perfectly normal. While I can withstand a temporary drop in pay or give into an impulse—thanks to savings and credit—people living in poverty lack a key resource for dealing with unexpected problems: what Mullainathan and Shafir call slack.

Mullainathan and Shafir use the term *slack* in a particular way. They ask us to imagine packing a suitcase for a business trip. If it's a big suitcase, we might start by casually throwing in the essentials. We then might start adding less-essential things: an umbrella (in case it rains), gym clothes (in case we work out), and so on. We might even close the suitcase with room to spare. Then, they ask us to imagine packing a small suitcase like the kind I usually pack for travel. We can't just throw things in that suitcase. Instead, we need to stick to the essentials, make choices, and pack carefully. Slack, to Mullainathan and Shafir, is that feeling of just being able to toss things in. Financially, it's the feeling that buying that latte or misplacing five dollars doesn't matter, but doesn't include the space that we create by saving for a rainy day or allocating money for contingencies. For my purposes, slack is a bit bigger: it also includes the ways that we create space. When we set aside money for the unexpected, we're creating slack. We are, as it were, buying a bigger suitcase.[14]

Not having slack means that people living in poverty need to think in terms of trade-offs. When we pack a small suitcase, this means understanding that packing the umbrella means not packing that extra—or essential—shirt or pair of socks. When we think about money, it means understanding that buying that latte means not being able to pay a utility bill. We all think in terms of trade-offs some of the time. We are all careful when the prices are high enough. We know that if we buy the pricey grill we'll have to find other money to use for the mortgage. The less money we have, the more often we think in these terms: buying this means missing rent, buying that means not eating out on Friday. Low-income families have to think in these terms a lot.[15]

This might sound like another mind-set thing, but it has important financial effects. First, it means that people living in poverty need to be financially savvy. Individuals in poverty are more likely to know where their money is going and how much things cost. They are also, as we've already seen, more likely to think in terms of trade-offs. And they're more likely to value things consistently across different contexts. For example, they're less likely to pay more for a beer at a hotel bar (where it's going to cost more) than they do at the local corner bar. Because of the absence of slack—because every dollar means something—people in poverty tend to know more about their finances than relatively wealthy people who have plenty of slack and therefore don't need to think about these things.[16]

Second, it means that there's less room for error. I've made plenty of dumb purchases, and those dumb purchases are evidenced by the things

14. Mullainathan and Shafir, *Scarcity*, 69–70, 73–75.

15. Mullainathan and Shafir, *Scarcity*, 70–73.

16. Davis and Cohen, "Three Myths about the Underbanked, Part Two," lines 45–56.

sitting in my house that I never (or almost never) use. A barely used Nintendo Wii U, countless half-read books (even more now that I don't need shelves to store them), bits of software, and so on. I also have unforeseen expenses. Car accidents happen and unexpected trips to the vet come up. My slack can absorb both of those things. I don't face a consequence for occasionally giving in to temptation or having an emergency. Low-income families, however, do face consequences. With little or no slack, every purchase means that another purchase can't be made. There's nothing to absorb an unexpected expense or the simple act of giving in to temptation.[17]

This can create a potentially vicious circle. Remember that part of the poverty mind-set is a reduction in fluid intelligence and executive control. People living in poverty have more difficulty focusing on consequences outside of the tunnel of their poverty and resisting temptation; and missing something outside the tunnel or giving into temptation have greater consequences for someone living in poverty. Poverty increases the chance of a mistake, and each mistake means more. That cycle of poverty can be difficult to escape.

Subir and Mumtaz cobble their meager income together from a variety of sources. Subir can spend a few days of the week driving a pedicab, but it's exhausting work. It's also dictated by weather, political conditions, and luck. Mumtaz works as a maid. Their sons, Iqbal and Salauddin, are a garment factory worker and a rag picker, respectively. In addition, they can sometimes take in a boarder, who can sleep in the corner of their small home. Together, they might earn $85 a month, or around $2.83 a day, or about $0.40 per person per day for their family of seven. Of course, none of this is reliable. Illness or injury, a factory closure, or job loss could reduce that income significantly. For Subir and Mumtaz, putting together something resembling a stable financial life is a major preoccupation.[18]

Because they have no slack and their circumstances can shift quickly, Subir and Mumtaz prize flexibility in their financial arrangements. Remember that Subir works as a pedicab driver. He would make more money if he owned his vehicle instead of renting one. His family could take out a microloan to do just that, but it wouldn't actually meet their needs. Their money would be tied up in a pedicab and loan interest. And they would have nowhere to store the vehicle. Instead, when they took out a microloan, they used the money for other things: rice, a cupboard (now one of two pieces of furniture), and to make a loan to a fellow pedicab driver. They may

17. Mullainathan and Shafir, *Scarcity*, 80–86.
18. Collins at al., *Portfolios of the Poor*, Kindle locations 521–31.

not have used the loan to start or expand a business, but they found it useful to take the loan and meet day-to-day needs (and earn some income from their own loan).[19]

In their landmark book *Portfolios of the Poor*—the culmination of ten years studying the actual financial lives of families like Subir and Mumtaz's—Daryl Collins, Jonathan Morduch, Stuart Rutherford, and Orlanda Ruthven tracked the finances of low-income families in Bangladesh, India, and South Africa. One of the things that they found was that low-income families made use of complex financial instruments—informal loans, savings clubs, money guards, and others—to navigate poverty. They also found that those families prioritized flexibility, even over reliability. Subir and Mumtaz illustrated this when they used a semi-formal microloan to pay for basic needs: they used the money in a flexible way instead of tying it up in a single asset.[20]

Other families—and Subir and Mumtaz's family—sought flexibility in another way: taking out informal loans that offered small payments on flexible repayment schedules. Small payments are important. It's easier for a low-income family to pay a small piece of their income frequently than it is for them to save up larger lump sum payments. Microcredit institutions have already recognized this, which is part of the reason that they use repayment plans with small frequent payments. They fit well with low-income cash flows. Informal loans also offer small frequent payments. They also offer flexible payment schedules. Borrowers don't have to pay loans back to friends and neighbors on a fixed schedule, meaning that unexpected expenses can be addressed without defaulting on the loan.[21]

It's important not to confuse the need for flexibility with irresponsibility. Credit cards are flexible. Yes, they need to be paid off, but not all at once or on a set schedule. If I have an unexpected expense that prevents me from paying my entire balance, I can pay a portion of it now and pay off the rest of it later. Low-income families—who have less slack to use to absorb an unexpected expense—make use of informal loans that allow the same kind of flexibility. And they use those loans for much the same reason that I use credit cards: they fit our cash flows better than inflexible financial tools.

Robert is a forty-eight-year-old man who works in IT for a nonprofit organization and makes $11.25 an hour, or about $22,000 a year. That puts him above the official poverty line, but he lives in New York City, so it's not

19. Collins et al., *Portfolios of the Poor*, Kindle locations 537–38, 776–86.
20. Collins et al., *Portfolios of the Poor*, Kindle locations 546–49.
21. Collins et al., *Portfolios of the Poor*, Kindle locations 945–77.

much to get by on. He pays $100 a month to live at his mother's apartment with his mom and five other members of his extended family. He's working hard to save money for his own apartment. Robert estimates that it will take him about $1,600 for his security deposit and first month of rent.[22]

Robert faces an interesting challenge: there are very few tools available to help him save that money. Most savings tools are designed for saving large amounts of money over a long period of time. When we save for retirement, for example, we try to put a good sum of money into a return-bearing account for years or even decades. Robert recognizes the importance of this kind of saving, putting $25 a month into his employer's retirement plan even though he knows that won't get him far. But a savings instrument that takes years to reach a goal isn't useful to him. He wants to save a limited amount of money over a short period of time.[23]

Robert is engaging in what some economists call high frequency saving. He has to make decisions to save every day—skipping the temptations of eating lunch away from his desk or paying to go to a movie—if he wants to reach his goal. In addition, that goal is relatively small, and he hopes to reach it quickly. Once he does reach it, he'll get an apartment, hand his savings over to his new landlord (depleting them), and begin saving for the next expense. This is in contrast to the slow and steady low-frequency saving that people use to fill their retirement account. This is common for low-income people, who often find themselves in a cycle of saving and spending. Sometimes, they're spending because their goals are short-term: a slightly nicer apartment, a slightly better car, and so on. Other times, they're spending because of an unforeseen expense. The absence of slack raises its ugly head again. Savings become a way of managing the day-to-day ups and downs of living in poverty.[24]

Since no formal instruments exist to help Robert save, he uses an informal one: what Jonathan Morduch and Rachel Schneider call the Bank of Mom. He gave his extra money to his mother, who held it for him. She would give him the money if he needed it, providing important flexibility, but would also warn him away from unnecessary withdrawals. Other people who Morduch and Schneider met in their research used similar methods, like the Bank of Far Away. The Bank of Far Away is simply a traditional bank that is a long way away and has inconvenient hours. The added difficulty of making a withdrawal makes it easier to avoid withdrawing the money. Subir

---

22. Morduch and Schneider, *The Financial Diaries*, 87–93.
23. Morduch and Schneider, *The Financial Diaries*, 92.
24. Morduch and Schneider, *The Financial Diaries*, 98–102.

and Mumtaz sometimes stand on the other side of a similar arrangement as money guards, watching over the savings of their friends and neighbors.[25]

The lack of tools for short-term savings isn't the only challenge that low-income families face when looking for financial instruments. Loans can also be difficult to obtain. As we saw above, informal loans are flexible. They're also available to people with little or no formal credit history. While a bank may not be willing to make a loan to someone, a friend or family member (or a payday lender) may be willing to. And, of course, there are plenty of other examples of low-income communities developing tools to fill in gaps in the formal financial sector. Low-income communities are constantly creating innovative tools to meet their financial needs in the absence of formal instruments.

In *Bridges Out of Poverty*—an excellent source for stories like this— Payne provides the reader with a scenario about a woman named Oprah. Oprah is a thirty-two-year-old widow who works as a "domestic" for a doctor, where she takes home about $300 every week. In Payne's scenario, Oprah receives a $400 Christmas bonus. After church one week, three different people approach her privately asking for money: $50 to have the electricity reconnected, $100 for food (for the asker's brother's family), and $60 to repair some glasses. Later, Payne frames this in terms of the hidden rules of poverty. According to Payne, middle-class people emphasize self-sufficiency, but people living in poverty believe that no one will ever get ahead, so extra money should be either shared or spent. She also recognizes that Oprah is part of a system: she needs to share the money with her community now so that can receive money from her community the next time she's in need. Finally, Payne asserts that this is part of poverty culture's understanding of people as possessions. Oprah's friends and neighbors have a claim on her and her money.[26]

There are plenty of assumptions here: that middle-class people prize self-sufficiency, that low-income people understand other people as possessions, and so on. All of these are based in Payne's idea of poverty culture and charity skepticism's broad conception of what poverty is. But once we start to understand the realities of the financial lives of people living in poverty, we can interpret this scenario in a different way: a way that takes the financial realities of poverty seriously.

---

25. Morduch and Schneider, *The Financial Diaries*, 103–4; Collins et al., *Portfolios of the Poor*, Kindle locations 833–36.

26. Payne et al., *Bridges Out of Poverty*, Kindle locations 274–87, 386–91.

The requests for money that people make of Oprah are excellent examples of the absence of slack in the lives of people in her community. All of them are examples of emergent expenses. No one plans on needing the electricity reconnected, or needing to find food for their brother's family, or needing to repair glasses. In the financial reality of poverty, however, there's no way to absorb these unexpected costs. These members of Oprah's community aren't asking for help because they're irresponsible, but because they've encountered an expense they didn't—and maybe even couldn't—plan on. Moreover, they are examples of expenses for which there aren't formal financial tools. These members of Oprah's community may not have the income or credit history necessary to secure a credit card, and no formal financial institution is going to make a loan that small. Informal systems are the only systems that will meet these needs. And, while their requests would take just over half of Oprah's bonus, she is the best resource for an informal system here: someone who has just come into unexpected income.

What Oprah and her acquaintances create through their sharing of resources is a kind of village insurance. As long as each member of the community participates in the system, each member can count on other members to help them out when they run into an unexpected expense. By sharing what she has now, Oprah can participate in a financial tool that helps her mitigate future risk. After all, an additional $400 may not last long anyway; not because no one will ever get ahead, but because it adds very little slack and that slack might be taken away in a moment. Sharing the wealth isn't just giving into social pressure or playing out an aspect of poverty culture. It's a rational economic decision given the financial realities of poverty.

And this, of course, is a key point. It's easy to imagine that people living in poverty have poor money management skills or are financially illiterate. In certain cases, that might even be true. But a closer look at how low-income families manage their money reveals a world of financial savviness, as well as diverse and complex financial instruments tailored to the financial realities of not having enough money. From money guards to informal loans to village insurance and beyond, people living in poverty are continuously developing systems to deal with the absence of slack, the need for flexibility, and the lack of formal financial institutions that meet their needs.

The Moral Price of Poverty

In 2008, Linda Tirado and her husband moved to Cincinnati, Ohio. They didn't have much money, so they rented the cheapest apartment they could find. It was a basement apartment, and when a summer storm came through southeastern Ohio, it flooded. Everything they owned was destroyed either by the flooding itself or by the mold that soon followed. Linda was eight months pregnant at the time, and all she wanted was somewhere to sit down. So, she started calling churches and charities, hoping to find one that would give her a cheap chair.

She reached a nonprofit organization that had a chair to give her . . . for a price: Linda would have to attend a resume writing class. "We need you to be looking for work and trying to better your situation," said the woman on the phone, "we don't just give charity to just anybody." The woman gave Linda two times for the class. Linda told her that she was scheduled to work during both of them. Missing work would certainly mean losing the pay from her low-wage job. It might even mean being fired. The woman on the phone just reiterated the importance of attending the class so that Linda "could find gainful employment." It's easy to see the irony in requiring someone to skip work to attend a resume writing class in order to get a cheap chair. Tirado also sees cruelty. She sees this kind of counterproductive demand as part of a system designed "to humiliate you as much as possible," because "what we need poor people to do in America more than anything else in the world is know their place." That might be a little extreme, but it isn't entirely wrong.[27]

So far, I've been talking about poverty in terms of psychology and finances. Not having enough money has real effects on how we think and how we manage the money we have. But there's also an important moral dimension to poverty. When the woman on the phone told Tirado that she needed "to make sure that . . . [people living in poverty have] some skin in the game," she was making a moral judgement about Tirado. And when charity skeptics say that people living in poverty are dependent, entitled, and feel that the world owes them a living, they are making moral claims about those people. In fact, a substantial part of modern philanthropy has been a project to reform people living in poverty in the name of middle-class morality. That is a project shared by charity skeptics. In this section, I'm going to look at a single example of the moral burden of living in poverty: the 2015 attempt by the state of Kansas to limit welfare withdrawals from ATMs to $25 per day.[28]

In 2008, Larraine Jenkins lived in Milwaukee, Wisconsin. She received $80 a month from the Supplemental Nutrition Assistance Program (SNAP,

27. Goldberg, "A Crowd-Sourced Escape from Poverty?"; Garfield and Gladstone, "'Busted' #5."

28. Garfield and Gladstone, "'Busted' #5."

also known as food stamps), money that was supposed to last her several weeks if not the entire month. She had lost the benefits for a while after missing an appointment with a county worker, but after getting them reinstated, she went to a grocery store and bought a feast: lobster tails, shrimp, crab legs, salad, and pie. She spent her entire monthly allowance on that one meal. You might even think that she represents everything wrong with poverty culture: the desire to throw away benefits that should last a month on a single luxurious meal.[29]

In 2015, and several states away, the Kansas legislature passed a law putting a new limit on people who received cash benefits. Recipients of these benefits were given a debit card, the benefits were deposited into an account each month, and the law limited recipients to withdrawing $25 of those benefits per day. Those benefits were supposed to be used on household necessities, and this law fit in with the tradition of laws in the United States that put restrictions on what low-income families can do with the money they're given. These laws are laws about morality and responsibility. They're intended to keep low-income families from spending their benefits on luxuries (like filet mignon and lobster tails).

This demand for frugality isn't one that legislatures put on everyone who receives benefits. As the *Washington Post*'s Emily Badger points out, we don't drug test farmers who receive agricultural subsidies, require Pell Grant recipients to stick to specific majors, or ask people who receive the mortgage interest deduction to prove that they don't use their home for illicit purposes. Part of the reason for this is that middle- and upper-class families don't always receive direct cash transfers. While most Americans receive some form of government assistance, relatively wealthy people receive those benefits in the form of not paying something: lower tax bills or bigger refunds (the home mortgage interest deduction), payments we don't make to hospitals (Medicare), lower tuition (college assistance programs like the GI Bill), and so on. For many people receiving these benefits, they are all but invisible.[30]

It's also worth noting that the Kansas law didn't serve any purpose other than punishing low-income families. Benefits in Kansas aren't deposited into a checking account, which makes sense since many low-income families cannot meet the minimum balance required to avoid account fees. This means that many families deal primarily in cash. In addition, most ATMs don't stock $5 bills, so the effective daily limit for withdrawals becomes $20

29. Desmond, *Evicted*, 215–18

30. Badger, "The Double-Standard of Making the Poor Prove They're Worthy of Government Benefits"; Thompson, "7 Facts About Government Benefits and Who Gets Them."

a day. And, of course, those same ATMs charge a fee for each withdrawal, meaning that benefit recipients must pay to access their own money. Someone attempting to get $200 in cash for rent would need to make withdrawals over ten days and pay $30 or more in fees. This law would not only prevent recipients from using their money on luxuries, but would require them to pay a hefty fee to use that money on necessities.[31]

Ultimately, the Kansas legislature scrapped this law, but laws that seek to control how low-income families use their benefits are statements about the moral status of those families. When we pass these laws, we are saying that those people cannot be trusted to make decisions for themselves. The same is true when nonprofit organizations set policies demanding that people in need attend a resume writing workshop, or show proof that they are seeking work, or meet some other behavioral requirement. And the same is true when we judge the person buying lobster tail or filet mignon with their SNAP benefits.

Larraine used to be involved with a man named Glen. One night, he came home drunk and high and grabbed a bottle of pills. Glen could fall deep into depression, and Lorraine was worried that he would take the whole bottle. In an attempt to save him, she wrestled the bottle away from him. But he slipped and hit his head on the refrigerator. The paramedics bandaged him up and took him to jail, where he later died of an overdose. The day Larraine had her feast was her and Glen's anniversary. Whatever glares she might have gotten when she slid her EBT card through the machine in the checkout lane were the moral price of her poverty: being judged by people who knew nothing about her situation.[32]

Poverty

Poverty is something that is both very simple and multifaceted. On the one hand, our intuitive definition is a good one. Poverty really does mean something like not having enough money. Even if we want to be more specific and look at poverty from different angles—absolute and relative poverty, income and asset poverty, and so on—those are just different ways of talking about not having enough money. On the other hand, the consequences of not having enough money are diverse. People living in poverty experience real psychological and cognitive consequences, communities in poverty develop financial instruments tailored to their needs, and individuals in

---

31. Ehrenfreund, "Kansas Has Found the Ultimate Way to Punish the Poor."
32. Desmond, *Evicted*, 118–19, 218.

poverty must bear the moral stigma that our society foists on them. A single root grows many branches.

Charity skeptics tend to focus on the multifaceted effects of poverty. To them, poverty is a culture that is characterized by a certain mind-set, specific financial instruments, and a moral stigma. There's a certain logic to that. What is a culture, after all, but a certain way of thinking and a set of institutions? And if poverty is a problem, then it follows that it is a problematic culture, and the solution must be to change that culture. The fault in this logic is that the culture—if we want to call it that—isn't a problem, it's a solution. Specifically, it's a solution to an underlying problem: not having enough money. Simply having more money would change mind-sets, allow access to new financial instruments, and remove the moral stigma. Not in every single case, perhaps. But in many. Charity skeptics are advocating for repairing the branches in order to improve the health of the root. But, as we'll see, it is far more likely that we can fix the branches by cultivating the root. Charity—in the sense of giving people money—might solve a host of problems.

3

Charity

In 2017, I was in downtown Baltimore for the United Church of Christ's General Synod, the denomination's biannual business meeting and celebration. Outside the convention center there were always several panhandlers. There was always someone telling me a story and presenting me with an outstretched hand. Sometimes, I would give them a few dollars. And that bore some similarities to something that happened inside the convention center. In several of the worship services I attended that weekend—it was a church conference, after all—someone stood at the front of the congregation, told us a story, and presented an outstretched hand in the form of an offering basket being passed through the rows. But the similarities were only on the surface. There's a difference between giving a few dollars to a homeless man trying to get something to eat and giving a few dollars to Howard University for a chair in Africana Religious Studies.

We don't often think of the different ways that we give (and receive). There are ways of giving that are deeply interpersonal, like a birthday gift to a spouse or a piece of macaroni art from a child. Other ways of giving are more thoroughly systematic. In Ancient Rome, patronage—a system of giving based on the reciprocal exchange of goods and services between social and economic unequals—permeated society. A military officer might provide goods for the clients who followed him into war; a wealthy man might provide comfort for a client who campaigned for him when he ran for election. But patronage wasn't just a relationship between individuals. A magistrate might give a library to a town in exchange for that town dedicating an inscription describing his generosity. And the emperor was the supreme patron: he provided protection, food, housing, entertainment, and so on to his clients and subjects; in exchange, they gave him gratitude, loyalty, praise, and (ultimately) worship. Patronage wasn't just a thing that happened in ancient Rome. It undergirded the whole social order.

Other forms of giving aren't as thoroughly ingrained in their society, but still reflect it. The word *philanthropy* was first used in its modern sense—the voluntary action of private people for public good—by the founders of London's Foundling Hospital in the mid-eighteenth century. The idea quickly made its way to America. It would take off when the reformational movements of the nineteenth century, like temperance, abolitionism, and sanitation, met the millionaire class that rose after the American Civil War. While originally dependent on the wealth of a few, the early twentieth century saw philanthropy open to the masses as large organizations collected donations and put them to work. While it started in Britain, philanthropy is, perhaps, the most American form of giving: it's based in volunteerism, the concentration of wealth (either in individuals like Andrew Carnegie or Bill Gates, or in organizations like United Way or Feeding America), a reformist spirit, and institutionalization.

Giving is multifaceted. Gifts aren't just transactions, but suggestions about how we should organize our families, friendships, and society. When patrons give, they are (in part) legitimizing their power, privilege, and prestige. When philanthropists give, they are (in part) legitimizing their wealth. When charity skeptics argue that loans and other market-based solutions are better than charity, they're trying to legitimize specific economic systems and delegitimize certain kinds of generosity. This makes it particularly important to be clear about what charity is. After all, charity skeptics aren't arguing against giving in general (grants are okay in some situations) and I'm not arguing for giving in general (though I tend to believe that the more tools we use to address poverty, the better). Instead, they are arguing against—and I am arguing for—a specific kind of giving: charity.

In this chapter, I'm going to define charity by focusing on three major traits. First, charitable giving is rooted in a connection to the divine. Second, it is directed specifically towards people living in poverty. Third, it is emphatically not about reforming the recipient, but transforming the donor. I'm going to look at these traits by telling a story about charity that's grounded in the history of Judaism, Christianity, and Western society. Telling the story of charity through that history makes sense. After all, the word charity itself comes to us from Latin (*caritas*), one of the two Latin words used to translate the Greek word *agape*. Both of these words mean love, and *agape* is an especially important term in Christianity, denoting the kind of love that God has for the world. As we'll see, in Christianity, charitable giving is a reflection of divine love. Etymology isn't an argument, but the practice of charity in the West has a history that traces the same route as the word.

But that doesn't mean that similar forms of giving haven't appeared in other places and other cultures. On the one hand, it is completely possible that charity, or something very much like it, has appeared with a different name and a different history in Australia or Africa or America. On the other hand, it is completely possible that charity is a uniquely Abrahamic form of giving. And while we should notice similar forms of giving, we should be careful to recognize the differences. Hindus worship their gods, but they do not go to church. Sikhs have a holy book—the Guru Granth Sahib—but it is not the Sikh Bible. Other religions and cultures have forms of giving, but that giving may or may not be charity. I am telling a particular story about charity, but we can recognize the similarities and celebrate the differences between this story and others.

The Divine Connection

In the first chapter, I wrote about Julian the Apostate, the last pagan emperor of Rome, and his attempt to import charity into Roman pagan religion. If you were to walk down the streets of an ancient Roman city, before the rise of Christianity, you would see a lot of things paid for by wealthy benefactors: theaters, government buildings, contests, feasts, and cash handouts, for example. But you wouldn't see the kinds of institutions we think of when we use the word *charity*. There were no soup kitchens, food pantries, or homeless shelters. As I wrote above, the dominant form of giving in the Empire was patronage. And providing help to people living in poverty does not make sense under the logic of patronage. Julian's experiment failed. And it failed, at least in part, because it didn't fit the worldview of the pagan priests.

What Julian's story tells us is that charity—even just the idea of giving to people living in poverty—isn't universal. While we don't often think about it, and while it might seem natural to us, charity as we know it has a specific history. It comes from a particular time, place, and culture. The charity that Julian tried to imitate originated in Judaism and spread alongside Christianity. The fact that charity seems so natural to us today is a result of Christianity's history as the dominant religion in the West.

In this section, I'm going to look at charity's connection to the divine. First, I'm going to look at the commands to care for people living in poverty—as well as other marginalized groups—that we find in Judaism and Christianity. Second, I'm going to suggest that these commands weren't understood simply as orders, but as statements about the fundamental nature of the universe. Charity is rooted in a connection to the divine, and that connection is more than a command; it's a moral framework that gives people the space to have charity make sense. This leads to the third piece of this section, where I'll look briefly at whether charity can exist without a moral framework that includes the divine.

"I am the LORD your God," opens the legal code in the book of Exodus, "who brought you out of the land of Egypt, out of the house of slavery; you shall have no other gods before me." This verse establishes God's position as the only god of the Israelites. That authority isn't based on the idea that God is the creator and sustainer of the universe or on God's overwhelming power. Instead, it's rooted in the fact that God liberated the Israelites from slavery in Egypt. It's not just a statement about God's power—although the surrounding verses that show thunder, lightning, smoke, and a trembling mountain make God's power clear—but a statement about God's character. God is merciful towards people who are weak and dispossessed.[1]

Compassion towards people who are poor and marginalized is a theme throughout the Bible. It would take far too much space to catalog every instance of God demanding this compassion in the law, the prophets, the Gospels, the epistles, and the other writings. In the legal code in Exodus alone, the Israelites are commanded not to oppress traditionally marginalized groups like resident foreigners, widows, and orphans; not to lend to fellow Israelites with interest; to return items taken as collateral when the borrower needs them; to make sure that people living in poverty receive justice; and to let their fields lie fallow every seven years so that the poor can eat what grows on its own. Similar codes in Leviticus and Deuteronomy command them not to harvest to the edges of their fields, but to leave food for the poor; to pay wages in a timely manner; and, as I mentioned in the first chapter, store a portion of their first fruits in their towns every third year for groups who were traditionally left on the margins of society. There is simply no getting away from God's commands to care for people living in poverty.[2]

Obviously, these commands to care for people living in poverty—as well as similar commands and teachings in other parts of the Bible—are nestled in among other commands. But they are also a central part of how Judaism and Christianity have traditionally understood themselves. By the time Jesus preached, for example, in the Galilean countryside, the word

---

1. Exod 20:2.
2. Exod 22:21–27; 23:6; 23:10–11; Lev 19:9–10; Deut 24:17–21; 24:24–25; 14:22–29.

mitzvah—which means commandment—had taken on an additional meaning: a generous act. Similarly, a bar mitzvah—a person obligated to obey the law—had come to mean a generous person. Anderson cites the Tosefta (a supplement to the Mishnah, a collection of Jewish oral traditions compiled in the third century) as saying: "Giving alms is equal to keeping all the commandments of the Torah."[3]

And this wasn't the case only in biblical times. In the middle ages, the Jewish scholar Nachmanides said that he didn't need to give specific references to caring for the poor in earlier rabbinic writings because there was a wealth of examples to choose from. Much later, Jim Wallis, the founder and editor of *Sojourners* magazine, would sit down with a seminary classmate and cut all references to the poor out of the Bible. The result was a Bible that "was falling apart in my hands. It was a Bible full of holes." With that, we've come full circle: The Bible is full of commands to give to people living in poverty, so the religions that the Bible is a part of are deeply sensitive to the needs of people living in poverty, and those religions, in turn, are drawn to the sources that emphasize the need to care for the poor.[4]

I'll write more about the theology of charity in the next chapter. For now, the important point is that Judaism and Christianity both recognize that charity isn't simply a nice thing to do, but a command from God. And it's not just a command from God, but a command that sits at the center of what God wants for humanity. Charity is, as it were, the whole of the law.

It's easy to think that God's commands are at least a little arbitrary. We might think of some of them, like the commands against murder and theft, as examples of natural morality or common sense. We might think of others, like the command to not make graven images, as cultural practices restricted to Judaism. We might think of still others as undergirded by deeper truths revealed by modern science, as when people interpret the command not to eat pork as a warning against trichinosis. We could imagine charity as a reflection of a universal impulse to care for people who are living in poverty even while modern sensibilities have superseded that particular way of giving. This seems to be what many charity skeptics are doing when they advocate for helping people living in poverty without simply giving money to them.

But there's another way of understanding these commands. In his book *Charity*, Gary Anderson tells a story about his wife and her swim class. Anderson's wife taught a swimming class that included some adults who

3. Anderson, *Charity*, 16–17.
4. Anderson, *Charity*, 16; Kuhn, "The Gospel According to Jim Wallis."

had survived near-drowning experiences and were incredibly scared of the water. One of the things that all swimming classes learn at some point is that you will float easily if you relax. Of course, these students were too scared to relax. Instead, they tensed up, and that made floating impossible. When Anderson's wife told her class to relax and float, she wasn't giving an arbitrary command. She was telling them something about the nature of their bodies and the water. Similarly, we could understand God's commands to be generous—specifically towards the poor and marginalized—as statements about the nature of the cosmos that God has created.[5]

If we think of charity this way, we can see an even deeper connection between charitable giving and the divine. Remember that God opens the legal code in Exodus with a statement about bringing the Israelites out of slavery in Egypt. Compassion for the poor and marginalized is a fundamental aspect of God's character, and God shows that character through acts of divine generosity: the creation of the universe, delivering the Israelites from slavery, entering the human word through the incarnation in Jesus, and so on. We can easily imagine that God molded a cosmic order that reflects the generosity of its creator. If that is the case, our own charitable acts are both ways of going with the flow of the cosmic order and reflections of divine generosity. Charity becomes a sacramental act, connecting the charitable person to God.[6]

We shouldn't be surprised that early Christians understood charity in these terms. For these Christians, communion and charity were inseparably linked. On the one hand, communion was a clear manifestation of God's mercy. By the second century, Christians understood that the bread and wine of the Eucharist were literally the body and blood of Jesus Christ and an instrument of conferring God's grace to the person who ate and drank them, a position still taken by Catholic and Orthodox Christians today. On the other hand, when Christians gave to people in poverty, they were giving directly to Christ himself. As Jesus said, "just as you did it to one of the least of these . . . you did it to me." By giving money to people living in poverty, Christians participated in a similar merciful act and completed the circle of generosity. A portion of the grace extended by God to the sinner is returned to God through the gifts that the communicant gives to the person in need.[7]

This adds an important layer to the connection between charity and God. Charity is not simply a command. It is an expression of the moral order of the universe, a way of matching the rhythms of the cosmos, a way

5. Anderson, *Charity*, 108–9.

6. Anderson, *Charity*, 7–8.

7. Anderson, *Charity*, 8; Matt 25:40.

of encountering and communing with God, and a way of participating in a divine economy of grace. Again, I'll write more about the theology of charity in the next chapter. For now, my point is more historical: Judaism and Christianity have traditionally understood charity not just as a way of obeying God, but as a way of connecting with God.

It's important to recognize just how utterly weird this understanding of the world was and is. Ancient Roman paganism, for example, didn't have the same moral framework. On the one hand, patronage—the dominant form of giving in their society—was based on an entirely different set of ideas. It was rooted in a clear social and economic hierarchy, an ethic of reciprocal exchange, and a deep concern about the worthiness of the person receiving gifts. A patron would give something to a client, but he expected to be paid back in some way. This means that there wasn't much sense in giving to someone who lived in chronic poverty; he would have nothing of value to give in return. On the other hand, there was no divine mandate to help people living in poverty. The Roman gods were concerned with sacrifices, purity, decorum, and ritual, but not with serving the least of these. Together, this meant that the idea of meeting the divine through giving to the poor was nonsensical.[8]

This understanding of the world is also strange to modern sensibilities. A major difference between our modern society and premodern ones is our tendency to see the world in naturalistic terms: a world where there are no gods, no transcendent moral laws, and no ultimate meaning. Ideas like moral facts or moral obligations don't really fit into that kind of universe. Thanks to the historical legacy of Christianity, many of us have a preference for and a commitment to caring for the poor and marginalized. But in a naturalistic world, it's hard to justify that as anything more than a preference for one option among many. While we can't decide whether to obey the laws or gravity or thermodynamics, we can choose whether to be charitable. And an important question is whether we can maintain commitments to things like benevolence, human rights, and equality in the face of competing ideals. As I implied in the first chapter, charity skepticism may be an example of this. It might be too hard to maintain a commitment to charity—or even generosity in general—when it exists alongside powerful forces like capitalism.[9]

8. Anderson, *Charity*, 17; Stark, *The Triumph of Christianity*, 118–20.

9. For an excellent discussion of benevolence, human rights, and naturalism, see Smith, "Does Naturalism Warrant a Moral Belief in Universal Benevolence and Human Rights?"

Charity, then, is more than the act of giving to people who are living in poverty. It's an expression of a certain way of understanding the world. It is, as it were, a way of lying back and floating on the waters of a generous cosmic order. Historically—in the West, at least—that has meant a deep connection between charity and the divine.

Loving the Poor

My family has a line in our budget for giving. A lot of that line goes to the places that my wife and I work. Some of it goes to other organizations like our alma maters. Some of it goes to people who ask, like the folks outside the Baltimore Convention Center with stories and outstretched hands. The United States government supports some of this giving. If we itemized our taxes, we could deduct the gifts to our workplaces, our alma maters, and other organizations. The government sees these gifts as charitable. The Internal Revenue Code has a definition of that word, which includes not only help for people living in poverty, but the advancement of religion, education, and science; maintaining public monuments; fighting prejudice and discrimination; and defining human rights.[10]

On the one hand, this is a very broad definition of charity. In the last section, I talked about helping the poor and marginalized as though that's the first thing that leaps to our minds when we think of charity. And it probably is. All of us would think of gifts to food pantries, homeless shelters, and other places that help people living in poverty as charitable. Similarly, we might think of gifts to groups that address racism, human trafficking, animal abuse, and other social justice issues as charitable. But other organizations don't fit into our intuitive understanding of charity. Symphonies, museums, and universities are all wonderful institutions, but very few are truly charitable.

On the other hand, it's an incredibly narrow definition of charity. The government is only concerned with donations to organizations, and gifts to individuals simply don't count. This is an effect of the institutionalization that's a trait of philanthropy. The sense of philanthropy is that money shouldn't be given haphazardly, person to person, but invested in professionally managed organizations that can reform both individuals and society. A gift to Harvard counts. A gift to a panhandler—no matter how much it might help him—does not. In fact, technically, that panhandler should claim any money that he collects as income on his own taxes!

10. Internal Revenue Service, "Exempt Purposes—Internal Revenue Code Section 501(c)(3)."

Our intuitive understanding of charity is that it helps people who are living in poverty—people who don't have enough money—whether that help is given through organizations or person-to-person. The Internal Revenue Code understands charity both more broadly and more narrowly. It sees charity as functioning only through organizations. And it sees charity as being used for any number of purposes, from housing someone who's homeless to providing a scholarship to an Ivy League school to the son of a president.

Of course, the IRS isn't trying to develop a precise definition of charity that differentiates it from other forms of giving. I'm only using it to illustrate that our intuitive understanding of charity focuses on gifts to people who are living in poverty or, if we choose to expand it, on those who are otherwise marginalized. And that intuitive understanding is rooted in the historical sources of charity—Judaism and Christianity—which recognize that charitable gifts are directed specifically towards people in poverty. In this section, I'm going to look at that purpose. First, I'm going to take a short detour back to our definition of poverty and expand it just a little. Second, I'm going to look briefly at what many theologians and biblical scholars call God's preferential option for the poor: the unrelenting focus on providing for people living in poverty. Finally, I'm going to look at a particularly important aspect of that preferential option for the poor: the idea that people living in poverty have a right to the gifts they receive through charity.

Before I talk about charity and poverty, I need to take a short detour back to the intuitive definition of poverty that I explored in the last chapter: poverty means something like not having enough money. That's a good definition, but we shouldn't be too narrowly pedantic about it. The Bible—and Jewish and Christian communities—often takes a broader view of what it means to be poor. For example, in the Gospel of Matthew, Jesus tells a parable about the Son of Man coming to judge the nations. The nations are gathered before him, and he separates them into two groups. He tells one group that they will inherit a kingdom that God has prepared for them because they fed him when he was hungry, gave him something to drink when he was thirsty, welcomed him when he was a stranger, gave him clothing when he was naked, cared for him when he was sick, and visited him when he was in prison. He then tells the other group that they are being sent into eternal fire for failing to do the same things. Similarly, when the prophet Isaiah talks about fasting, he tells his audience that God would prefer it if people would share their food with the hungry, house the homeless, clothe the naked, and free the oppressed.[11]

The word *poor* isn't in these lists, but the idea lurks in the background. Some of these groups obviously have a close relationship with poverty. When hunger, thirst, homelessness, and nakedness is a major part of someone's lived reality, she is poor. For others, the relationship is less obvious. Someone who is a stranger, or sick, or imprisoned, or oppressed isn't necessarily poor even if she is cut off from her community and struggling to meet her basic human needs. But we also shouldn't dismiss the relationship between these problems and poverty. Isolation, illness, imprisonment, and oppression are all worse when someone also doesn't have enough money. Not having enough money can still be at the center of our definition of poverty even as we recognize that poverty can be expressed in more robust ways.

A short look at language in the Bible might be useful in helping us understand this. In Hebrew, there are multiple words for poor. Two especially important ones are *'any* and *'evyon*, and *'any* is the word that's usually used in the Hebrew Bible. In Greek, there are also multiple words for poor. Again, two fairly common ones are: *penēs* and *ptōchos*. *Penēs* means something like working poor: a person who has to do manual labor, doesn't have much leisure time, and so on. *Ptōchos* means something more like destitute: someone who is reduced to begging because he has no resources. When people translated the Hebrew Bible into Greek in the third century before Christ, they translated both *'any* and *'evyon* to *ptōchos*. The biblical poor—regardless of their particular circumstances—became the destitute.[12]

That point about Hebrew and Greek is important for a few reasons, but the biggest one right now is that people who are *ptōchos* really have to rely on others. And while it makes sense to put people who are desperately poor at the center of that group, we can also think of that in other ways. Someone can be alone in a foreign country where they have to depend on other people, someone can be so sick that they depend on other people to care for them, and so on. Not having enough money is the archetype of poverty—the example that forms the core of the definition—even if poverty can be understood a little more broadly.

In the last section, I wrote about the connection between God and charity in Judaism and Christianity. In the Bible, this connection often takes one of two forms: command and judgement. The command to be generous is what we see in the legal codes in Exodus, Leviticus, and Deuteronomy. God

---

11. Matt 24:31–46; Isa 58:6–7.
12. Rhee, *Loving the Poor, Saving the Rich*, Kindle locations 1172–88.

commands the Israelites to share what they have with people who are living in poverty. The judgements against people who have failed to be generous are what we see in the psalms and the prophets. Amos, for example, has a message specifically about what will happen to those who oppress the poor and hurt the needy. These commands and judgements are so common that some theologians recognize a preferential option for the poor in the Bible: a tendency for God to prioritize the well-being of the poor and powerless.[13]

In the first chapter, I gave one example of this emphasis on the poor and marginalized. In Deuteronomy, the Israelites are commanded to pay a tithe from their first fruits on a seven-year cycle. In the first, second, fourth, and fifth years, they take their tithe to the temple in Jerusalem. In the third and sixth years, though, they keep the tithe in their towns, "giving it to the Levites, the aliens, the orphans, and the widows, so that they may eat their fill within your towns." That list is important. Levites (a tribe that had certain religious and political responsibilities, including the priesthood), foreigners, orphans, and widows were groups that had no, little, or limited access to land. They couldn't grow or raise their own food, so they relied on support from their neighbors.[14]

For example, in the book of Ruth, Naomi is an Israelite who moves with her husband and sons to the land of Moab. Her sons marry Moabite women, Ruth and Orpah. Over time, Naomi's husband and her two sons die. While Orpah stays behind in Moab, Naomi and Ruth return to Israel, setting up the story. What's significant for us is how Naomi and Ruth survive. As women who are not connected to a man—they are both widows—they can't own land. Instead, they have to glean. That is, they can rely on God's command not to harvest to the edge of a field and to leave whatever isn't harvested behind for aliens, orphans, and widows. In effect, Naomi and Ruth can pick up what farmers leave behind. This is the core of the list we see in Deuteronomy and elsewhere: Levites, foreigners, orphans, and widows are excluded from normal economic life and must rely on others. Of course, these aren't the only people in that position. I've already talked about the lists that Isaiah and Jesus provide: the oppressed, the hungry, the homeless, the stranger, the sick, and so on. What all of these groups have in common is that they can't meet their most basic needs on their own.[15]

This focus on people living in poverty continued in early Christian communities. Early preachers were obsessed with the importance of giving specifically to the poor. For example, the fourth-century Greek bishop Basil

13. Amos 4:1–5.
14. Deut 25:1–15.
15. Ruth 2:2–3; Deut 24:19–20; Lev 19:9–10; 23:22; Isa 58:6–7; Matt 25:31–46.

of Caesarea is well known for his sermons on social justice and his emphasis on a distributive mandate: the idea that anyone who has extra also has a responsibility to restore the balance of things by sharing with those who do not have enough. In one of his most famous sermons, he even implies that the extra belongs to the people who are living without. The bread we hold back, the clothes we have in storage, the shoes that are rotting away, and the money that we are saving are for the hungry, the naked, the unshod, and the poor.[16]

Similarly, early Christian communities put an emphasis on alleviating suffering. Sociologist Rodney Stark provides a powerful example of this emphasis in the Christian reaction to the Antonine Plague. In the mid-second century—and again a hundred years later—a terrible epidemic ravaged the Roman Empire, killing a quarter to a third of the population. No one knew how to cure it, but they did know that it was contagious. Roman pagans avoided contact with the sick. And the Roman elite—including the famous physician Galen—left the crowded cities for the countryside, where they hoped to wait out the plague in safety. Christians, however, risked their own lives providing care for their neighbors. And while many Christians contracted and died from the disease, they also saved lives in a situation where even elementary nursing could help a patient survive long enough to get better on their own.[17]

Treating the sick during a plague isn't necessarily the same as helping people living in poverty in a narrow sense. Certainly, many of the people suffering from the plague would have been poor. Others might not have been. But if we draw on a broader understanding of poverty—if we draw on the idea of someone not being able to meet her own basic needs—then we can see that the impulse to care for the sick comes from the same place: a desire to care specifically for the poor and marginalized.

Of course, it seems obvious to us that we should care for people who are poor, whether in the narrow sense of not having enough money or in the broad sense of not being able to meet their own basic needs. To us, the preferential option for the poor might look like a specific application of a universal impulse to altruism. But it's important to recognize that this isn't a universal idea. As I've already written, for example, ancient Romans didn't see any particular point in helping people living in poverty or helping people suffering from disease. Similarly, modern philanthropy recognizes the value of helping people who are struggling with meeting their own basic needs, but also places that as one cause among many. A person can be a philanthropist towards museums, operas, Ivy League schools, and hundreds

16. St. Basil, *On Social Justice*, Kindle locations 308–15, 1175–77.

17. Stark, *The Triumph of Christianity*, 114–20.

of other institutions, all while leaving the poor on their own. It is charity that puts God's preferential option for the poor at its center.

The biblical mandate to care for people in need doesn't distinguish between the deserving and the undeserving poor. When Ruth goes to glean from the field, no one makes sure that she's tried to find a legitimate job. Jesus and Isaiah don't suggest that the hungry or homeless need to prove anything before someone gives food or housing to them. God's preferential option for the poor has one, and only one, criterion: need.

Really, though, it goes further than that. Charity skeptics often complain that low-income people have an unearned sense of entitlement. As Ruby Payne puts it, these families—and especially families who experience generational poverty—feel that society owes them a living. Payne and other charity skeptics see this as a problem. For centuries, Jews and Christians understood it as a fact. They believed people living in poverty (or any other kind of need) really were entitled to help from others.[18]

Ruth, for example, really was entitled to the grain she collected from the field; it belonged to her. The eleventh-century French rabbi Rashi interprets the command that Ruth was relying on quite literally. The command tells the Israelites, "you shall not reap to the very edges of your field . . . you shall leave them for the poor and for the alien." Rashi interpreted this to mean that the owner of a field couldn't even help someone who came to glean, because doing so would imply that the owner of the field also owned what the person was collecting and was giving it to them. Instead, Rashi understood that the collector was simply gathering what was already hers. Ruth owned the grain she was collecting.[19]

Basil of Caesarea takes a similar view. In one sermon, Basil anticipates his audience's reaction to being told to share what they have with people who live in poverty: "Whom do I treat unjustly," he asks for them, "by keeping what is my own?" He goes on to tell his audience that everything that they have has been entrusted to them by God so that they can give it to people in need. According to Basil, when people keep more than they need, they are no better than thieves and robbers. This is context for the passage I referred to earlier: the bread we hold back, the clothes we have in storage, the shoes we have that are rotting away, and the money we keep safely in banks literally belong to the people who need it. Failing to give to people living in poverty is no different from stealing from them.[20]

---

18. Payne et al., *Bridges Out of Poverty*, Kindle locations 699–700.

19. Lev 23:22; Rashi, "Rashi on Leviticus 23:22"; *Mishnah Peah* 5:6

20. St. Basil, *On Social Justice*, Kindle locations 1161–78.

An entitlement is simply something that someone has a right to. In the United States, we have government programs that are entitlements: Social Security (you pay into it during your working life, so you have a right to the payout when you need it), for example, or Medicaid (we've agreed as a society that low-income families should have access to necessary medical care). Rashi and Basil didn't know about those programs, of course, but they carried the idea of entitlement further. For them, people living in poverty really are entitled to a living. The excess that others have belongs to the poor. They have a right to it.

Again, I need to point to how weird this idea is. I've already talked a bit about ancient Roman patronage and its lack of concern for people living in poverty. Ancient Roman society didn't focus on the poor for a couple of reasons. First, the ethic of reciprocity was ubiquitous in Roman society. And that meant that giving to the poor, whether the working poor or the destitute—people who, by definition, could never repay the gift—was nonsensical. The poor could benefit from patronage, entire cities or provinces might receive gifts from a powerful benefactor, but they were never the focus of patronage. Second, the Roman elite looked down on the poor. In literature, they might romanticize the rural poor, like the thrifty and industrious farmer. In practice, the actual poor were largely ignored, and poverty was seen as a problem of moral degeneracy.[21]

Modern philanthropy takes a different approach. While some philanthropists focus on helping people living in poverty, philanthropy is historically grounded in a reformist spirit. In the eighteenth century, this meant that early British philanthropists saw the creation of London's Foundling Hospital as an opportunity to save abandoned children and to create "useful hands" and "good and faithful servants" of the British Empire. When philanthropy came to America, no less a figure than Benjamin Franklin wanted to use it to end poverty: something as simple as teaching a poor man to use a razor could begin his journey out of poverty. During the late nineteenth century and into the twentieth, philanthropy took on an effort to reform both individuals and societies. Scientific philanthropy believed that it could provide immediate assistance, promote moral reform, and reimagine entire social systems to do everything from eliminate poverty to end war. Helping people in poverty was one philanthropic cause, but philanthropy has never just been about helping people in poverty. It's also about transforming them.[22]

21. Rhee, *Loving the Poor, Saving the Rich*, Kindle locations 946–1026.
22. Gross, "Giving in America," 37, 39; Sealander, "Curing Evils at Their Source,"

Both patronage and philanthropy—and countless other forms of giving—can include giving to people who live in poverty. Two things make charity distinct in this regard. First, an unrelenting focus on the poor, whether we mean that in the narrow sense of people who don't have enough money or a broader sense of people who can't meet some basic human need. Second, a belief that people living in poverty have a right to what they are given. Charity doesn't expect the person who receives a gift to repay it in some way (like patronage) or to change in some way as a result of receiving the gift (like philanthropy). Charity simply gives the recipient what is theirs.

Saving the Rich

In *Charity*, Anderson asks us to consider something like the following scenario. A distant relative passes away and leaves you a huge sum of money. Suddenly, you have a fortune. Your first impulse, like any newly minted millionaire, is to spend it. But you push that impulse down and start thinking about how you can invest that money in a way that will provide for your future. You consult with two advisors. One is a wealth management professional, who develops an investment plan that will let you live in comfort for the rest of your life. The other is a saint, who tells you to give your money to people who need it more than you do and ride the waves of generosity that propel the world forward. Both the professional and the saint are telling you to act in your own self-interest. But each is telling you to do that in a very different way.[23]

For my purposes here, that saint is Basil of Caesarea, who we met in the last section. Like many Jews and early Christians, Basil had an economic metaphor for charity: giving a gift to someone in poverty was like making a loan to God. In one sermon, he tells the wealthy people in his audience that a gift to a poor person is also a loan. It's a gift because the giver doesn't expect to see it returned. It's a loan because God—"the supreme repayer of debts"—will repay on behalf of the person who received the gift. In another sermon, he tells the poor people in his audience the same thing. "Lend, you who lack," he says, "to the rich God. Have faith in the one who always personally undertakes the cause of the oppressed, and makes recompense from his own resources." He even goes so far as to tell his listeners that even if they asked for their loan to be returned while they were at sea, they would receive principal and generous interest "in the very middle of the ocean."[24]

227–28.

23. Anderson, *Charity*, 4.

24. St. Basil, *On Social Justice*, Kindle locations 1623–36, 1376–93.

The loan metaphor is a common one, and is even found in Scripture. Proverbs, for example, says that "whoever is kind to the poor lends to the Lord, and will be repaid in full." This is just an example, though, of an idea I think of as charitable self-interest: the idea—proposed by the saint in the scenario above—that charitable giving somehow protects the giver. The loan to God, made by giving to the poor, funds a heavenly treasury that the giver can draw on in times of trouble.[25]

I have to be careful here. This idea that a charitable gift to someone in poverty is also a loan to God that will be repaid generously sounds a lot like prosperity theology, which teaches that if you give your money freely—usually to one televangelist or another—and make "positive confessions" about the things you want in life you can have great material wealth. Want a new BMW? Give to the church and ask God in faith! But Basil and other early Christian preachers and theologians are being subtler. They aren't suggesting the generosity will lead to material wealth. Instead, they're saying two important things. First, that in a generous society, no one would be in need (I'll come back to that in a couple of chapters). Second, that people can secure their salvation by being generous towards the poor.[26]

As I wrote above, charity isn't concerned with the character of the person who receives it. Its only criterion is need. But charity is concerned with the character of the donor. Remember what I said earlier about Judaism and Christianity believing that divine generosity is part of God's character, and about those religions seeing that generosity reflected in the cosmic order. Charitable giving is a transformative act that brings the donor more in line with that divine generosity. It changes the donor.

In this section, I'm going to explore that idea. First, I'm going to look at the extreme version of charitable self-interest embraced by the earliest Christians. This version saw wealth itself as a threat to people's souls and advocated for believers to give up their possessions and give whatever they could to the poor. Second, I'll look at the softer version of charitable self-interest that developed as the Christian community grew to include more wealthy members. This version saw wealth as a tool, and charitable giving as a discipline that could reform the soul of the donor. Finally, I'll look at charity as a way for donors to build up a good habit; to move from being a person who gives charitable gifts to being a charitable person.

Modern Protestant Christians like me are usually uncomfortable with the idea that anything we do might affect our salvation. We tend to agree

---

25. Prov 19:17.
26. St. Basil, *On Social Justice*, Kindle locations 1164–66, 1442–53.

with the author of Ephesians, who writes that we are saved by grace through faith, and that our salvation "is the gift of God, not the result of works, so that no one may boast." Early Christians, though, had a different view. They saw wealth as inherently dangerous, and radical—even reckless—almsgiving as a way for the rich to secure their salvation in the face of their wealth. Redemptive almsgiving was a major theme for early Christian theologians and preachers.[27]

To get this, we need to start with a tradition that Christianity inherited from the Hebrew prophets and Jewish apocrypha (remembering that the earliest Christians were themselves Jewish): what historian Helen Rhee calls the idea of "the pious poor and wicked rich." We can see this tradition in the parable of Lazarus and the Rich Man. In this parable, the rich man is, unsurprisingly, wealthy and powerful. Lazarus, meanwhile, sits at the rich man's gate and is so hungry that he longs for crumbs from the rich man's table. When they die, Lazarus is carried off to heaven to be with Abraham while the rich man goes to Hades to be tormented. When the rich man begs for Lazarus to bring him some water, Abraham tells him why he's in his current situation: "Child, remember that during your lifetime you received your good things, and Lazarus in like manner evil things; but now he is comforted here, and you are in agony." The moral of the story couldn't be put in starker terms: wealth in this world means torment in the next; poverty in this world means comfort in the next.[28]

For the earliest Christians, wealth was a problem to be solved, and the solution was for the wealthy to sell what they had and give the money to the poor. In Matthew, for example, a man asks Jesus what he must do to be saved. When Jesus tells him to keep the commandments, the man replies that he has done that and asks what else he should do. Jesus tells him to sell what he has, give the money to the poor, and follow him. When the man walks away dejected—because he has many possessions—Jesus turns to the disciples and says, "It is easier for a camel to go through the eye of a needle than for someone who is rich to enter the kingdom of God." Again, the moral of the story is clear: the way for the wealthy to find comfort in the next world is to give up their wealth in this one. And, Peter implies in the same story, this is exactly what the disciples have done.[29]

This is the extreme version of charitable self-interest. Material wealth is dangerous; it imperils the soul of the person who has it. But the wealthy person can overcome that danger by giving their wealth away. While doing

---

27. Eph 2:8–9; Rhee, *Loving the Poor, Saving the Rich*, Kindle locations 2071–72.

28. Rhee, *Loving the Poor, Saving the Rich*, Kindle location 519; Luke 16:19–31.

29. Matt 19:16–27.

that might help the person who receives it—a person who can now get food, drink, shelter, or whatever—early Christians believed that it definitely helped the person who gave it away. By giving up his material wealth, the donor could receive something far more valuable: eternal life.

It's easy to see why this message might become less appealing as the Christian community grew to include more people who were themselves rich and powerful, and who didn't want to give up everything they had. After all, how many people are going to join a movement if the price for entry is destitution? In order to accommodate this part of the early church, theologians like Clement of Alexandria—who taught in the late second and early third centuries—had to make some adjustments. I don't mean anything as cynical as the idea that these theologians changed their message for the sake of the wealthy. But they did soften the dichotomy between the wicked rich and the righteous poor, while maintaining the kernel of charitable self-interest.

First, they internalized wealth and poverty, making these words statements about the spiritual health of believers. Someone could be materially wealthy and use those riches in faithful service to God. Similarly, someone could be materially poor and lead a life of sin. For example, in his homily on the man who asked Jesus what he had to do to be saved, Clement suggested that Jesus' command to sell everything wasn't a call to material poverty, but to giving up the "alien possessions" in his soul. Clement believed that someone could be rich and still be saved.[30]

Second, they focused on how someone should use the wealth they had. Someone could be rich and still be saved . . . as long as they used their wealth in Godly ways. Clement, like many early Christians, believed that cultivating virtue was an ongoing project for believers. Being saved was a beginning; believers had to work to overcome their passions and desires, to build up their purity and self-control, and to attain a sort of passionless state of imitating God. Almsgiving was one way to cultivate virtue. By giving freely to the poor—especially the Christian poor—the rich person demonstrated both detachment from his wealth and concrete love for his neighbor (who, being poor, also embodied Christ). Clement even proposed that wealthy Christians should have trainers who would hold them accountable for their giving![31]

It's worth noting that this echoes some ideas found in Greek and Roman culture—ideas that informed patronage as a form of giving—and that

30. Clement of Alexandria, "Who is the Rich Man That Shall Be Saved?," XIX.

31. Rhee, *Loving the Poor, Saving the Rich*, Kindle locations 2124–32, 2195–97, 2207–12.

Clement was a convert. While Greeks and Romans generally didn't care about the poor, they were very concerned with the ethics of wealth. There were several different viewpoints, but there was also a general idea that wealth should be used to cultivate virtue. In a way, Clement imported some of these ideas into Christian charity. And, of course, the internalization of wealth and poverty shows up in charity skepticism as well. We've already seen how Corbett, Fikkert, Lupton, and Payne internalize wealth and poverty through ideas like poverty of stewardship and poverty culture; and how charity skeptics prioritize change within a person over changes in financial circumstances.

But Clement was doing more than restating pagan ideas about wealth and virtue. He was building on the same tradition of building up a heavenly treasury that I mentioned earlier. Clement's economic metaphor in his homily is more direct—"One purchases immortality for money," he says, "and, by giving the perishing things of the world, receives in exchange for these an eternal mansion in the heavens!"—but based on the same general idea: when someone gives in this world, they will receive more in the next. This is a softer version of charitable self-interest.[32]

Again, I have to be careful here. It would be easy to read this as a crass appeal to selfishness: give now so that you can be rich later! But there's something deeper going on here. It might help us see the deeper angle if we fast forward a millennium and a half to the work of the French thinker Blaise Pascal. You might be familiar with Pascal's wager, where he presents us with a bet that we have to make. Either we bet that God is real or we bet that God is not. On the one hand, if we bet that God is real and God is, then we gain everything; if God isn't real, we lose nothing (or very little). On the other hand, if we bet that God is not real and God is, we lose everything; if God isn't, we lose nothing. As Pascal presents it, the best move is to believe in God. If we're right, we win big. If we're wrong, it's no big deal.[33]

But there's another part to this argument that often gets overlooked. Pascal tells the person who doesn't believe, but who wants to, to imitate believers. He implores the reader to take holy water, have masses said, and so on, saying, "even this will naturally make you believe." At worst, he writes, "you will be faithful, honest, humble, grateful, generous, a sincere friend, truthful." In other words, fake it 'til you make it; and even if you never make it, you'll be better off for the effort.[34]

---

32. Clement of Alexandria, "Who is the Rich Man That Shall Be Saved?" XXXII.

33. Pascal, *Pensées* (*Thoughts*), 41.

34. Pascal, *Pensées* (*Thoughts*), 42.

Charitable self-interest isn't about a simple exchange: the gift to a person living in poverty now for a mansion in the world to come. It's about a transformative experience for the donor. And, of course, that experience doesn't come from a single gift, but from a habit of generosity. At first, that generosity might be forced—the giver might have to think about each gift and talk herself into giving it—but, over time, it becomes second nature. As the habit is built up, it transforms the person who gives charitably into a charitable person.

While we might not have the same end goal that Clement had in mind—most of us probably aren't hoping for an existence of dispassionately contemplating God—there is certainly something about cultivating virtue or building character here. And, again, this makes charity distinct: it isn't necessarily about a person who is already generous following their natural inclination, but about a person who wants to become generous—or, if they're already generous, even more generous—in imitation of divine generosity. Charity is not concerned about the worthiness of the person who receives it. Instead, it is a practice that helps the person who gives it become worthy.

Charity

Sometime in the middle of the fourth century, according to legend, a young Roman soldier and catechumen—someone who is studying for baptism but who hasn't yet been baptized—named Martin was approaching the city of Amiens in what is now northern France, a little more than seventy miles north of Paris. It was an unusually cold winter. At the gates to the city, Martin met a scantily clad beggar. The beggar had been asking everyone who passed by for help, but no one gave him anything. Martin, however, was moved. He took his cloak, cut it in half, and gave half of it to the beggar. That night, Martin saw Jesus in a dream. Jesus was wearing the part of the cloak he had given to the beggar and bragging to the angels, "Martin, who is still but a catechumen, clothed me with this robe." Martin went to be baptized as quickly as he could. He became a monk, then a bishop, and eventually a saint.[35]

This is an archetypical example of charity. First, when Martin sees the beggar, he doesn't evaluate the man. Martin doesn't ask whether the beggar will be responsible with his cloak, whether he is playing the part of a beggar in hopes of playing on the compassion of others, or anything else. He responds to the need he sees by meeting it. Second, when Martin gives

35. Severus, "On the Life of St. Martin," chapter III.

the beggar part of his cloak, he is literally giving to Jesus. Third, the experience of giving was transformative for Martin. He was already considering baptism. He had also developed a habit of giving; his biographer notes that he gave part of his cloak because he had already given away his other clothes under similar circumstances. And his experience of his connection to the divine led to his baptism.[36]

These three traits—the divine connection, the focus on the poor without concern for their worthiness, and the transformation of the donor—make charity distinct from other forms of giving like patronage and philanthropy. I looked at these briefly at the beginning of this chapter and I've occasionally returned to them to contrast charity with them. But there are many forms of giving, from philanthropic gifts to museums to chocolates given on Valentine's Day. Different gifts mean different things, reinforce different social arrangements, and imagine the world in different ways. And just as not every box of chocolate is a Valentine's Day gift, not every gift—even if it's aimed at helping people who live in poverty—is an act of charity.

One final note. This might make it sound like charity is purely interpersonal, but we shouldn't overlook the larger social ramifications that even Martin's single act of charity had. In the middle ages, his cloak—the *cappa Sancti Martini*—became a relic that was carried into battle. The priests who carried the cloak were called *capellanu*, which became the word *chaplain* in English. The small temporary churches where it was kept were called *capella*, which became *chapel*. Martin's simple act of generosity echoes through the church. I'll return to the social power of charity in chapter six. For now, I just want to note that our interpersonal acts ripple through society.

---

36. Severus, "On the Life of St. Martin," chapter III.

4

The Heart of Christianity

The first time I encountered charity skepticism was when my parents sent me a copy of Robert Lupton's *Toxic Charity*. A group in their church was reading it and my parents wanted to know my thoughts. At the time, I had been a nonprofit fundraiser for around five years and I was working at a church-related organization that provided services like emergency assistance and housing rehabilitation for low-income families. I was amazed not only that a congregation would read Lupton's book, but that so many of its members would base their personal giving on Lupton's suggestions.

Since then, of course, I've come across charity skepticism in any number of church settings. *Toxic Charity*, *When Helping Hurts*, and *What Every Church Member Should Know about Poverty* are all aimed at church audiences. Other books, articles, talks, and media aren't specifically for churches, but are eagerly consumed by Christians who want to adopt the best new strategies for addressing real social problems. And their ideas show up in conversations, book groups, grant applications, sermons, and dozens of other settings. Charity skepticism has a surprisingly large influence in the church. And that would be fine . . . if charity were something that Christianity had just happened to adopt at some point in its history. Well, maybe not fine, but understandable.

But as we saw in the last chapter, charity isn't just a random way of giving that the Christian church just happened to pick up somewhere. It is a specific form of giving that has deep roots in Judaism and Christianity. It is possible that charity would exist without those religions, but historically it is those religions that led to charity becoming a major form of giving in the West. In this chapter, I'm going to look at the inverse of that idea: it isn't just that charity is rooted in Christianity; Christianity is rooted in charity. Without charity, Christianity as we know it—Christianity as it has existed for 2,000 years—would not exist.

That's a deliberatively provocative statement. It's also an important one. While I'm sure that charity skeptics and the people who are embracing their ideas usually have the best of intentions, adopting charity skepticism means questioning a core facet of Christianity. Charity is the heart of the Christian religion. First, in the sense of sitting at the center of Christian faith and practice. Second, in the sense of being the way that Christians are commanded to care for—to love—our neighbors. In this chapter, I'll look at this idea by beginning to sketch a theology of charity, both in the sense of a theology about charity and in the sense of a theology rooted in charity.

A Charitable God

Christian theology begins with the life and ministry of Jesus of Nazareth: a Jewish preacher and teacher who was executed by the Roman Empire in Jerusalem when Tiberius was the emperor of Rome and Pontius Pilate was the governor of Judea. Beyond those bare facts, there are a lot of ways to interpret his life. People understand the picture painted by the Gospels and other canonical—and noncanonical—works in many different ways. Depending on who you ask, Jesus is a violent political revolutionary, a cynic philosopher, a proto-Marxist, a proto-feminist, a Pharisee, an Essene, or a member of any number of other groups. To put it simply, Jesus doesn't seem to fit into our modern categories. But he does fit into an ancient one: Jesus was an apocalyptic prophet. He taught that the world as he knew it would soon be overturned in favor of the kingdom of God. The miracles that he performed were signs of that kingdom breaking through into the current age. Christian theology begins with the life of a social, economic, political, and cosmic revolutionary.[1]

Of course, Christians don't stop with the life and ministry of Jesus. We understand this life as the meeting point between the human and the divine; the human life in which we see God. This becomes very important when we consider two biblical passages: the beginning of Genesis and the beginning of the Gospel of John. "In the beginning," writes the author of Genesis, "God created the heavens and the earth." John echoes this idea and inserts Christ—the Word—into the scene. "All things came into being

---

1. Ehrman, *Did Jesus Exist?*, 11–12.

through him," writes John, "and without him not one thing came into be-ing." Christians believe that God creates the universe through Christ. If the universe reflects God's character, and if Jesus of Nazareth is where we see God most clearly, then we can understand the character of the universe by looking at an apocalyptic prophet who was executed by the machinery of empire and who rose again on the third day. Jesus of Nazareth shows us the moral character of the cosmos.[2]

One of Jesus' most visible characteristics—and a major theme through-out the Bible—is generosity. In this section, I'm going to look at God's gen-erosity through four stories from the Bible: Jesus's healing of a woman with hemorrhages, the creation stories from the first two chapters of Genesis, and a brief passage from Revelation. A crucial part of my interpretation of these narratives is that they are about more than God, they are about the world that God creates. Generosity is baked in to the moral structure of the universe.

Mark, Matthew, and Luke give us a powerful illustration of Jesus' generosity in a story about a woman with a chronic hemorrhage. In this episode, Jesus is on his way to the home of a man named Jairus—a leader in the local synagogue—to revive his daughter. On the way to Jairus's house, a woman who has been suffering from hemorrhages for twelve years touches the hem of his cloak. In Matthew, this is almost a non-event: Jesus sees the woman, declares that her faith has made her well, and moves on. But in Mark and Luke, there's a bigger production: Jesus is aware that something has happened, but he does not know what. He only learns that he has healed the woman when he asks the question.[3]

Like a lot of things in the Gospels, there are many layers to this story. One particularly important aspect of this episode is that Jesus is both cur-ing a disease and healing an illness. In medical anthropology, the difference between a disease and an illness is a difference between a physical problem and a social one. A disease is an issue with a body that a doctor might be able to treat. An illness includes that, but also captures the psychological and social dimensions of having the disease. For example, Hansen's Dis-ease, more commonly known as leprosy, is a single disease caused by a spe-cific kind of bacteria. The illness, however, depends on the time, place, and culture. An ancient Israelite would live alone outside the camp, wear torn clothes, and shout "unclean." A modern person might undergo multi-drug

---

2. Gen 1:1; John 1:3.
3. Matt 9:20–22; Luke 8:43–48; Mark 5:25–34.

therapy to cure the disease and no one would be the wiser. Same disease, two very different illnesses.[4]

The woman with hemorrhages has both a disease and an illness. There is a tradition of interpreting her story as a story about cultic impurity and social rejection; the story of a woman whose illness was that she was unclean in the eyes of her community. That interpretation seems unlikely: it doesn't really follow the Jewish laws around discharges of blood, the crowd didn't scatter when they saw her, and physicians had been willing to treat her. But there is a social dimension to being a woman who has suffered from hemorrhages for twelve years and who has spent all of her money on ineffective treatments. She may not be perpetually unclean, but she is certainly destitute and on the margins of her community.

And the critical piece of Jesus' healing act is that it happens without him knowing about it. Generosity towards someone in need is so natural for Jesus that it's all but unavoidable. In the same way that a stone naturally falls to the ground, Jesus' power naturally overflows in response to the woman's need and faith. And because Jesus provides an interpretive lens through which we can understand God and the world that God creates, this episode also tells us that overflowing generosity is there, too.

The story of the woman with the hemorrhages shows us the overflowing generosity of Jesus' divine nature. As I just said, if we understand that Jesus is our clearest image of God and that God's character is reflected in the nature of the universe, then we have reason to believe that the cosmic order in fundamentally generous. But it's also true that divine generosity is visible in the first chapter of Genesis, which tells the story of God creating the heavens and the earth.

It's important to recognize that the first chapter of Genesis is not about the material origins of the universe. While we care deeply enough about those kinds of questions—enough that we'll spend huge amounts of time and money probing the primordial past in search of answers—the ancient people who wrote the Bible simply didn't tell those kinds of stories. They cared much more about the functional origins and underlying moral nature of the cosmos. The story in Genesis 1 is about the character of the world, not its manufacturing process.[5]

According to John H. Walton, the story in Genesis 1 is a story about God setting up and inaugurating a cosmic temple. We tend to focus on the first six days of creation, when God forms the cosmos out of an earth that's

4. Lev 13:45–46.
5. Walton, *The Lost World of Genesis One*, 23–37.

formless and void. But the critical moment of the story is on the seventh day, when God rests. As Walton points out, God resting brings two important facts into the picture. First, gods rest in temples, and God resting marks the universe itself as a temple. Second, rest means something specific when it comes to gods. God doesn't need a nap after a hard week of creative work. In this context, rest means that God is making the transition from setting up the cosmic order to beginning the day-to-day work of running the universe. Creation isn't just a one-time act spanning a few days, but the first phase of an ongoing and dynamic process that God is engaged in all the time.[6]

It's also important to recognize that this story doesn't give any reason for God to create the universe. As literary critic Terry Eagleton writes, "God appears to create, simply for the love and delight of it . . . as gift, superfluity, and gratuitous gesture." God's act of creation is as much an act of unrestrained generosity as Jesus' act of healing the woman with hemorrhages. And that's not just true of God's creative work over those six days. God's generosity is shown permeating the world throughout the bible. In the Psalms, God makes springs so that animals can drink, grass so that cows can eat, and other plants so that people can use them. In Job, God gives prey for lions, provides food for ravens, and gives land to wild asses. In the New Testament, Jesus echoes that image when he asks the disciples to consider the ravens, who neither reap nor sow, but who God feeds; the lilies, who neither toil nor spin, but who God clothes.[7]

Remember that the ancient authors of the Bible weren't as concerned with the material origins of the universe as they were about its fundamental moral nature. In the opening chapter of Genesis—and throughout the Bible—those authors are telling us that God is generous and that God's generosity is embedded in the universe. To be overly poetic, God creates the world as a gift to itself. And God continues to sustain a cosmic order that is as naturally generous as the divine power that overflowed in response to the need of the woman with hemorrhages. The cosmic order is a fundamentally generous one.

The second chapter of Genesis tells a very different story about creation. This version doesn't pay much attention to God creating the universe. Instead, it focuses on God planting a garden in Eden. In this garden, God plants every tree that is "pleasant to the sight and good for food," along with the tree of life and the tree of the knowledge of good and evil. There is also

6. Walton, *The Lost World of Genesis One*, 72–77.

7. Eagleton, *Reason, Faith, and Revolution*, 8; Ps 104:10–11,14; Job 38:39–41, 6; Luke 12:24–27.

a river that flows out of the garden and splits into four branches. God puts the first man in the garden and, after God decides that the first man needs a partner, puts animals and the first woman there, too.[8]

The end of the book of Revelation mirrors this image when it describes a new heaven and a new earth. While a city—the new Jerusalem—takes center stage here, there is also the river of the water of life and, on either side, the tree of life. God is also present in this new creation just like God was present in the garden in Eden: not in some clichéd sense where God is present everywhere, but in a far more literal sense. The city doesn't even need a sun and a moon because God's glory provides light. Finally, in an interesting reversal of Genesis 1, the new earth is not a cosmic temple. Instead, God is the temple in the new Jerusalem.[9]

It might be tempting to treat these two passages as bookends. After all, one is so very close to the beginning of the Bible and the other right at the end. I don't want to make that much of the similarities, but there are two notable things. First, that both of these passages about a paradisiacal world illustrate that world with themes of abundance: a river, a tree, many kinds of fruit, and so on. Second, that these passages don't present a world that we only hope for. Instead, they show us the world as God intends it, as it was in the beginning (before sin entered the world) and will be in the end (after sin is abolished). And the world as God intends it to be is defined by a lush garden or paradisiacal city, a flowing river, and the tree of life. Obviously, that's not how things are now. The garden in Eden and the new Jerusalem of Revelation are not the world we live in. I'll address that in the next section. For now, it's enough that these passages continue a theme of divine generosity.

As I wrote at the beginning of this section, God's generosity is one of the Bible's major themes. We see it in the passages I've looked at here and in countless others, including important episodes in the life of Jesus like the feeding of the multitude and the wedding at Cana. We might even put God's generosity alongside other divine attributes like omnipotence, omniscience, and omnipresence. Generosity is a defining aspect of God's character and a fundamental aspect of the cosmic order.[10]

As we've already seen, though, not all generosity is charitable. Ancient Roman patrons and modern philanthropists can be generous without being

8. Gen 2:4b–24.

9. Rev 22:1–5, 21:22–23; Gen 3:8.

10. Mark 6:31–44; 8:1–9; Matt 14:13–21; 15:32–16:10; Luke 9:10–17; John 6:5–15; 2:1–11.

charitable, and we could imagine a god who is like them. For example, the citizens of the Roman Empire imagined their emperor as the patron *par excellence*. He benefitted and protected "his friends, clients, and subjects." And they, in turn, gave him the highest form of honor: they worshipped him as a god. We could imagine that God's generosity works in a similar way. We could imagine that God is generous towards people who worship and honor God (and, especially, we could imagine that God is generous only towards people who worship and honor God in just the right way).[11]

But that isn't the image that we get from the Bible. In the ancient world, worship—including worship by ancient Israelites—was dominated by the logic of the temple. Remember, gods rule over their domains in temples. They live in them. The altar in the temple has a special purpose: it's where the priests prepare meals for their gods. In a strikingly literal sense, the temple altar was where people put food that would be transferred to God. And while that logic might seem very strange to us—after all, we're used to the idea of God being completely self-sustaining—the ancient Israelites took it very seriously. Violating the temple could be deadly.[12]

We've already seen how the Bible subverts these expectations a little. Remember that when the Israelites paid the tithe from their crops in certain years, they did not take it to the temple altar. Instead, they distributed it to people who didn't have the resources to raise their own food. Already in Deuteronomy—and in a part of Deuteronomy that is talking about the temple—the logic of the temple is being played with. Giving to the poor is equated with giving to God! The prophets take this even further. Isaiah, for example, tells us that God never asked for the burnt offerings of temple worship, and that the entire logic of the temple—the offerings, animal blood, appointed festivals, solemn assemblies, and so on—has become a burden that God is tired of bearing. What God wants is not worship, but imitation: "Wash yourselves; make yourselves clean; remove the evil of your doings from before my eyes; cease to do evil, learn to do good; seek justice, rescue the oppressed, defend the orphan, plead for the widow."[13]

That last clause is especially important. Again, these are the groups who have nothing to offer in return and who stand on the edge of the community. God is not generous because God wants something in return—the people (and, as we saw in Job and the Psalms, the animals) who God gives to have nothing to offer in return—but because that generosity is a reflection of God's nature. God is charitable precisely in the sense that God gives most

---

11. Rhee, *Loving the Poor, Saving the Rich*, Kindle location 865.

12. Anderson, *Charity*, 25; Lev 10:1–3.

13. Isa 1:12–17.

generously towards those who cannot reciprocate and without any apparent concern for the worthiness of those recipients.

A Broken World

It's hard to believe that this is a world that is created and sustained by a charitable God. There is a reason that the problem of evil—the mere existence of suffering in the face of God's supposed love—is considered one of the most powerful arguments against God's existence. If the world was created as a reflection of God's charitable nature, then it's obvious that the world as it is right now is not the world that God intended. The Christian word for the distance between the world-as-it-is and the world-as-God-wants-it-to-be is *sin*.

The Bible imagines sin in a lot of different ways. Sometimes, it's a weight that must be carried. Other times, it's a stain that must be washed away. Still other times, it's a debt that must be paid. Each of these ways of thinking about sin brings other ideas along with it. For example, a scapegoat makes sense if we imagine sin as a weight that can be put on the back of an animal and carried out into the desert. It doesn't make sense if sin is a debt that has to be paid. But in that case, giving money to people in poverty—people who can be imagined as a kind of altar—makes sense as a way to alleviate sin. While the Bible imagines sin in a variety of ways, there is a common thread between them: sin is a condition.[14]

All of these ways are very different from how we often imagine sin. We tend to think of sin in legal terms: God has given us a list of laws or rules, and when we break one of them, we sin. In these terms, sin is a discrete act: a thing we do. That's very different from understanding sin as a condition: a statement about something being wrong with our lives and our world.

We can understand this better is we look at how Corbett and Fikkert describe the problem in *When Helping Hurts*. They describe sin in terms of four foundational relationships—with God, with self, with others, and with the rest of creation—being broken. Corbett and Fikkert find the origin of this brokenness in the third chapter of Genesis, which I'll write about below. I don't know how literally they take Genesis, but the story itself makes an important point about the nature of sin: we are not the people who originally broke these relationships; from our perspective, they were always already broken. The problem isn't that we broke the law. The problem is that we live in a world that is already broken.[15]

14. Anderson, *Sin*, Kindle Locations 572–77.
15. Corbett and Fikkert, *When Helping Hurts*, 55–58.

In this section, I'm going to look at this condition of brokenness through the lens of three biblical stories: the exile from the garden in Eden in the third chapter of Genesis, the parable of the Rich Fool, and Jesus' saying that person cannot serve both God and Mammon. I'll also take a quick detour into Paul to look at how life and death work in the Bible. The theme that I'll draw out of these stories—and others that I refer to—is that the condition of sin is caused by and reinforces itself through idolatry, and that the most threatening idol, according to the New Testament, is wealth.

I've already looked at the first two chapters of Genesis, so I'll finish the cycle with the story about the origin of sin in the third chapter. The first man and the first woman live together in the garden in Eden. One day, the serpent tempts them into eating from the tree of the knowledge of good and evil. As soon as they eat from it, the man and woman's eyes are opened, they see that they're naked, and they use fig leaves to make clothes for themselves.[16]

That evening, God discovers the man and the woman and what they've done. God responds to this transgression by cursing the serpent, the woman, and the man. The serpent loses its legs and is cursed to live at war with humanity. The woman's pain in childbearing is increased and she's cursed to be ruled over by her husband (a good reminder that patriarchy is a result of the fall). The man is cursed to work to feed himself and his family, eating only by the sweat of his brow. Even the ground is cursed to grow thistles and thorns to make farming more difficult for the man. Finally, God sends the man and the woman away from the garden, but not without making them clothes from animal skins.[17]

Like the other chapters in Genesis I've looked at, this isn't a story about what really happened. There never was a garden in Eden, the evolutionary development of snakes is more complex, and so on. Instead, it's a story about the way that the world is: the world is broken by humanity's tendency to have a disoriented faith.

We often think about faith in terms of intellectual assent. In this sense, faith is believing something without evidence, or even in the face of evidence to the contrary. Traditionally, though, faith—and the related words in Hebrew (*emunah*), Greek (*pistis*), and Latin (*fides*)—means something more like trust or loyalty. Remember the story about Anderson's wife's swimming class? Those students were asked to have faith that the water would hold them if they relaxed. They were asked to trust the water. Similarly, having faith in God is trusting in or being loyal to God. That trust must be lived.

16. Gen 3:1–7.
17. Gen 3:6–24.

Faith isn't just knowing that you'll float if you relax; it's actually relaxing so that you can float.

Of course, not all faith is the same. I have faith in the restaurants that I visit: faith that the food will be good, that the cooks are using quality ingredients, that they won't accidentally poison me. But the faith that I have in a restaurant is faith that I hold lightly. I can have faith in more than one thing. I can hold on to or let go of faith in a restaurant without it having a big impact on my life. Faith in God—at least in monotheistic religions like Judaism, Christianity, and Islam—is weightier. We can only have this kind of faith in one thing at a time, and what we choose to put this faith in has an unparalleled effect on our lives.

In this story, the man and the woman put their faith in the serpent who tempts them toward the one and only forbidden tree. Their faith is disoriented; it's aligned with someone other than the God who provided all of the trees in the garden. The result of that disoriented faith is a broken world where humanity cannot enjoy the world-as-God-wants-it-to-be: the paradise of a lush garden.

Eating from the tree of the knowledge of good and evil isn't just a matter of breaking a rule. It's a matter of trading faith in God for idolatry. And the curses aren't just punishments for breaking a rule. They are changes to the way that the world works. The wages of sin, as Corbett and Fikkert point out, are broken relationships and broken systems. The man and the woman—and all of the rest of us—no longer enjoy their natural relationships with God, with each other, with themselves, and with creation. And those broken relationships lead to broken political, social, religious, and economic systems.

When the serpent tempted the woman, it asked whether God told her not to eat from any tree in the garden. The woman replied that she could eat from any tree except for the tree of the knowledge of good and evil, "or you shall die." Much later, Paul echoed this when he wrote that "the wages of sin is death." Many modern readers will immediately interpret these statements as saying that the result of sin is physical death and, perhaps, eternal torment in hell. That may not be wrong, but it's also a particularly legalistic way of understanding sin. The writers of the Bible had a much more flexible concept of death. It included physical death, but also severe disease, exile, and other things that created a rift between people and their community, their land, and their God. While we tend to focus on biological life and death, the authors of the Bible were focused on what I'll call capital letter—spiritual and communal—Life and Death.[18]

When we think about life and death, we think about them as digital and one-way. A person who is alive is alive no matter how healthy they are. A person at the apex of health and a person barely clinging to life are both alive. And they're both alive until they're dead. And once someone dies, there's no coming back.

Life and Death are different. First, they're on a spectrum. In the Bible, childlessness is bad, childlessness and severe illness (risking the future possibility of children) is worse, childlessness and severe illness while in exile (and removed from the land that God has given) is still worse. Someone moving along that scale is constantly moving closer and closer to—or maybe further and further into—Death. Second, a person can move back and forth along the spectrum. For example, the psalmist says that God has "brought up my soul from Sheol, restored me to life from among those gone down to the Pit." Sheol is the traditional place of the dead, but the psalmist can talk about being in Sheol—or, at least, very close to and gravely threatened by Sheol—in the past tense. It is where he was, not where he is now. Death isn't the binary opposite of Life, but something that creeps into and constantly surrounds Life.[19]

The idea of Life and Death can help us understand what the woman was getting at when she spoke to the serpent. It isn't that she and the man immediately died; according to the Bible, Adam lived to the ripe old age of 930! But Death did enter the world: suffering became a real and unavoidable possibility. As a result of sin, Death is now part of the human condition. Paul gets at something similar when he writes that we are in slavery to sin. We are constantly presenting ourselves to sin as instruments of wickedness and the world that we live in is the result of that slavery. It's a vicious circle. In order to enjoy success in a world broken by sin, we sell ourselves deeper into slavery to sin; in selling ourselves deeper into slavery, we become better instruments of wickedness; and in becoming better instruments of wickedness, we break the world even more. We become, as it were, well-adjusted to living in the valley of the shadow of death. And, by doing that, we take ourselves further and further away from Life.[20]

Today, the risk of anyone turning away from faith in God on the advice of a talking snake is pretty low. But there are still a lot of things that compete

18. Gen 3:1–3; Rom 6:23; Anderson, *Charity*, 79.

19. Ps 30:3.

20. Rom 6:13–17; Ps 23:4.

with God for our faith. One of those things was also recognized by Jewish communities during Jesus' ministry: material wealth. And wealth—or, maybe a little more accurately, the love of money—played a central role as a source of disoriented faith in early Christianity.

Matthew captures the competition between God and wealth in a series of three sayings. In the Sermon on the Mount, Jesus tells the crowds who are listening to him not to store up treasures on earth, but to store up treasures in heaven. He then tells the crowd that the eye is the lamp of the body, and that if the eye is healthy, the whole body is healthy; but if the eye is unhealthy, the whole body is full of darkness. Finally, he tells the crowd that "no one can serve two masters . . . you cannot serve God and wealth." The parts form a sort of sandwich where each part helps us interpret the others: when we serve God and store up treasures in heaven, we are full of light; when we serve money by storing up treasures on earth, we are full of darkness. "Where your treasure is," Matthew has Jesus say, "there your heart will be also."[21]

Luke expands on this idea with the parable of the Rich Fool. In this parable, a wealthy land owner has a larger yield of crops than he knows what to do with. He tears down his barns, builds bigger ones, and uses them to store his crops and goods. He believes he's set for years to come and says to himself, "Self, you have ample goods laid up for many years; relax, eat, drink, be merry." God confronts him, saying, "You fool! This very night your life is being demanded of you. And the things you have prepared, whose will they be?" The parable ends with Jesus underscoring the point: "So it is with those who store up treasures for themselves but are not rich toward God." After a short discourse on worry, he repeats Matthew's advice to build up "an unfailing treasure in heaven . . . for where your treasure is, there your heart will be also."[22]

In both of these passages, Jesus is laying out a choice: we can put our faith in God, or we can put our faith in material wealth. The rich fool showed us where he put his faith when he chose to build bigger barns and store more treasures. He was, to use a phrase that Jesus uses elsewhere, a lover of money. The New Testament repeatedly holds up love of money as a major threat to faith in God, and the phrase "lover of money" is used as a pejorative in Luke, 1 Timothy, and 2 Timothy. The author of Hebrews even admonishes the reader to keep herself from the love of money. And the author of 1 Timothy makes the power of the love of money all too clear: "love of money is a root of all kinds of evil, and in their eagerness to be rich

21. Matt 6:19–24.
22. Luke 12:16–34.

some have wandered away from the faith and pierced themselves with many pains."[23]

To get a clear picture of the problem, let's go back to an illustration I used in the last chapter. You have inherited a large sum of money and you have a choice between the advice of two experts. A wealth management professional has an investment plan that will keep you comfortable for the rest of your life. A saint tells you to give your money away to people who need it more than you do right now. This is, more or less, the situation that the rich fool faced. He didn't have any control over how much his land produced—just like you don't have control over whether you inherit a large amount of money—but he did have a choice about where he put his faith. And, as the parable illustrates, putting his faith in his material wealth was a bad choice: it couldn't protect him against the great equalizer that is death (and it led him closer and closer to Death).

As I wrote near the beginning of this section, we tend to imagine sin in legal terms. We imagine that we have to follow the universal laws that God has created just like we have to follow the laws that our government passes. And, just like we can break the laws our government creates—and be punished for breaking them—we can break the laws that God has created. According to this metaphor, sin is the act of breaking one of God's laws. This isn't necessarily a bad way of imagining sin, but it is an incomplete one.

The Bible imagines sin in a variety of ways. Sometimes, it might imagine sin as a discrete act like breaking a law, but more often it imagines sin as a condition. Specifically, it is the condition we live in when we exchange our faith in God for faith in something else. In the biblical story of the garden in Eden, that something else is the advice of a serpent. In other stories, that something else is a foreign god like Baal or Moloch. In much of the Bible—and especially in the New Testament—that something else is material wealth.

It might help to think of sin as having two natures. On the one hand, it's the condition of living in allegiance to something other than God. This is what Paul is getting at when he writes about living in slavery to sin, and it's part of what I'm getting at when I write about capital letter Death. On the other hand, it's the things we do because of that allegiance. That's what Paul is getting at when he talks about being instruments of wickedness. Sin (the condition) works through us to commit sin (the acts). And, by doing that, it increases the distance between the world-as-it-is and the world-as-God-wants-it-to be. Whenever we exchange our faith in God for faith in

23. Luke 16:14; 1 Tim 3:3; 2 Tim 3:1–5; Heb 13:5; 1 Tim 6:10.

something else, we take the world a little further away from the world God created.

A Redeemed Life

So far in this chapter, I've told two parts of a story. The first part tells us that the God who creates and sustains of the universe is generous, and that the universe reflects that generosity. The second part tells us that, while charity is part of the fundamental moral order of the world we live in, that world is also broken. And, while it might not be the only cause of that brokenness, human idolatry—our tendency to put our faith in things other than God, and especially our tendency to put faith in material wealth—is a major contributor.

Fortunately, that isn't the end of the story. Christianity proposes a solution to the problem of cosmic brokenness and promises a restoration of the fundamental moral order of the universe. Somehow, Jesus Christ made the world whole again. Like sin, this is often put in legal terms. When we imagine sin as a violation of God's law, and when we imagine that people who break the law have to be punished, then it makes sense that everyone who has broken the law—that is, everyone, for "there is no one who is righteous, not even one"—must be punished. The legal solution to the legal problem of sin is the crucifixion: Jesus Christ—God in human form—taking the punishment that we so richly deserve. This version of the story tells us that we can avoid our punishment by putting our faith in the fact that Jesus was crucified for our sake. By taking the punishment that we deserve, Jesus saves us from God's rightful wrath. It's the story of salvation.[24]

In this section, I'm going to look at the Christian proposal and promise through another lens: the story of redemption. In this version of the story, God doesn't just save the world from God's own wrath. God regains possession of the world and reorients it. God changes the world to be more in line with the world that God intends it to be. Specifically, I'll explore the responsibility that Jesus put on humanity to participate in the reorientation of the world: to reorient our faith towards God, rely on God's generosity, and trust—as Jesus says—that "it is God's good pleasure to give us the kingdom."[25]

The Gospel of Luke is widely recognized as emphasizing both concern for the poor and disapproval of the rich. According to this Gospel, near the

24. Rom 3:10.
25. Luke 12:32.

beginning of Jesus' ministry he went to his hometown of Nazareth. On the Sabbath, he went to the synagogue and read from the scroll of the prophet Isaiah:

> The Spirit of the Lord is upon me, because he has anointed me to bring good news to the poor. He has sent me to proclaim release to the captives and recovery of sight to the blind, to let the oppressed go free, to proclaim the year of the Lord's favor.[26]

When he sat down, everyone was staring at him, and he said, "Today this scripture has been fulfilled in your hearing."[27]

This is a remarkable way to begin a ministry, and one that puts Jesus firmly in Judaism's prophetic tradition. Isaiah doesn't hold back in his criticism of the powerful who "serve [their] own interests on fast day and oppress all [their] workers" instead of fasting by "loos[ing] the bonds of injustice . . . shar[ing their] bread with the hungry, and bring[ing] the homeless poor into [their] house." In the passage that Jesus reads, Isaiah is looking forward to the restoration of Israel, when the oppressed will be comforted. And he draws a firm line, with the powerful on one side and the oppressed on the other. In the coming days, according to Isaiah, God will be on the side of the oppressed.[28]

Jesus would have read this passage in Hebrew or Aramaic, but the Greek translation narrows the potentially big group of the oppressed down to the poor. Remember the Greek, like Hebrew, has different words for the poor. The two that are important for my purposes are *penēs* (the working poor) and *ptōchos* (the destitute). During the Second Temple period—the long span of time during which the Second Temple of Jerusalem existed— Jewish apocalyptic literature connected wealth with wickedness and poverty, specifically *ptōchos*, with righteousness. Good news for the *ptōchoi* (the plural of *ptōchos*) was, pretty much by definition, bad news for the wealthy. And Jesus would cement the opposition between rich and poor later when provided blessings to the poor, the hungry, the sorrowful, and the hated— explicitly saying that the kingdom of God belongs to the *ptōchoi*—while declaring that woe is coming to the rich, the full, the joyful, and the reputable.[29]

It's tempting to extend the idea of poverty to include all of us. For example, when Corbett and Fikkert talk about poverty in terms of the four broken relationships, they write that "every human being is poor in

26. Luke 4:18–19.
27. Luke 4:21.
28. Isa 58:3–7; 61:1–2.
29. Luke 6:20–26.

the sense of not experiencing these four relationships in the way that God intended." In a broken world, of course, it's true that everyone suffers; that, as Paul puts it, "all . . . are under the power of sin." But when Jesus is talking about the *ptōchoi*, he is talking exclusively about the materially destitute: "the afflicted and humble ones," as Helen Rhee puts is, "whose confidence rests only in God."[30]

Whatever else Jesus may preach—and he does have a message for the wealthy—the gospel begins here, with the promise of good news for the poor. To take that further, it begins with the promise of good news for the *ptōchoi* who are—in the most literal understanding of the word—bent over begging, with nothing to their names, and completely dependent on the generosity of others. A gospel that is anything less than good news for the least of these is no gospel at all.

In the last section, I wrote that sin is the condition of living with a disoriented faith, a faith that draws the world farther from being the world that God intends. The solution to a disoriented faith is a reoriented faith. And the Christian word for that reorientation is *repentance:* a change that leads to a new way of living. In the Gospel of Mark, Jesus opens his ministry in Galilee not with a visit to a synagogue and a reading from Isaiah, but with a simple proclamation: "The time is fulfilled, and the kingdom of God has come near; repent, and believe in the good news." Good news to the poor is one pillar of the gospel. A call to repentance is another.[31]

And just as there's a temptation to say that everyone is poor, there's a temptation to say that everyone needs to repent. It's true that everyone is suffering from a disoriented faith, but Jesus is clear that his call for repentance isn't for everyone. For example, when the Pharisees and scribes chide him for eating with sinners, he tells three parables that draw a distinction between people who need to repent and people who don't, explicitly saying that "there will be more joy in heaven over one sinner who repents than over ninety-nine righteous persons who need no repentance."[32]

The question this raises is: who are the sinners and who are the righteous? The answer—in this episode, at least—is in the parable of the Prodigal Son. In this parable, a man had two sons. The younger son asked his father for his share of the estate and, after receiving it, left for another land where he squandered the money. Once he had spent his inheritance,

---

30. Corbett and Fikketi, *When Helping Hurts,* 59; Rom 3:23; Rhee, *Loving the Poor, Saving the Rich,* Kindle location 1280.

31. Mark 1:14–15.

32. Luke 15:7.

a famine swept through the land and left him desperate. After struggling to survive on his own, he went back to his father's house and asked to be treated as a hired hand. His father saw him, greeted him as a son, and ordered his servants to prepare a celebration. The older son—the responsible one who stayed with his father through all of this—is understandably upset. His father explains to him, "you are always with me, and all that is mine is yours," but that he had to celebrate his younger brother's return to life.[33]

It's easy to read this parable as though Jesus is telling the scribes and Pharisees that they are the righteous—perhaps even the self-righteous—older son and that the sinners who Jesus is eating with are the prodigal younger son. After all, the Pharisees are famous for following the Torah. But pay close attention to what's happening in the parable. The younger son is like the rich fool (and, maybe, like the first man and the first woman): he trades the abundance of his father's estate—even his "hired hands have bread enough and to spare"—for the pleasures and security of material wealth. And, like the rich fool, he discovers that material wealth cannot really protect him from the uncertainties of life. He ends up in a foreign country, thinking longingly about the food that he's giving to pigs. He is capital letter Dead, and all he can do is repent: reorient his faith towards his father and hope for a share of his father's abundance.[34]

Behind the idea of the righteous poor and the wicked rich—a natural continuation of God's preferential for the poor—was the idea that the *ptōchoi* were the rightful heirs to God's kingdom precisely because they had no choice but to rely on God alone. They are the ones who, like the older son who had never even had a young goat of his own, have a share in all that God has. It's the people who rely on the material wealth that they have now—the inheritance that they've received before its time—who need to reorient their faith. In a shocking reversal, Jesus is asking the scribes and Pharisees to repent and join him with the *ptōchoi* who are already a part of God's kingdom.

So, what does a reoriented life—a repentant life—look like? In both Matthew (after he talks about serving two masters) and Luke (after the parable of the Rich Fool), Jesus tells us what that kind of life is like. A faithful life is characterized by trusting that God will provide what we need. Even material things like what we eat and drink and wear.[35]

---

33. Luke 15:25–32.
34. Luke 15:17.
35. Matt 6:25–34; Luke 12:22–34.

In a passage sometimes called the "discourse on worry," Jesus points to how God's generosity is reflected in the natural order:

> Look at the birds of the air; they neither sow nor reap nor gather into barns, and yet your heavenly Father feeds them . . . Consider the lilies of the field, how they grow; they neither toil nor spin, yet I tell you, even Solomon in all his glory was not clothed like one of these.[36]

Then, he goes on to point out that if God cares for the birds who neither sow nor reap, and the lilies who neither toil nor spin, then God will surely care for us: "But if God so clothes the grass of the field, which is alive today and tomorrow is thrown into the oven, will he not much more clothe you—you of little faith?"[37]

This might sound like the kind of invitation to not worry that you can find in any self-help or self-improvement book, but it's more than that. Like the parable of the Prodigal Son, this is an invitation to have a living faith in the God who provides all things; and a living faith is a faith expressed through generosity. Luke makes this clear when he adds a moment where Jesus says, "Do not be afraid, little flock, for it is your Father's good pleasure to give you the kingdom. Sell your possessions, and give alms." This is Jesus' message to the wealthy: when we give our material wealth away, we're able to take on the righteousness of the *ptōchoi* —putting our confidence in God alone—and be a part of a divine economy of abundance.[38]

This cannot be overstated. A life that is faithful to God is not concerned with material wealth; and a life that is not concerned with material wealth is characterized by generosity. Charity is a way to help people living in poverty, but it is also more than that. It's also a way to demonstrate that our faith is in the generous God who creates and sustains the universe.

The idea that charitable giving is a demonstration of faith in God is perfectly illustrated in the parable of the Judgement of the Nations. I've already talked about this parable a couple of times. As a reminder, in this parable, the Son of Man separates the people of the world into two groups: the sheep and the goats. The sheep are all the people who gave food to the hungry, drink to the thirsty, and so on. The goats are all of the people who

---

36. Matt 6:26, 28–29.

37. Matt 6:29–30.

38. Luke 12:32–33.

failed to do those things. The sheep are destined for the kingdom of God. The goats are destined for eternal fire.[39]

Earlier in this chapter, I wrote about two different kinds of faith. On the one hand, there's the kind of faith that we hold lightly: the kind of faith I have that a particular restaurant will serve good food at a reasonable price, for example. On the other hand, there's the kind of faith that we hold more tightly: the kind of faith we have in God. Unlike the faith I might have in a restaurant, the faith I have in God can't be shared with other things. This kind of faith is reserved for one thing. And the reason that this kind of faith is in one thing is that this is the faith we have in the thing against which we will ultimately be judged. We could put that faith in money; an old boss of mine used to joke (or, at least, I hope he was joking) that whoever dies with the most toys wins. As Christians, though, we put that faith in God.

In this parable, that power to judge is put firmly in the hands of the poor. The Son of Man might sit on a throne of glory, but he *is* the poor: the hungry, the thirsty, the stranger, the sick, and so on. How we treat those in need—how we treat the Son of Man—is *the* criterion for entry into the kingdom.

We need to be careful with this scene. It's tempting to think that this parable is just asking us to be kind to people in need, as though we can live in fantastic wealth as long we meet some minimal obligation to the poor. There is a big problem with this kind of interpretation. If feeding one hungry person is enough to earn a place among the sheep, then failing to feed one is enough to earn a place among the goats. Given the huge number of people in need, earning a place among the sheep is impossible.

This parable simply isn't about helping some people or being generally nice towards people in need (though we should do that). It's about the general attitude towards wealth and poverty that the sheep have and that the goats do not have. The sheep are generous—maybe they're even foolishly generous—towards people in need. Their natural inclination towards a hungry person, for example, is to feed her. And the sheep can be so generous precisely because they don't see wealth as something to hold onto, whether for the sake of greed or for the sake of financial security; they see it as something to be shared.

I need to end this section by being clear about two things that I am not saying. First, I'm not saying that the only way for the wealthy to repent is to sell everything, give the proceeds away, and be destitute. Second, and related, I'm not saying that redemption depends on our generosity, as though

39. Matt 25:31–46.

we can buy our way into the kingdom by giving money to Christ through the poor. As the author of Ephesians writes, we have been saved from capital letter Death by grace through faith. No matter how much we give away, our charity doesn't redeem us. God's grace—itself an act of charity—does. What I am saying is something more subtle: charity is an act of repentance and an expression of faith in God. When we give, we show that our faith is not in material wealth, but in God.[40]

There's another important piece here: charitable giving has the power to reorient our faith. In the last chapter, I touched briefly on the part of Pascal's wager that we often overlook. Remember that Pascal suggests that the person who doesn't believe, but who wants to, should imitate the faithful. Doing the things that people of faith do will naturally make the non-believer into a believer. And, at worst, that non-believer will become more honest, humble, grateful, and so on. Similarly, we don't have to reorient our faith first. We can behave as though our faith is where it should be. Even if we worry about money, we can give it away. And by doing that, we might find that our worries are unfounded, that we have less and less faith in money, and that we have more and more faith in God.

The problem of sin is a problem of disoriented faith, and one of the most faith-disorienting forces in the world is material wealth. It can lull us into having faith that it can protect us from life's uncertainties. It can exert "an almost eerie power over its possessor such that it is nearly impossible not be possessed by it." As much as charitable giving is a way to help people living in poverty, it is also a refusal to be possessed by wealth. And when we take on charitable giving as a practice, it can help us abandon faith in money—service to Mammon—and embrace faith in God.[41]

The Heart of Christianity

In this chapter, I've sketched out a rough theology of charity that shows how charity is a thread that runs through the Christian story. First, the Christian God is a generous God, and that generosity is reflected in the cosmic order that God creates and sustains. Second, the problem of sin is a problem with a disoriented faith, and that disoriented faith is often oriented towards material wealth. Third, God redeems the world in part by inviting us to participate in the generosity that forms the moral foundation of the universe. This is a story about a creation, a fall, and a redemption. And, ultimately, that redemption is God returning the world to what it was meant to be: a

40. Eph 2:1–8.
41. Anderson, *Charity*, 59.

place of divine abundance. That is, a place ruled by charity. Charity is the heart of Christianity.

Here's what I mean by that. First, charity is a critical attribute of God and the cosmic order that God creates, sustains, and redeems. God's nature is to give to the poor without thought of return or concern for their worthiness. And charity is divine love and divine grace. As I've already written, our word charity comes from the Latin *caritas* (meaning love), one of the two words used to translate the Greek word *agape* (traditionally meaning the love that God has for the world). "God," as we might translate 1 John, "is charity."[42]

Second, charity is the way that God provides for the care of the poor and the redemption of the wealthy. Of course God wants us to *feel* love for people in need. God also wants us to *show* that love through charitable giving: leaving crops in the field and grapes in the vineyard, feeding the hungry, clothing the naked, caring for the sick, and so on. Our charitable giving is a reenactment of God's charitable love in the world. Again, from 1 John, "if we love one another, God lives in us, and his love is perfected in us." So charity is the heart of Christianity in two ways. On the one hand, charity is at the core of Christianity. On the other hand, it is the way that Christians care for the world.[43]

This is especially important in light of what I wrote at the beginning of this chapter. Many of the books, talks, articles, and other media that promote charity skepticism are aimed specifically at churches and other Christian organizations. The unspoken argument behind those works is that Christians can let go of "toxic charity"—and take on other forms of giving—while holding onto the rest of Christianity. So, for example, we could stop giving money to people who stopped by the office and still celebrate communion. Or we could close the food pantry (and maybe open a food co-op) and still sing praise songs. Or we could invest in micro-lending and still pray.

And maybe we could do those things. But that doesn't change the fact that charity is a central thread that runs through the Christian understanding of God, the world, and the relationship between the two. If we gave up that central thread, what would be left would be a version of Christianity so hollowed out that it wouldn't deserve the name "Christianity" at all. We could still take communion, sing praise songs, pray, and practice all the other trappings of Christianity . . . but it would be play acting. Christianity without charity simply does not exist.

42. 1 John 4:8.
43. 1 John 4:12.

5

Charity Works

Jane is a Kenyan woman in her late fifties. She makes most of her meager income through farming, and she sometimes has to sell her cattle to make ends meet. She had a small home that was in poor condition, with no toilet and no kitchen, where she lived with her three children. In early 2017, she received her first payment from GiveDirectly, a nonprofit organization that specializes in giving unconditional cash transfers to low-income households in Kenya and Uganda. GiveDirectly identifies people in very poor communities and gives them roughly $1,000—an entire year's household budget—through an app on their phone. Recipients can use the app to transfer money to other people or withdraw physical money at shops, gas stations, supermarkets, and other places (basically, anywhere we would find an ATM).[1]

Jane's first transfer was $97, which she spent to cultivate her land and buy food for her family. She spent her second transfer of $484 on school fees for her daughter. Normally, she would have had to sell some of her cattle to cover the cost. This time, she didn't have to do that, and those cattle can continue to provide her with income. She also began building a kitchen so that she doesn't have to cook in the cowshed. Her third and final transfer, which she received about eight months after the first one, was $466. She finished her kitchen, bought a small bull that she can use to work her land, and paid

---

1. GiveDirectly, "Jane's Profile"; World Bank Group, "Kenya"; GiveDirectly, "Operating Model Overview."

86

more school fees. Over all, she received just under $1,050 and invested that money in her business, home, and family.[2]

We'll probably never know the long-term outcome of GiveDirectly's payments to Jane. Fortunately, GiveDirectly is passionate about collecting data on its activities and impacts, and several other organizations have taken an interest in studying cash transfers like this. Research into giving people money is a growth industry, and rigorous studies and experiments are readily available. GiveDirectly, for example, uses third party researchers and randomized trials—giving to some people and not to others—to learn about the impact of their gifts. They announce studies once they're in progress, so they can't hide the results of studies that aren't favorable, and they report the outcomes of those studies. This rigorous self-evaluation, and the host of other studies that have been conducted, gives the rest of us the chance to learn whether cash transfers like this work.

Jane's story and hundreds of others like it demonstrate, counter to the story that charity skeptics tell, that giving people money can be a viable way to address poverty. That doesn't mean that it works in every case, but it does mean that charity can work. It also means that we can look at the cases where it doesn't work and ask why it isn't working. In this chapter, I'm going to look at charity in the real world. First, I'll review some of what we learned about the poverty mind-set in chapter two. Then I'll look at two ways of putting cash in the hands of people living in poverty: microloans and cash transfers. Finally, I'll outline why the research that I'm looking at in this chapter strongly suggests that charity works.

Before I go any further, I want to be clear about the stakes of this chapter. Charity skeptics and I have two important things in common. First, we want to help people who are experiencing poverty in the most effective ways possible. Second, we both have prior commitments. As I outlined in the first chapter, charity skeptics tend to be committed to a sort of compassionate capitalism. They believe that exploitative social systems might play some part in poverty, but the mind-sets and cultures of people living in poverty are far more important. Similarly, they believe that the solution to poverty can be found in helping people overcome those mind-sets and cultures, join the economy, and work their way into the middle class. Charity skeptics want to help people who are experiencing poverty, but not at the expense of normal, American, middle-class values.

I outlined my biggest commitment previously: I believe that personal challenges might play a role in poverty, but that social and economic

2. GiveDirectly, "Jane's Profile."

systems are the root cause; and that the mind-sets of poverty are a response to poverty, not its cause. Giving people money can not only solve the financial problem of poverty, but address the other challenges that we often associate with living in poverty. Most importantly, charity lies at the heart of Christianity: it is both a central part of the way that Christians understand God and the world, and the way that we are called to care for people who are experiencing poverty. If charity doesn't work—or, worse, if it really does hurt people—a central part of my Christian faith has a very big problem.

In a sense, we're both betting our faith here. If charity is effective—and especially if it's more effective than more capitalism-friendly ways of helping people overcome poverty—then the faith that the charity skeptics have in capitalism is called into question. If charity doesn't work, then a core tenet of historical Christianity is called into question. Of course, either of us might be able to tweak our faith to suit new information. Still, the stakes are high. Whether or not charity works has an impact on how we choose to help people in need, and on how we can imagine that the world works.

Great Expectations

I used to work for a nonprofit social services organization in Mississippi. One day, during a staff meeting, one of our program managers told the staff a story about James (his name, and some facts, have been changed to protect his identity). James was a veteran who spent many years living in homelessness. He was a regular visitor to our food pantry when we approached him about joining one of our permanent supportive housing programs. Permanent supportive housing is a bit of a misnomer. These programs do provide affordable housing, and James was given an apartment that would never cost more than 30 percent of his income and never cost less than $50 a month. They also provide support, and James received intensive case management through the local VA, as well as connections to other organizations that could help him. But these programs are not permanent. That word differentiates them from temporary housing programs that provide housing for a defined time period. Instead of having a year to get back on his feet before getting kicked out, James would have as long as he needed to prepare for independent housing. As long as he was following the rules and making progress, he could stay; and his case manager would let him know when it was time to go.

Several months after he moved into his apartment, the staff at our food pantry noticed that he wasn't coming in anymore. They got in touch with James and asked him why they hadn't seen him. He told them that he had come to realize that he wasn't always responsible with the money that he had, and that he used to use the food pantry to make up for his own poor choices. Now that he had the physical space to make his own food, the financial ability to buy ingredients, and the mental space to think about his situation, he was buying groceries and making his own food. Thanks to this permanent supportive housing program, he didn't need the food pantry anymore.

James's story is a good example of what we learned about the poverty mind-set in chapter two. To people on the outside, homelessness often looks like a single problem. To James, it was a collection of individual puzzles that he had to solve every day. These ranged from where he could sleep that night and how to protect his few possessions to how he could keep himself and his clothes reasonably clean. Each of these puzzles used some of James's mental resources, making it harder to solve problems, plan for the future, and control his impulses. When we gave him an apartment, that took a lot of those puzzles off the table and freed up mental space that he could now use to think about things like his budget and his eating habits.

In this section, I'm going to review some of what we learned about the poverty mind-set in chapter two. Then, I'll look at why the things we learned should cause us to expect charity—whether it's a program like permanent supportive housing or something simpler like giving a few dollars to a panhandler—to work.

In chapter two, we learned about three major facets of Sendhil Mullainathan and Eldar Shafir's research into scarcity. First, scarcity has real effects on two parts of our mental toolkit called fluid intelligence and executive control. Fluid intelligence is the ability to do things like think about abstract concepts and solve problems that don't depend on specific knowledge. When you apply something you learned to a new problem, you're using your fluid intelligence. Executive control is the ability to do things like plan, pay attention, take action, and refrain from taking action. When I see *queso fundido* on a menu and don't order it, I'm using my executive control. Mullainathan and Shafir use the term *bandwidth* to capture both of these ideas, and one of their key findings is that scarcity taxes our bandwidth, and that makes it harder to do things like think abstractly, solve problems, and control impulses.[3]

Second, scarcity tends to focus our attention. For example, it's easier to focus on a writing project and resist the temptations of social media and television when there's an impending deadline. When we experience

3. Mullainathan and Shafir, *Scarcity*, 39–66.

consistent scarcity, that focus can become tunneling: we can become so focused on the project that we need to finish this week that we forget the one that needs to be finished next week. One project falls inside the tunnel and the other falls outside it. This can become a major problem if, when we finish the project that needs to be finished this month, we lift our heads only to see the next project barreling through the tunnel like an oncoming train.[4]

Third, one of the resources that people who face scarcity are missing is slack. Mullainathan and Shafir use the term *slack* in a very specific way, but I'm defining it as having the resources to absorb the unexpected. For example, I keep a certain amount of flex time on my calendar. It isn't devoted to any particular project but exists as a kind of empty space that I expect to be filled, either by something new being put in that spot or by something that was already scheduled but that had to be moved. When we think about money, it means having the money to absorb an unexpected expense (like a car repair), an impulse buy (like movie tickets when a friend wants to go to the new Marvel movie), or something else we didn't budget for.[5]

Poverty is a specific kind of scarcity, and these three facets of the poverty mind-set have two big financial effects. First, there's less room for error. Without slack to take care of unexpected bills, a single shock to a delicate financial situation can make things much worse. Second, and related, people living in poverty tend to be financially savvy. They're more likely to think in terms of trade-offs, meaning that they know that paying for one thing means not being able to pay for something else. They're also more likely to value things consistently across different contexts. For example, the same beer at a hotel bar tends to cost more than it does at the local corner bar. People living in poverty know this and take it into account. Because every dollar means something, people living in poverty usually know more about their finances than relatively wealthy people who have plenty of slack and who don't need to think about these things.[6]

They also lead to what we might think of as a habit that's bad, but necessary: juggling. Imagine that you've been very busy and utterly focused—tunneling, really—on a project that absolutely needs to be done today. You get it done, and as the day ends you give yourself a congratulatory pat on the back. But once you catch your breath, you realize two things. One, that another project is due tomorrow. Two, that you forgot to buy tickets for a show you've been thinking about for ages. Neither of these things came out

4. Mullainathan and Shafir, *Scarcity*, 19–38.

5. Mullainathan and Shafir, *Scarcity*, 69–86.

6. Mullainathan and Shafir, *Scarcity*, 147–64; Davis and Cohen. "Three Myths about the Underbanked, Part Two."

of the blue, but you were so focused on that project that you forgot all about them. Now you have to jump from one pressing responsibility to another. That's juggling.[7]

Not having enough money means having to deal with all of these problems. People who live in poverty tunnel on the expenses that have to be paid now, which reduces the ability to plan, budget, and control impulses. That tunneling can lead to a cycle of using limited resources to pay the most immediately pressing bill, only to discover that there aren't enough resources left to pay the next one. Each choice makes the next one more complicated as resources have to be redeployed, debts need to be considered, and predictable expenses that were once outside the tunnel (and, therefore, all but invisible) reenter with a vengeance.[8]

In one part of their book, Mullainathan and Shafir describe fruit vendors at Koyambedu market in Chennai, India. These poor vendors buy about $20 of fruit in the morning and sell it throughout the day for a gross profit of about $2. Most of the vendors have to borrow the money to buy the fruit, and half of their profits go just to paying the interest on the loan. As Mullainathan and Shafir point out, a vendor could get out of debt by saving just a small portion—maybe ten cents—of her earnings each day and using that to buy her stock. As she bought more and more fruit with her own money and borrowed less and less, she would reduce her debt and improve her situation. In fact, thanks to the power of compounding, it would only take thirty days for her to become debt free![9]

As they point out, though, there are problems with this plan. First, the fruit vendor is preoccupied with too many things that use up valuable bandwidth. Since she doesn't have any slack to deal with mistakes like buying too much or too little stock for that day, every decision is a big one. And that makes the burden even harder to bear. Second, the plan probably isn't as simple as Mullainathan and Shafir make in out to be. Saving a few cents a day sounds easy, but there are bound to be days when she can set aside more and other days when she really needs to use that money. Finally, with no slack, any unforeseen expense will throw off her plan. And with little bandwidth, she's more likely to have an expense that she didn't anticipate; even something entirely predictable will catch her by surprise.[10]

7. Mullainathan and Shafir, *Scarcity*, 127–30

8. Mullainathan and Shafir, *Scarcity*, 127–130.

9. Mullainathan and Shafir, *Scarcity*, 123–25.

10. Mullainathan and Shafir, *Scarcity*, 130–32.

Mullainathan and Shafir decided to do a little experiment. Working with another economist, they studied hundreds of fruit vendors. For some, they just followed their finances. For others, they bought their debt, turning them from debtors into potential savers. And the vendors who were now debt free did exactly what Mullainathan and Shafir wanted. They didn't spend the money unwisely and they didn't go back to borrowing. But, as the year went on, they fell back into debt one by one. By the end of the year, the vendors whose debt had been erased has just as much debt as the ones that Mullainathan and Shafir had left alone. And the reason was surprisingly simple. During the year, each vendor experienced shocks—unexpected expenses like needing to buy a gift for a relative's wedding—that used up her savings and pushed her back into debt. While the vendor was debt free, she didn't have enough slack to absorb the shock.[11]

Mullainathan and Shafir are economists, and their proposals tend to be in the form of policy initiatives and financial instruments. They point out that there are solutions to the problem that the vendors faced that don't involve giving them more money. If they had access to low-cost loans, liquid savings accounts that could only be accessed in an emergency, or some kind of insurance, they wouldn't have fallen back into poverty.[12]

Of course, the same result could have been attained by giving them more money. Here, we can see the power of exchange rates at work. Remember that a fruit vendor might take out a loan of about $20 to cover stock for the day. At the end of the day, she makes about $22 gross profit, paying $21 in loan repayment plus interest and pocketing $1 for herself. Repaying one of these loans is cheap for someone from the United States. If Mullainathan and Shafir had not only bought the loan, but provided an additional $20— enough to pay for an additional day's stock if necessary—would that have given the vendors enough slack to weather the shocks they encountered? Quite possibly. In fact, that additional gift could provide the basis for the emergency savings account!

As I pointed out in chapter two, the important thing here is the direction of causality. It isn't that people with low fluid intelligence, low executive control, poor money management skills, and so on naturally end up living in poverty. It isn't even that most people who experience poverty began with traits like that. Instead, poverty itself uses bandwidth and makes it more difficult both to plan a way out of poverty and to stick to that plan. We should expect that taking the problem of scarcity away—giving people

---

11. Mullainathan and Shafir, *Scarcity*, 133–36.
12. Mullainathan and Shafir, *Scarcity*, 137–38.

enough money or other resources—should result in an increase in available bandwidth, less tunneling, less juggling, and better money management. We might even expect people who come out of poverty to be better at financial management than people who were never in it. After all, they already had good habits—trade-off thinking, value consistency, and so on—that can carry over to a new life.

We see this in Mullainathan and Shafir's example of the fruit vendors at Koyambedu. If they had simply been bad at managing money, we would expect them to fall back into debt pretty quickly. They would have spent their windfall on things they didn't need and started borrowing money again. Instead, what we see is that they managed their money well until they hit a shock that their little bit of slack—if they have any at all—cannot absorb. If they were able to absorb those shocks, we could expect that they could continue to manage their money well, build up their own savings, and get themselves into a position where they could weather those shocks.

We also see this in James's story. When James was homeless, his bandwidth was consumed by the everyday reality of homelessness and the problems that come with it. Once he had an apartment, those bandwidth-eating problems disappeared. Now he knew where he could sleep every night, where he could safely keep his stuff, where he could take a shower, and so on. He applied that newly free bandwidth to managing his budget through making his own meals.

There are a couple of caveats to my claim here. First, obviously, the effectiveness of giving people money depends on how much money we give them. Giving enough money to buy a meal lets the person who receives it buy a meal. But if we want someone to be lifted out of poverty—to the point that they have free bandwidth to apply to other problems—it will take considerably more. Enough to buy a burger wouldn't be enough to transform James's life, but an apartment just might be. My contention is that even a large amount of money would be a worthwhile investment. Second, there's value in identifying the point of leverage where help will do the most good. For the fruit vendors, that might be loan forgiveness and savings accounts. For James, it was housing. In both of these cases, people who were outside of the situation identified those leverage points and applied money to them. But, as we'll see, it's reasonable to imagine that people living in poverty might know best where their leverage points are. These two caveats, though, don't change the central points: given what we know about how poverty affects behavior, we should expect charity—or, at least, giving money to people living in poverty—to work.

The Microfinance "Revolution"

Lindiwe is a twenty-two-year-old juice and soda maker in rural Zimbabwe. She used to make a little over five gallons of her beverages each week. Thanks to a $500 microloan—crowdfunded through Kiva—and training from the Campaign for Female Education, she now makes more than fifty gallons each week, which she sells at her own small shop. She also has a small poultry business, and all of her businesses—the beverage making, the shop, and the poultry—are organized under her own umbrella corporation, Lee Investments. She doesn't pay interest on the loan that she took. Instead, she serves as a mentor and teacher for other women in her area, a form of social engagement that she loves. This small loan helped her grow her business, and now she's making a difference in her community.[13]

Many people in Lindiwe's situation find it extremely difficult to get the credit they need to invest in their own businesses, and there are two big reasons why. First, one way that lenders protect themselves against intentional default is by asking for collateral: something that the creditor can take in the event that the borrower doesn't pay. For many of us in the first world who take out large loans, this might be the very thing we're taking out the loan for. The collateral on a mortgage can be the house, on a car loan it can be the car, and on a business loan it can be all of the business's assets. But someone living in poverty, who has nothing to put up as collateral, cannot secure a traditional loan.[14]

Second, lenders want to know things about their borrowers. These include things that indicate whether the borrower is likely to repay the loan and things that will help the lender track down the borrower if they don't pay: things like how much money the borrower has, what their income is, whether they usually pay bills on time, where they live, and so on. In the United States, a lender can learn these things by looking at a credit report. But for people who have irregular incomes, poor payment histories, unstable housing, and other challenges, it may be more trouble for the lender to find this information than it is worth to make the loan.[15]

Microloans like the one that Lindiwe received ingeniously overcome both of these challenges. First, one common model makes a loan to a group of people. Since the group as a whole is responsible for the loan—if one member defaults, the remaining members have to pick up their share—each person has an interest in making sure everyone else makes their payments.

---

13. Miller, "She's 22, from Rural Zimbabwe, and a Mogul in the Making."

14. Banerjee and Duflo, *Poor Economics,* 162–63.

15. Banerjee and Duflo, *Poor Economics,* 162–63.

Second, loans are repaid as a fixed amount on a regular and often rigid schedule. The loan officer can simply collect the money from the group, make sure it's the correct amount, and move on to the next group. There's no need to track individual borrowers, deal with fluctuating repayment amounts, or track anyone down. These practices make the loans more cost-effective for lenders and keep default rates low: the portfolio at risk for loans in South Asia in 2009—the loans that might default, even though not all of them will—was less than 4 percent.[16]

It's not surprising that charity skeptics embrace microcredit. Steve Corbett and Brian Fikkert refer to a "microfinance revolution," although they do highlight a few challenges. At the time that Corbett and Fikkert were writing, few microfinance institutions offered savings accounts, reached the extreme or rural poor, or allowed loans for things other than businesses. Despite these shortcomings, microcredit puts money into the hands of people living in poverty while pressing all of the right buttons for charity skeptics: it doesn't give anyone anything, it's profitable for the people making the loans, it encourages entrepreneurship, and it uses a perfectly normal practice—lending money—that doesn't threaten the modern economic order. All that borrowers have to do is put their social capital—their relationships and reputations with other people in their communities—up as collateral.[17]

There's some evidence that microcredit works, but charity skeptics—and many microfinance organizations—are probably promoting it with too much optimism. In 2015, a group of economists published six evaluations of microcredit programs, and a summary of those evaluations, in Bosnia and Herzegovina, Ethiopia, India, Mexico, Mongolia, and Morocco. They found that borrowers tended to use their loans to invest in businesses and that those businesses expanded. But microloans appeared to have few, if any, transformative effects. On the one hand, microloans didn't appear to reduce poverty or improve living standards. There was also little evidence that social indicators—things like how empowered women felt or whether children were in school—improved. On the other hand, there was some evidence that borrowers had more choice in what their work was like and what they bought, women claimed more decision-making power, and families

16. Banerjee and Duflo, *Poor Economics*, 166–68.

17. Corbett and Fikkert, *When Helping Hurts*, 189–91; Lupton, *Toxic Charity*, 120–23.

managed risk better. As economists Abhijit Banerjee and Esther Duflo put it, microcredit isn't miraculous, but it works.[18]

There are any number of reasons that microloans might not deliver on the biggest promises of their supporters, even if they're directed to businesses. Families who make money from their small business might give up income from another job, the focus on business might discourage people who need money for other things, the group lending model might discourage people who don't want to be involved in other people's business, and the strict repayment schedule might discourage people who expect lumpy incomes or who have projects that will take time to produce money. Right now, though, I'm going to focus on the reason that's close to the heart of why charity skeptics are such vocal proponents of microcredit: entrepreneurship.[19]

The basic idea behind microcredit is that it will allow people to live stories like Lindiwe's: a young woman uses a microloan to start or expand a business, increasing the business's profits and her own standard of living; eventually, she hires people in her village; and some other people are inspired to start their own businesses. With enough microloans and enough entrepreneurs, a village that has been mired in poverty for generations can develop a robust economy and begin growing its way out of poverty.

But there are two big reasons that relying on entrepreneurship to lift people out of poverty is problematic. First, the businesses owned by people living in poverty are rarely profitable enough to do that. In the United States, politicians spend a lot of time talking about small businesses. The businesses run by people living in poverty tend to be very small. A little shop run out of a home is a standard example. In their book *Poor Economics*, Banerjee and Duflo tell us about a typical home store in rural India with a total stock of 431 items. Not 431 different items, but 431 items total, including things like individual tea bags. In one day, that store sold a handful: a single cigarette to one customer and a few sticks of incense to another. That is not a small business so much as a tiny one.[20]

Tiny businesses are usually too small to make enough of a profit to lift someone out of poverty. For example, when Banerjee and Duflo looked at the sales and profits of tiny businesses in Hyderabad, India, they found that the median business has sales of 11,751 rupees and profits—not including the time that family members put into it—of 1,035 rupees. That's

18. Banerjee et al., "Six Randomized Evaluations of Microcredit"; Banerjee and Duflo, *Poor Economics*, 172.

19. Banerjee et al., "Six Randomized Evaluations of Microcredit"; Banerjee and Duflo, *Poor Economics*, 173–74.

20. Banerjee and Duflo, *Poor Economics*, 216–18.

enough profit to pay one family member about 34 rupees, or about $2, per day. When they looked at similar numbers in Thailand, they found that the median family run business made so little profit that it could only pay a single family member less than $1 a day. This creates a paradoxical situation. On the one hand, it might be good for an investor to lend to that business if it already exists; the marginal return on the investment could be high. On the other hand, that investment still wouldn't make the business profitable enough to support a family. It would be better to make money a different way.[21]

Let me unpack that a little, since it can be difficult to understand how it could be worthwhile to lend to a business that isn't even profitable enough to keep someone out of poverty. There are two different kinds of return on a business: the overall rate and the marginal rate. The overall rate is easy: it's the total revenue minus the operating expenses. If this isn't high enough to cover the value of the time that the owner is putting into the business, it would be better to do something else. The marginal rate is a bit harder: it's what happens to the overall rate when the owner invests another dollar. For many tiny businesses, the marginal rate of return is good: investing another dollar results in more than a dollar of overall revenue. The problem with tiny businesses and microloans is that the growth in overall revenue isn't fast enough. So the business gets a little bigger and the lender gets back his money plus interest, but the business still isn't worth the time that the owner is putting in. The loan is good for the lender, and it may even help the borrower a little, but it won't help the borrower make her way out of poverty.[22]

If the first problem is that these tiny businesses aren't profitable enough, the second problem makes perfect sense: most people don't want to be entrepreneurs. As Robert Lupton points out in *Toxic Charity*, there are many people operating tiny businesses in developing economies. But those businesses aren't the result of a general entrepreneurial drive; they're the result of need. If the only way to make money is to be a shopkeeper, a fruit seller, or a craft maker, people will do it. But, as Banerjee and Duflo found, what most people want is the stability and security of a regular job. Steady jobs have real effects: besides providing a steady source of income that allows families to pay for things they couldn't afford otherwise, employment opens up new avenues of credit, educational opportunities, and access to healthcare. In addition—and drawing on what we know about the poverty mind-set—knowing that income is regular and expected opens up the mental space that a family needs to make good decisions. A family with a steady

---

21. Banerjee and Duflo, *Poor Economics*, 212–18.
22. Banerjee and Duflo, *Poor Economics*, 214–16.

income can imagine the future in a different way than a family that is unsure where the next dollar is coming from or when it will show up.[23]

Neither of these problems is a problem with microcredit itself, or even with microcredit that's aimed at entrepreneurs. People who want to take on the challenge of starting and growing their own business should have access to the credit they need to do so, and microcredit provides that access. But creating an army of passionless owners of unprofitable businesses is not going to end poverty. Banerjee and Duflo put it bluntly: microcredit is valuable because these tiny businesses are often the only way for people living in poverty to make any money at all, but "we are kidding ourselves if we think that they can pave the way for a mass exit from poverty."[24]

Of course, there are success stories about entrepreneurs, like Lindiwe, who have used microcredit to expand their businesses. A microloan really did help Lindiwe invest in her business and increase output. Maybe it will lead to real increases in profitability and a steady climb out of poverty for her and her community. And microloans have uses beyond entrepreneurship. As Mullainathan and Shafir point out, small loans are often used to pay off other debts, buy durable goods, and pay bills. As people living in poverty juggle in order to make ends meet, a small loan can help people solve the puzzle of how to pay the bills. At least, it can do that temporarily, until it comes due. Then it becomes another puzzle to solve.[25]

The problem with best-case scenarios like Lindiwe's is that it undercuts the logic that prefers microcredit over charitable giving. After all, would Lindiwe—who already had three businesses under an umbrella corporation—have done anything differently if Kiva had simply given her $500 and pointed her in the direction of a volunteer opportunity? Perhaps. Maybe she would have used part of the loan for additional training, home maintenance, or savings. But it's hard to believe that she would have done anything with it that wasn't wise. Maybe giving her the money would have worked just as well. Maybe it would have worked even better.

Cash Transfers

Hellen is a thirty-five-year-old dry grain seller in Kenya. In 2017, she began receiving unconditional cash payments from GiveDirectly. Over three payments, she received just under $1,050. Like Jane, she used some of the

23. Banerjee and Duflo, *Poor Economics*, 225–30.

24. Banerjee and Duflo, *Poor Economics*, 234.

25. Mullainathan and Shafir, *Scarcity*, 168.

money to cultivate her land, repair her house, pay school fees (including university fees for her daughter), and buy food. Like Lindiwe, she also expanded her business, which is not making enough to cover what she spends on food for her family. Since she received the money, she's joined a local savings and credit cooperative. She wants to use the credit she can get through the cooperative to diversify her business.[26]

Cash, whether it's provided by a microloan or a cash transfer, is an important resource. Not just because it lets people buy things, but because it offers flexibility. Sociologist Kathryn Edin and social work professor Luke Shaefer ask us to imagine being offered a job with two options for our salary. Option one is a cash salary of $55,000. Option two is a cash salary of $53,000 plus $4,000 in scrip that can only be spent on food. Almost all of us—and almost all of the people who Edin and Shaefer asked—would take the first option over the second, even though option two is more money overall. The reason is simple: the flexibility that cash provides has a value. While we can only spend the scrip on food, we can spend the cash on anything. If we end up in a situation where we're willing to give up a meal or two in order to afford rent, a car repair, or medical care, the cash lets us make that choice. The flexibility of cash is more useful than additional but inflexible purchasing power.[27]

The unconditional cash transfer that Hellen received gave her a lot of flexibility. She used some of that flexibility to meet short-term goals like buying food for her family. She used some of it to meet long-term goals like paying her daughter's university fees. The money gave her choices that she wouldn't have had without it, and the choices she made were good ones. And recent research suggests that Hellen is fairly typical. People living in poverty are likely to make good investments when they have the money to do so.

In this section, I'm going to look at three studies of cash transfers like the one that Hellen received. First, a study in Uganda that used a model similar to the microloan model that I described above, but with a gift instead of a loan. Second, a study in Kenya that simply gave people money. Third, a study in Morocco that compared a conditional cash transfer program—a program that requires recipients to do something in order to get the money—and an unconditional one. After I look at those studies, I'll write a little bit about why they suggest that charity works.

---

26. GiveDirectly, "Hellen's Profile."
27. Edin and Shaefer, *$2.00 a Day*, 106.

In 2008, the Ugandan government experimented with an unconditional cash transfer initiative. Young people between the ages of sixteen
and thirty-five applied to the program in small groups. Each group had to
submit a proposal for how they would spend the money to develop a trade,
but it was clear that no one would enforce that proposal. The money was
completely unconditional. To simplify administration, the grants were distributed to the groups, which divided the money among members. In the
end, thousands of young people in very poor areas received cash payments
equal to about a year's income. The question that a program like this poses
is simple. When a group of young people working an average of ten hours
a week for less than a dollar a day are suddenly flush with cash, what will
they do? Will they invest that money in things like education and business
development? Or will they blow it on temptation goods like alcohol and
tobacco?[28]

Three economists worked together on a major research project to
answer those questions and others. Christopher Blattman, Nathan Fiala,
and Sebastian Martinez looked at a large group of the young people in this
program at three different points in time: before they received the money,
two years after they received it, and two years after that (or four years after
they got the money). They also looked at a control group of young people
who had applied for the grants, but who didn't receive them. In all, they
surveyed more than 2,600 people from both groups to find out whether the
cash transfers made a difference. The study was rigorous, randomized, and
carried out by trained professionals with no stake in its outcome. The results
of this study can give us a good idea of whether unconditional cash transfer
programs can work.[29]

A large majority of the grant recipients did exactly what the people
who ran the program wanted them to do: they invested the money in training for jobs like tailoring and carpentry, and in business assets like tools.
Those investments led participants to work more hours, take on more
skilled work, have higher incomes, and have more wealth. After four years,
program participants were 65 percent more likely to be in a skilled trade,
and had earnings 41 percent higher, than the control group. Recipients also
thought of themselves as being in a better economic position than they
were before they received the grant. To put it simply, while this grant didn't
immediately propel anyone out of poverty, it did have definite economic

28. Blattman et al., "The Economic and Social Returns to Cash Transfers," 4.

29. Blattman et al., "The Economic and Social Returns to Cash Transfers," 4; Yglesias, "The Best and Simplest Way to Fight Global Poverty."

benefits. Grant recipients created wealth for themselves by investing in education and entrepreneurship.[30]

In 2011, GiveDirectly conducted a trial of an unconditional cash transfer scheme in Kenya. The organization gave unconditional cash payments of $404—twice the amount that the average household in the area consumed in a month—to 503 poor households in sixty-three of the poorest villages in the country. In some cases, the households received the money in a lump sum; in others, they received it in payments over nine months. In addition, 137 households were selected to receive an additional large payment. The only requirement for the participating households was that they live in homes with thatched roofs.[31]

Psychologist Johannes Haushofer and political scientist Jeremy Shapiro surveyed the households who received payments and a control group who did not. They also took physical measurements of children and saliva samples to test for cortisol, which is related to stress. I should point out that Shapiro was a founder and ex-director of GiveDirectly, so he may have had an interest in the outcomes. But the study was well-designed, rigorous, and randomized, so—just like the Ugandan study—we can have confidence in its results.[32]

Among families who received the payments, consumption was 23 percent higher than they were before the payments, investments were 58 percent higher, and revenues (though not profits) from income-generating activities were 34 percent higher. Those same families were happier, more satisfied with life, less stressed, and less depressed. In addition, there was no increase in spending on temptation goods. Moreover—in case you were wondering why households had to have a thatched roof—many of the participants used the money to replace their thatched roof with a metal one. This will save those households money over time, since they won't have to replace their roof every year or so.[33]

That last point is an especially important one. Imagine the difference between buying a cheap pair of shoes that you have to replace every year and buying a more expensive pair that can last for years or decades. If you can only afford the cheap pair, you will need to buy them again every year,

30. Blattman et al., "The Economic and Social Returns to Cash Transfers," 4, 19–21.

31. Haushofer and Shapiro, "Household Response to Income Changes," 7–9; Innovations for Poverty Action, "The Impact of Unconditional Cash Transfers in Kenya," lines 31–51.

32. Haushofer and Shapiro, "Household Response to Income Changes," 12–13.

33. Innovations for Poverty Action, "The Impact of Unconditional Cash Transfers in Kenya," lines 53–89.

and that may prevent you from ever having the capital to buy the expensive pair. But you will also end up spending more money as you replace the shoes over time than you would have if you had been able to buy the expensive shoes in the first place. The same principle applies to thatched roofs versus metal ones. Households with thatched roofs have to replace them regularly. By buying a metal roof—or making any number of other investments—the households in the study were making a money-saving investment that freed up future money for other purposes.

From 2008 to 2011, researchers from Innovations for Poverty Action helped the government of Morocco evaluate a pilot version of a cash transfer program called *Tayssir*. This program gave cash payments, equal to about five percent of annual household expenditures but variable depending on the age of the children, to households with children between the ages of six and fifteen, as long as those children were enrolled in school. The researchers modified the program so that it had two tracks. On one track (the conditional cash transfer), families received payments as long as their children didn't miss more than four school days in a single month. On the other track (the labelled cash transfer), the payments were unconditional, but the program was clearly labelled as being tied to education.[34]

The researchers looked at several things, and there were other variables, but the important piece for my purposes is the difference between the conditional cash transfer and the labelled cash transfer. The researchers called the first program a "shove" and the second a "nudge." Conditional cash transfers try to shove recipients into desired activities by providing cash incentives that the families will miss if they disappear. The labelled cash transfer program tried to nudge recipients into the activities—in this case, education—by using the cash transfer to endorse them. Both the shove and the nudge had significant positive impacts on school attendance, dropout rates, and re-enrollment. What was surprising was that the nudge had a higher impact! The labelled cash transfer program did more to encourage education—and got better results—than the conditional one![35]

We don't know exactly why the labelled cash transfer program was so effective, but one theory is that it didn't discourage students who might have been edge cases. While a family with a child who was likely to have more than four absences in a month might not bother with the shove—because they wouldn't think they were going to get the money anyway—they might

34. Benhassine et al.,"Turning a Shove into a Nudge?"; Innovations for Poverty Action, "Conditional Cash Transfers for Education in Morocco."

35. Benhassine et al., "Turning a Shove into a Nudge?"; Innovations for Poverty Action, "Conditional Cash Transfers for Education in Morocco."

enroll in the labelled program. And simply being involved in the first place has positive effects. A shove might discourage people who aren't confident in their ability to meet the requirements. A nudge lets those same people try something without the pressure . . . and maybe even surprise themselves.[36]

The studies in Uganda, Kenya, and Morocco are just three data points. Unconditional cash transfers worked in these cases, and GiveDirectly can be confident in their impact. More importantly, these studies fit in with the growing research literature on cash transfers. That literature strongly suggests that cash transfers—both conditional and unconditional—have positive impacts on people's lives. And that, in turn, suggests that charity might be a surprisingly good thing.

GiveDirectly summarizes the collective findings on cash transfers in three key areas. First, as we saw in each of the studies above, cash transfers can have an array of positive impacts on the people who receive them. Transfers are associated with increased birth weight, reduction in HIV infections and psychological distress, increased schooling, and decreased child labor. Second, cash transfers have long-term effects. People who receive transfers invest the money in ways that lead to increased income in the years that follow (like getting vocational training or investing in a business) and that increase future savings and flexibility (like replacing a thatched roof with a metal one). Third, people who receive cash transfers don't tend to abuse them. Recipients don't spend the money on temptation goods or reduce their work hours. Some studies even show that transfer recipients are less likely to spend money on temptation goods and more likely to work more hours (especially as they move into skilled work)![37]

Of course, none of this guarantees that people living in poverty will use windfalls—whether in the form of cash transfers or lottery winnings—wisely. But the research does strongly suggest that low-income families will use money from cash transfers to invest in things that will improve their lives. For some families, that will be entrepreneurship. For others, it might be education, home improvement, or any number of other things. Those investments will have long-term effects that will increase the health, income, and wealth of those families. And that, again, fits in with what we know about the poverty mind-set.

Unconditional cash transfers aren't terribly different from charity. While the cash transfers that I examined here weren't rooted in a connection to the divine, they were directed specifically towards people living in

36. Benhassine et al., "Turning a Shove into a Nudge?," 117.
37. GiveDirectly, "Research on Cash Transfers."

poverty and they didn't involve reforming their recipients. The first of those points—that they were directed to people experiencing poverty—is obvious. The second point might be a little more subtle. Obviously, these gifts were given in the hope that people would steward that money effectively and make investments that helped them improve their financial situation. The Moroccan experiment even hoped that people would invest in education. But these transfers drew upon the resources that the recipients already had. There was no expectation that recipients would adopt another way of speaking, thinking, or behaving. Instead, there was the belief that people in poverty are already capable of using money effectively.

This should give us some hope that charity works. After all, if giving people money through unconditional cash transfers has positive effects on people's lives, then it should also have those effects when it is given out of a connection to the divine. This also provides some insight into one of the two caveats I gave earlier in this chapter. These cash transfers may look small to American eyes, but they were huge in terms of average household income and consumption in the areas where they were given. Whether smaller gifts would have been as effective is an open question. However, the evidence suggests that large gifts are effective, and it's not much of a leap to suppose that smaller gifts might serve a purpose as well.

Charity Works

One of the reasons that I've spent so much of this chapter focused on research is to provide a contrast to the work that charity skeptics usually do. In *Toxic Charity*, for example, Robert Lupton speaks from personal experience and quotes a handful of other experienced people. His opinion is an informed one, but in the end *Toxic Charity* is composed largely of assertions backed up by anecdotes. Similarly, in *A Framework for Understanding Poverty*, Ruby Payne talks about conducting a naturalistic longitudinal study of poverty. But what she is describing is the fact that her husband's family lived in a low-income neighborhood and that she made casual observations when she was there. Again, she has an informed opinion, but her work is not the result of rigorous study. If we're going to accept big claims like "charity is dangerous" or "poverty is about culture," then we want those to be based on more than impressions. The same is true if we're going to accept equally big claims like "charity works."[38]

38. Payne, *A Framework for Understanding Poverty*, Kindle locations 132–44; Ng and Rury, "Poverty and Education," paragraph 4.

That means that I don't want to get too far ahead of the research, so I want to be clear. None of the research that I've looked at in this chapter proves that charity works in every case, and it certainly doesn't do so if what we mean by "works" is something like "lifts people out of poverty forever." My claim is more tentative than that. The research that I've presented here—and the larger literature that it is a part of—strongly suggests that charity tends to have positive effects on the people who receive it. As I end this chapter, I want to summarize exactly why I find this research so suggestive.

First, Mullainathan and Shafir's research into scarcity in general—and poverty specifically—suggests that one of the major reasons that people living in poverty struggle to get out of it is that poverty itself uses a lot of mental resources. As we've seen, those mental resources include things like the ability to think abstractly, plan ahead, and control impulses. Poverty certainly makes it harder to do things that rely on money, like pay bills, see a doctor, or get an education. It also makes it harder to remember to pay those bills, follow through on going to the doctor, or focus on studying. Poverty means not having enough money, but not having enough money means not having enough bandwidth. But that also means that alleviating poverty can increase bandwidth; or, maybe more accurately, it can free up bandwidth that was previously being used. Giving money to people experiencing poverty can make bandwidth available, and the people who receive that money can then use that bandwidth to improve their situation.

Second, the research conducted by organizations like GiveDirectly suggests that this is exactly what happens. When people living in poverty receive a large sum of money, no strings attached, they tend to spend that money in ways that improve their financial situation. It is at least possible that being given enough money to take the immediate stress of poverty off of the table frees up enough bandwidth that people can reimagine their situation, plan to make changes, and adhere to that plan. Importantly, we see these results with gifts (and an unconditional cash transfer is a gift) and not with loans. After all, loans grant access to money at the price of interest, they don't improve the balance sheet.

These two pieces strongly suggest that large gifts can make a real difference in people's lives. Through cash transfers, Jane and Hellen were able to make significant investments in their homes, families, and businesses. Some of those investments will pay off right away. For example, Hellen's business now makes enough money to cover the cost of food for her family, and that has eased tensions between her and her husband. Some of those investments will pay off over time. Through the in-kind gift of an affordable apartment and intensive case management, James had been able to make small improvements to his life that will pay off in the coming years. While

there are always exceptions to the rule, it appears that charity—at least inso-
far as giving large amounts of money to people in poverty is charity—works.

As far as I'm aware there's no research on the effects of smaller gifts,
and nothing that I've looked at here means that giving a few dollars to a
panhandler works. But we shouldn't overlook the idea that anything can
help. Remember that part of poverty is juggling: moving quickly from one
pressing need to another. A small gift that takes even one need off the table
not only provides immediate relief—a meal eaten, a utility bill paid, rent
made—but can free up a small amount of bandwidth and help someone
solve the next puzzle. And in a charitable world, those small gifts can add
up. Charity works.

6

The Generosity Dividend

In *When Helping Hurts*, Steve Corbett and Brian Fikkert tell a story about Creekside Community Church. Creekside is a white church in the downtown of an unnamed American city. Nearby is a predominantly African American housing project with massive social problems ranging from high unemployment to drug abuse. In Corbett and Fikkert's story, the people of Creekside decided to reach out to the residents of that housing project by buying Christmas presents for their children. For the first few years, this worked wonderfully, and the people of Creekside Community Church were proud of the work they were doing. But after a few years, they grew resentful: every year they delivered Christmas presents, but the residents of the housing project never improved their lives.[1]

Robert Lupton tells a similar story about well-meaning church members delivering Christmas presents to families in the inner city. Like Lupton, Corbett and Fikkert tell us that this kind of giving hurts the families who receive the gifts. Having to rely on white families to deliver Christmas presents contributes to a deep sense of shame and inadequacy, especially for black men, which in turn makes it more difficult for those low-income families to find work. Corbett and Fikkert also tell us that this kind of giving hurts the people who give the gifts! As I wrote above, while the members of Creekside were proud of their work at first, they came to resent the people they were helping. Remember that Corbett and Fikkert believe in many

---

1. Corbett and Fikkert, *When Helping Hurts*, 62–63.

different kinds of poverty; this resentment contributed to the poverty of being and poverty of community of the Creekside members.[2]

It's important to note that the problem that Corbett and Fikkert see here isn't that the members of Creekside Community Church had unrealistic expectations for their Christmas project. Giving Christmas presents to the children in low-income families wasn't going to lift those families out of poverty. Instead, Corbett and Fikkert use this story as an illustration of how charity in general hurts everyone involved. "One of the biggest problems of many poverty-alleviation efforts," they write, is that they "exacerbate the poverty of being of the economically rich . . . and the poverty of being of the economically poor."[3]

In the last chapter, I pushed back against the idea that charity hurts the people who receive gifts and argued that emerging research strongly suggests that giving money to people living in poverty helps them. In this chapter, I'm going to push back against the idea that giving hurts the people who give charitable gifts and argue that the research strongly suggests that generosity is good for us. I'm going to do this by looking at two research trends. First, I'll argue that being generous has direct benefits by looking at research by sociologists Christian Smith and Hilary Davidson. Second, I'll argue that generosity has indirect—but no less important—benefits by arguing that generosity is a key part of community, which has its own set of benefits.

Again, it's important to be clear about the stakes in this chapter. An important part of the theology that I sketched out in chapter four was that charity is good for the person who gives as well as the person who receives. Generosity towards people living in poverty—even to the point of foolishness—is a way for Christians to live their faith in a generous God. To return to the metaphor that I borrowed from Gary Anderson in chapter three, living a generous life is how we relax in the waters of the cosmos and float. It is a way of riding the currents of the universe that a generous God creates and sustains. If charity doesn't help the people who give—or, worse, if it hurts them—then that undermines part of my Christian faith. Similarly, if charity helps the person who gives—and especially if it does something that the kinds of relationships of exchange that charity skeptics advocate for cannot do—that undermines the skeptics' faith in compassionate capitalism.

2. Lupton, *Toxic Charity*, 31–33; Corbett and Fikkert, *When Helping Hurts*, 63–64.

3. Corbett and Fikkert, *When Helping Hurts*, 62.

Getting More Than You Give

Before I became a pastor, I spent about twelve years as a professional fund-raiser. One of the things I learned about during that time—something that I picked up from a blog somewhere—is the power of the post-gift glow. The fact is that you feel good when you give, and a skilled fundraiser can keep that glow going from the time you give a gift through the thank-you letter that you receive and on to the next time that they ask you for money. Keeping that post-gift glow going means you'll be more receptive to the next appeal. You can look at that as a neat trick that fundraisers know or a nasty trick that fundraisers pull, but the point stays the same: fundraisers know that giving makes you feel good.

And giving doesn't just make people feel good. It's actually good for us. In their book *The Paradox of Generosity*, Christian Smith and Hilary Davidson look at what they see as a paradox. It seems like giving should be a zero-sum game. For example, someone who gives ten dollars to their local homeless shelter should simply be ten dollars poorer while the shelter is ten dollars richer. And yet, as reported by people who give money, volunteer, spend time and energy taking care of their families and neighbors, and so on, people who give end up receiving things in return. Similarly, people who hold onto what they already have miss out on opportunities to get other things that they don't have. Giving isn't a zero-sum game. The person who gives ten dollars is in fact ten dollars poorer, and the shelter is in fact ten dollars richer, but the donor is also happier and healthier (among other things). We get back more than we give.

Of course, Smith and Davidson aren't relying on intuition to come to this conclusion. They conducted a survey of almost 2,000 Americans, asking questions about their giving and volunteering as well as questions about their health, happiness, sense of purpose, and more. They also conducted interviews with more than sixty of the people who responded to the survey. Those interviews were carefully analyzed to get a fuller picture of these respondents' lives. Finally, they took thousands of pictures of forty of the households that they studied and collected hundreds of pages of field notes to get an even fuller picture. In this section, I'm going to take a brief look at Smith and Davidson's research, focusing specifically on the ways that donors and volunteers benefit from their generosity.[4]

Smith and Davidson firmly establish the link between generosity and well-being. They examined several different kinds of generosity: regular

4. Smith and Davidson, *The Paradox of Generosity*, 5–6.

financial giving, occasional financial giving, volunteering, relational generosity (giving attention to loved ones, listening to people's problems, and so on), neighborly generosity (visiting others, babysitting for neighbors, and so on), organ donation, lending out personal possessions, and giving through estate planning. They also looked at how people think about their own generosity in two ways. First, in terms of whether people think they are generous in the ways I just listed. Second, in terms of how important people believe it is to be generous. Finally, they compared generosity and attitudes towards generosity with five measures of well-being: happiness, physical health, sense of purpose, avoidance of depression, and interest in personal growth.

Smith and Davidson's deep dive into happiness provides a powerful example of the effects of generosity. They found that people who regularly gave away at least ten percent of their income, volunteered, were relationally generous, and were neighborly were consistently—and considerably—more likely to report that they were very happy and less likely to report that they were very or somewhat unhappy. The same was true about people who thought of themselves as generous and who thought that generosity was important, regardless of whether they were actually generous. And the findings were similar across physical health, sense of purpose, avoidance of depression, and interest in personal growth.[5]

But not every form of giving had that effect. While financial giving, volunteering, relational generosity, and neighborly generosity increased happiness and other indicators of well-being, four forms of giving did not. Occasional financial giving, organ donation, lending out personal possessions, and giving through estate planning had no significant impact. Smith and Davidson offer a compelling explanation for these differences: habitual generosity has a positive impact on well-being, non-habitual generosity does not. And that makes sense. Habitual practices are repeated and meaningful. They become part of who we are in a way that a one-time experience does not. And by becoming part of who we are, they have a greater effect on our lives.[6]

For example, an occasional donation to the Salvation Army, dropped into a red bucket outside a store at Christmas time, doesn't have a major effect on the donor. It's a generous act, but it's also a single moment that can be forgotten by the next day. Regularly giving away ten percent of your income is different. It requires ongoing commitment, planning, and action. It's a generous habit, and it can't be forgotten. That habitual act of regularly

5. Smith and Davidson, *The Paradox of Generosity*, 13–44.

6. Smith and Davidson, *The Paradox of Generosity*, 27.

giving away ten percent of your income takes you past a single generous act to making generosity part of who you are. It changes you from being a person who has done a generous thing, to being a generous person. And it is people who cultivate generosity—who strive to be generous people—who reap the benefits of that generosity.

The direction of causation matters here. Smith and Davidson note that well-being probably has some effect on generosity. Some people are healthier and happier, and are more likely to have a positive outlook, more energy, more money, and more social connections. And it makes sense that people who have those things would also be more generous. However, they also point out that the arrow of causality cannot go in only one direction. After all, if well-being were completely responsible for generosity, then people who are healthy and happy would also be more likely to donate blood or organs. The fact that well-being isn't related to every form of generosity tells us that the causal arrow must also point in the other direction: even if well-being has some effect on generosity, being generous must also have an effect on well-being.[7]

Smith and Davidson lay out nine interrelated ways that generosity improves well-being. I'm going to put these under two broad umbrellas, even though that will leave a couple of ways out. First, generosity tends to improve how we think about ourselves and the world we live in. This includes reinforcing positive emotions, reducing stress, giving us a sense of personal agency, creating positive self-identities, and reinforcing a perception of living in a world of abundance. Second, generosity tends to improve how well integrated we are in our social networks. This includes reducing self-absorption, expanding personal networks, and strengthening relationships. Both of these umbrellas—and the individual ways of improving well-being that they cover—have been shown to improve health, happiness, and other indicators of well-being.[8]

While these two broad umbrellas cover most of the ways that Smith and Davidson explain generosity's effects on well-being, there are two specific ways that are particularly important for my purposes. First, that "generosity expands the number and density of social-network relational ties, which tends strongly to lead to greater happiness and health." Basically, people who practice generosity tend to know more people and have more meaningful relationships. Generosity creates and strengthens communities.

7. Smith and Davidson, *The Paradox of Generosity*, 49–52.
8. Smith and Davidson, *The Paradox of Generosity*, 53–85.

And that idea will be important as I move into the more complicated argument of the next section.[9]

Second, "practicing generosity requires and reinforces the perception of living in a world of abundance and blessing, which itself also increases happiness and health." There are two sides to this idea that Smith and Davidson focus on. On the one hand, believing that the world is a place of scarcity and vulnerability is bad for us: it triggers biological fight or flight responses, closes off social relationships, and causes us to avoid risks and threats. On the other hand, believing that the world is a place of abundance and safety is good for us. Smith and Davidson write that the generous people they spoke to felt a sense of liberation—a freedom to enjoy what they had instead of worrying about not having enough—when they thought of the world as a place of abundance. We are built, they write, so that we thrive when we "experience the liberation, enjoyment, gratitude, confidence, and openness that accompany life in a perceived world of abundance." This idea will be important as I conclude this section below.[10]

As I wrote at the beginning of this section, Smith and Davidson see all of this as a paradox. It seems like someone who gives away money, energy, time, or attention should experience that giving as a loss; and only the person who receives should experience a gift. But—as anyone who has given or volunteered can tell you, and as Smith and Davidson's research shows—people who are generous receive far more than they give. Regularly giving away ten percent of your income means losing money, but it also means gaining happiness, healthiness, a sense of purpose, and an interest in personal growth. "In letting go of some of what we own for the good of others," they write, "we better secure our own lives, too."[11]

The fact that we receive more than we give away is paradoxical . . . from a secular sociological point of view. But there is no paradox if we look at this from a Christian perspective. As I've written repeatedly, the Christian understanding is that the world we live in reflects the generosity of the God who creates and sustains it. Living a generous life is a way of tapping into that generosity. It is a way of relaxing, leaning back, and floating on the natural currents of a generous cosmic order. Of course generosity makes life easier. Of course people who are generous—not simply people who commit an occasional generous act, but people who cultivate generosity as a habit—are happier, healthier, and have a greater sense of purpose. They are

---

9. Smith and Davidson, *The Paradox of Generosity*, 78–82.

10. Smith and Davidson, *The Paradox of Generosity*, 74–78.

11. Smith and Davidson, *The Paradox of Generosity*, 11, 224.

being who they are called to be and living in the world in the way that they are called to live in it. And, of course, people who choose to be generous experience the world as a place of abundance and blessing; they are seeing the world as it really is.

Smith and Davidson aren't writing from a Christian perspective, and it would be unfair to claim that their research into how generosity affects people proves that a Christian understanding of the nature of the universe is right. But their research does do two important things. First, it demonstrates that generosity is good for the generous person. People who give—including people who give to people who are experiencing poverty—are better off in a variety of ways. Second, the relationship between generosity and well-being is built into the human experience. The fact that generosity is good for us isn't a fluke. It is part of how we are made. Generosity is part of being most fully human. We could even go so far as to say that generosity is part of having an abundant life.

Generosity and Community

The story that Corbett and Fikkert tell about well-meaning church members delivering Christmas gifts to low-income families is a story about charity and community. Like many churches that take on this kind of project, Creekside Community Church almost certainly saw their project as an opportunity to build community with their low-income neighbors. As the project went on, and as the church members failed to see improvement in their neighbors' financial circumstances—again, a lot to demand from Christmas present delivery—their trust in those neighbors deteriorated. It's not simply that the church members saw their efforts as a failure; they started seeing their neighbors as part of the problem. If giving Christmas gifts wasn't working, it must have been because the people receiving those gifts weren't doing their part to change their lives.

Smith and Davidson make a compelling case that generosity is good for generous individuals. Individuals who cultivate a habit of generosity are happier, healthier, and have a greater sense of purpose. It seems like the same should be true of communities. This theory hinges a little on what we mean by community. Sometimes, we use that word to mean a group of individuals. In this sense, a community is healthy and happy when all—or some, or a majority, or some other threshold—of its members are healthy and happy. Other times, we use the word *community* to mean that a group of individuals is greater than the sum of its parts. In this sense, a strong community isn't strong because its individual members are strong. It's strong because something about those individuals coming together makes it strong. Either way, it seems like communities that cultivate generosity as a social habit—that teach their members to be generous and that embody generosity as a community—should enjoy a host of benefits that are rooted in that generosity.

In this section, I'm going to argue that generosity provides benefits for communities. I'm going to do that by looking at three things. First, I'll argue that a community is something more than a collection of individuals. I'll draw on two influential works by philosopher Charles Taylor and political scientist Robert Putnam to make a historical argument for community. Taylor explores the gradual and centuries-long shift from premodern social imaginaries to modern ones. This is a shift that includes big changes in how people have thought about themselves as individuals and how they have thought about communities. Putnam explores a faster and decades-long decline in social capital in the United States, eroding the sense of community that modern Americans have shared. Together, these two stories can help us understand how the idea of community has changed over time. More importantly, they can help us imagine community in a new and more robust way.

Second, I'll draw on Putnam to argue that community is good for us. When Putnam argues this, he means that places with large amounts of social capital enjoy benefits like health, education, safety, and economic prosperity. I will go beyond that and argue that reclaiming aspects of the premodern idea of community would be benefit us. While it would be impossible—and undesirable—to return to premodern ways of thinking, there are ways that we can adapt those ways of thinking to strengthen our modern communities.

Third, and finally, I'll draw on the work of anthropologist David Graeber to argue that generosity plays a key role in community. Community—at least in the sense that it is something bigger than the sum of its individual parts—is rooted in the act of sharing what we have with each other. Not only our money, but our personal possessions, time, energy, attention, and, to some extent, our identities. Extravagant generosity is the basis for a deep sense of community.

In *A Secular Age*, Charles Taylor tries to answer a question about the nature of modern Western society: how did we go from a society where it was almost impossible not to believe in God—in, say, the year 1500—to one where many people find it easy not to believe in God? If I'm right that charity is rooted in Judaism and Christianity, and that charity is at the heart of Christianity, then I have a similar question: how did we go from a world where charity was a privileged way of helping people living in poverty to one where charity skepticism is not only possible but increasingly popular (and even popular in church settings)?[12]

To answer his question, Taylor looks at the centuries-long shift from premodern social imaginaries to modern ones. A social imaginary is a collection of all of the things—institutions, traditions, symbols, practices, and so on—that help us think of ourselves as . . . well, as an "us." Social imaginaries make us more than a collection of individuals; they make us a community. They aren't rational. We don't think about them. We don't decide on them. They're simply shared, often unspoken, understandings of how things are and how things should be. Taylor identifies many differences between premodern social imaginaries and modern ones. I'm going to focus on three of those that have a particular impact on how we imagine communities: disenchantment, the buffering of the self, and lowering the bar of human flourishing.

First, modern social imaginaries are disenchanted. Our premodern ancestors saw the world as a living place; relics and holy places had both power and agency. Taylor uses complicated language to describe this, but philosopher James K. A. Smith summarizes him nicely: for premodern people, things could do stuff. Not only could the bones of a saint heal someone, they could, in a way, want to heal someone. In the modern world, we tend to imagine the world as a machine. If we're religious, we might believe that there are supernatural creatures—gods, spirits, demons—pulling the levers. But even if we believe that, those supernatural creatures are still working a machine. In general, people are the only agents, and the world is something that can be dominated, controlled, and used.[13]

Second, and related to the first point, modern people imagine themselves as buffered. In the premodern world, a person was open to the world around him. That openness is what made it possible for demons to possess him or a relic to heal him: power could flow freely between the enchanted world and the person. In the modern world, we imagine ourselves as closed off. We are each the consciousness that lives in our heads, separate from the outside world, and even separate from the bodies that we control. So, for example, a premodern person who was depressed was in the grip of melancholy, a black bile that literally filled his body and affected his soul. And it could be treated with light, gardens, and warm baths. A modern person who is depressed has depression; it doesn't possess him, he possesses it. And that

12. Taylor, *A Secular Age*, 25.
13. Taylor, *A Secular Age*, 31–37; Smith, *How (Not) to Be Secular*, 28–29.

can be treated with pills that change his brain chemistry, releasing the real person who lives underneath.[14]

Third, modern social imaginaries focus on our well-being in the here and now. Premodern people lived in a tension. On the one hand, they lived in this world and they were concerned about many of the same things we are today. They cared about having a decent place to live, enough to eat, loving family and friends, and all of the things that make up ordinary life. On the other hand, there was a call to reach towards something beyond that ordinary life. Premodern people sought something beyond ordinary well-being; something, maybe, like heaven. Without getting into details, what's important is that they lived with this tension, and they had a variety of ways for letting off the steam that built up. In modern social imaginaries, we don't deal with that tension. Instead, we've found ways to resolve it, usually by giving up on anything beyond our well-being in the here and now. We don't try to reach out to something beyond this world; we often don't even believe there's anything beyond this world to reach out to. Smith describes this shift from premodern ideas about human flourishing to modern ones as lowering the bar for flourishing.[15]

These three strands come together in how we imagine community. In the premodern, enchanted, porous, other-world-seeking social imaginaries of our ancestors, community was extremely important. And everyone who was a part of a community affected everyone else who was a part of that community. For example, say that a community had a special rite that they believed guaranteed a good harvest: they would gather in a field at the beginning of the planting season to read passages from the Bible and take communion. A single person who doubted the power of that rite could make it less effective, increasing the chances of a famine and endangering the whole community. On the one hand, those kinds of stakes meant that communities enforced orthodoxy and punished heresy. These weren't just private opinions, but affected the entire village or kingdom. On the other hand, those kinds of stakes must have meant that members of the community had responsibilities towards each other. Keeping the community strong and safe could mean getting rid of members who posed a threat, but it could also mean restoring and redeeming them.[16]

In our modern, disenchanted, buffered, here-and-now social imaginaries, communities are a very different thing. Communities are collections of individuals who come together for some common good. Otherwise, we

14. Taylor, *A Secular Age*, 37–43; Smith, *How (Not) to Be Secular*, 29–30.
15. Taylor, *A Secular Age*, 43–54; Smith, *How (Not) to Be Secular*, 31–34.
16. Taylor, *A Secular Age*, 41–43; Smith, *How (Not) to Be Secular*, 30–31.

tend to live our own private lives. For example, whether I shovel my sidewalk matters to my neighbors, and whether they shovel theirs matters to me, so everyone shovels for the good of the neighborhood. But my religious beliefs don't affect my neighbors, and theirs don't affect me, so we don't bother each other about them. Sidewalk clearing is part of the public sphere, religious beliefs are part of the private sphere, and those two spheres are kept as separate as possible. On the one hand, this means that we aren't nearly as concerned about orthodoxy and heresy. A person can have weird—even obnoxious or bigoted—private views and still participate in their society. On the other hand, we are less concerned about each other. Our neighbors' problems, as long as they don't affect us directly, aren't our concern.[17]

Taylor's story about the shift from premodern social imaginaries to modern ones is also a story about a shift from premodern communities to modern ones. We might think about premodern communities as super-organisms composed of individuals. That kind of community loses something when an individual part of it leaves. And each individual loses something when they aren't a part of the community. Modern communities are different. We aren't part of a super-organism anymore. Instead, our communities are places where self-sustaining individuals come together for some common project. And those communities are thinner—more tenuous—than their premodern counterparts. Beyond that, modern communities have been going through another substantial change over the last several decades: they've become even weaker versions of themselves.

In *Bowling Alone*, Robert Putnam looks at the erosion of community over the second half of the twentieth century. He does this through the lens of social capital. The fact that he can think of community in that way is important: social capital is an economic way of thinking about community. Capital is anything that increases a person's ability to contribute to the economy. For example, screwdrivers and hammers are physical capital for a carpenter. Similarly, a degree in accounting or economics is human capital for a financial analyst. Each of those things helps the person who has them be more economically productive. Social capital is a way to imagine that social networks are something that a person can use to increase their economic productivity. Our premodern ancestors would never have been able to think about their communities as economic tools. Not only can we think of them that way, it's easy for us to do that. We even have large corporations—social media networks like Facebook and Twitter—whose entire business model

---

17. Taylor, *A Secular Age*, 41–43; Smith, *How (Not) to Be Secular*, 30–31.

is based on monetizing our social networks. That's a major shift in how we think about community.[18]

Putnam doesn't look at that shift. Instead, he's focused on the decline in social capital in the United States over the second half of the twentieth century. Basically, even our modern communities have gotten thinner. For example, by the end of the twentieth century, a substantial number of Americans had opted out of political life (even if they were involved in specific elections): a smaller percentage of people voted, went to political rallies, worked for political parties, ran for office, signed petitions, wrote to their representatives, sent letters to the editor, made speeches, and so on. And the decline in social capital wasn't confined to politics. Putnam found similar trends in civic participation, religious life, workplace connections, informal social connections, altruism (including giving and volunteering), and social trust.[19]

One of the measures of social capital that Putnam looks at is philanthropy. While Putnam uses that word to refer to almost any kind of giving, he also recognizes that philanthropy became more professional and organized in the early twentieth century. And you might remember from chapter three that philanthropy is a particularly modern form of giving rooted in voluntary giving, the concentration of wealth (either in individuals or organizations), a reformist spirit, and institutionalization. In practice—when directed towards people living in poverty—philanthropy tends to mean individuals voluntarily pooling their money and paying professionals to help people experiencing poverty change.

Putnam shows two things about philanthropy in the United States. On the one hand, the absolute number of dollars has increased. In constant 1996 dollars, giving grew from $280 per capita in 1960 to $522 per capita in 1995. A more recent statistic shows that, in constant 2016 dollars, giving rose from $333 per capita in 1954 to $1,204 per capita in 2016. On the other hand, though, Americans are spending more money on almost everything, and giving as a fraction of our income has decreased over that same time period: from 2.26 percent of income in 1964 to just 1.61 percent in 1998. Americans are spending more across the board, but giving hasn't kept its share of that spending. Despite the growing number of absolute dollars, Americans spent the second half of the twentieth century becoming stingier, not more generous.[20]

---

18. Putnam, *Bowling Alone*, 18–24.

19. Putnam, *Bowling Alone*, 31–47.

20. Philanthropy Roundtable, "Statistics on U.S. Generosity"; Putnam, *Bowling Alone*, 122–27.

Putnam also looks at social trust as a measure of social capital. Social trust is the kind of trust that a person might put in a family member, neighbor, or even a stranger. And it's different from the kind of trust that a person might put in government or social institutions. For example, the trust that lets a tourist in New York City hand their phone to a stranger so that stranger can get a photo of them in front of a landmark is social trust. And we can further divide social trust into thin trust (the kind of trust we have when we trust that stranger we just handed our phone to) and thick trust (the kind of trust we share with someone we've known for years). Putnam shows that both thin and thick social trust steadily declined over the second half of the twentieth century. People just don't trust each other as much as they used to.[21]

Social trust is obviously important to any idea of community. Everything from potluck dinners with neighbors to multi-billion-dollar business deals rely on two basic beliefs. First, that other people are going to do what they say they're going to do (like bringing a dish for the potluck). Second, that no one is going to take unfair advantage of the situation (by always bringing a small dish while eating the most food). As social trust has declined, Americans have turned to other methods to enforce those social contracts. Putnam notes that we increasingly use preventative lawyering: we hire lawyers, draft contracts, and use the courts to document and enforce what used to be informal agreements. Without social trust, civility is a matter of law.[22]

In part, the stories that Taylor and Putnam tell are stories about community becoming thinner. In Taylor's case, it was about the shift from a community that was a kind of super-organism to a community that is nothing more than a collection of individuals working on a common project. In Putnam's case, it's a story about the shift from those individuals being deeply engaged with each other on a regular basis to those individuals being less engaged with each other. That's true both in the sense of being more lightly engaged and being engaged less often. And there's no reason to believe that this shift—this decline in social capital—stopped at the end of the twentieth century. Even in terms of our thin modern sense of community, our communities are becoming even more tenuous.

We shouldn't be surprised that our ideas of community—and our communities themselves—have changed over time. Ideas, institutions, and all of the things that make up our social lives are always changing. Sometimes

21. Putnam, *Bowling Alone*, 134–44.
22. Putnam, *Bowling Alone*, 146–47.

that change is for the better; sometimes it's fairly neutral; sometimes it's for the worse. Putnam makes a powerful argument that the decline in social capital has left us worse off. And there are good reasons to believe that the thinning of community from the premodern world to the modern one has also left us in a worse position than we used to be in.

In the second part of *Bowling Alone*, Putnam introduces the Social Capital Index. The Index uses fourteen criteria—things like the percentage of people who served as an officer for an organization in the last year and the percentage of people who think that other people can be trusted—to assign a single number that measures social capital. Putnam looked at the Index on a state-by-state level and assigned each state a score. North Dakota had the most social capital with a score of 1.71, while Nevada had the least amount of social capital with a score of -1.43. Other states filled in the spaces between those two extremes. It shouldn't be surprising that states with high scores on the Social Capital Index also score better on other measures of well-being. Among other things, they score better on the Kids Count Index and Index of Educational Performance, have lower rates of violent crime, score higher on the Healthy State Index, and have lower age-adjusted mortality rates. Overall, states with high levels of social capital are better off when it comes to education, children's welfare, public safety, economic prosperity, health, happiness, and democratic participation.[23]

Putnam offers a few reasons for this relationship between social capital and well-being. One of those reasons is especially important for my purposes. Besides allowing community members to solve collective problems and advance the common good, facilitating the exchange of information, and helping us cope with trauma, social capital helps people see the ways in which our lives are intertwined. On the one hand, people who join communities and organizations are "more tolerant, less cynical, and more empathetic to the misfortunes of others." On the other hand, people who aren't connected to their communities are more likely to give in to their worst impulses. And beyond those specifics, people who believe that their well-being is linked to the well-being of other people are more likely to support things like quality education and responsible policing that help communities have all the other benefits that come along with high social capital.[24]

Putnam gives us good reasons to believe that social capital declined during the second half of the twentieth century and, because social capital is good for us, that we lost something important during that decline. It's much harder to make the case that we also lost something in the shift from

23. Bowling Alone, "Research"; Putnam, *Bowling Alone*, 298, 300, 309, 330.

24. Putnam, *Bowling Alone*, 288–89.

premodern social imaginaries to modern ones. We don't have the same kind of empirical data. Even if we did, too many other things have also changed. Our ideas about community have changed over the last few centuries, but so have forms of government, legal systems, scientific knowledge, technologies, and hundreds of other things. The link between slowly changing social imaginaries and human well-being isn't clear cut.

But there's still a case for that link. Remember the three features of premodern social imaginaries that I outlined above: people lived in an enchanted world, were open to the powers of that world, and reached towards something beyond ordinary human flourishing. This meant that people understood that their lives were interconnected. Each person really was their neighbor's keeper. On the one hand, as I wrote above, this meant that communities were very concerned about orthodoxy and heresy. That concern—especially when it turns into a demand for conformity—isn't something that we want to reclaim. On the other hand, though, it must have also meant that communities were concerned with the well-being of their members. After all, the well-being of the community was inextricably tied up with the well-being of each of its members. If this is combined with the idea that my eternal fate is directly linked to how I treat people living in poverty, then I have to accept that my well-being—both here and now and in the hereafter—depends on my generosity towards people experiencing poverty now.

In the world of our modern social imaginaries, we don't have many reasons to look out for our neighbor's well-being. Perhaps we will do that if we can see some obvious personal benefit to helping them. For example, we might argue that a strong education system is important because it means that the teenager at the checkout counter will be able to make change when the computers go down. But outside of those benefits that come back to me in the here and now, there just aren't many reasons to support big social programs or take personal action to help people in our communities. I am suggesting that reclaiming a deeper sense of interconnectedness and a belief that there is some kind of flourishing beyond the here and now would benefit us all. It would allow us to take on big social projects that might not benefit us personally, but would benefit the community in generations to come. Super-organism communities might be even better off than strong modern communities.

So far in this section, I've established two things. First, that our ideas about communities—and our communities themselves—have changed both over the last several centuries and the last several decades. In the broadest terms, we've gone from imagining ourselves as fundamentally embedded in communities to imagining ourselves as individuals who can choose to be part of a community when and how we want to be. And even in that second understanding, we've become less engaged with our communities over the last seventy years or so. Second, that being engaged in community is good for us in a variety of ways. Among other things, strong communities are safer, healthier, happier, and more prosperous. If we want to be better off, we should build communities. If we want future generations to be better off, we should reclaim a deeper sense of community. And at this point of the book it shouldn't surprise you that one of the best ways to do that is through generosity.

Generosity plays two big roles in building community. First, generosity is at the root of our most basic social relationships. There's a common myth—common enough that it shows up in economics textbooks—that communities that haven't developed money use a barter system. If one person has some cloth and wants an egg, she needs to find someone who is in the opposite situation: who has an egg and wants some cloth. If she can't do that, she needs to find a string of trades that begin with her having cloth and end with her having an egg. But according to anthropologist David Graeber, there's no real support for this theory. People in societies that haven't developed money don't barter among themselves. Some communities store goods in a common space and allocate them based on criteria like need. Others expect members to share with each other: the person with an egg gives it to his neighbor, knowing that if he ever needs some cloth, his neighbor will return the favor. Regardless of how they handle things among themselves, they only barter with strangers.[25]

This isn't just true of pre-monetary societies. It's true in our daily lives, too. Most of our relationships—especially our closest relationships—work according to a principle like "from each according to their ability, to each according to their need." When someone asks for something, as long as the request is small enough or the need big enough, we give them what they ask for. On one end of that spectrum, that might mean giving a guest a glass of water, a coworker some help on a project, or a stranger directions to where they're going. On the other end, it might mean giving a refugee a safe place to stay, an accident victim a blood transfusion, or a hurricane survivor the money to start rebuilding their life. Like the sharing economy I mentioned above—where members are expected to share what they have with people who ask, knowing that their neighbor will return the favor if asked—we might keep track of who owes us one, and we might refuse to share with someone who abuses our generosity, but we start by sharing. In fact, we

25. Graeber, *Debt*, 96, 28–36.

usually don't even keep score. And, when you think about it, we only stop sharing and start demanding payment under pretty specific conditions.[26]

Second, as we learned from Smith and Davidson, generosity creates new social connections and strengthens existing ones in the communities that we're already a part of. Anyone who has volunteered knows this. When I worked for a community organization that had volunteers from across the country come on mission trips to work with our staff and the people we served, I saw firsthand how those volunteers built relationships with each other and with our clients. Groups from different churches would come on mission trips at the same time and develop long-term relationships with each other. And I regularly heard from volunteers who would ask how the family whose house they repaired—or the person who they assisted in the food pantry, or the person who they talked to in the day center—was do-ing. According to Smith and Davidson, volunteers learn about and develop social ties with the people they serve.[27]

Giving money also strengthens relationships. Smith and Davidson write that giving money almost always requires donors to get involved with a local organization or research a non-local one. After giving a gift, smart organizations will tell those donors what their gift did, and many donors will want to know who their gift helped. Even giving directly to a person helps build relationships. Striking up a conversation with a panhandler, or taking a few minutes to talk to someone you see every day, creates a new relationship. And financial giving is an even more powerful community-building tool when it's combined with neighborly generosity. In a virtuous cycle, generosity helps us get to know each other, and getting to know each other gives us permission to be more generous—to give as we are able to our friends and neighbors who are in need—with each other.[28]

I've already mentioned that people in societies that haven't developed money tend to share among themselves and barter with strangers. Even in our society—where money is everywhere—we only use money under cer-tain conditions. And this is important. Being generous keeps relationships going. On a basic level, if you invite me over for a meal, I owe you one. Our relationship will go on at least until I've repaid that debt. Of course, real life is more complex. In the kind of relationship where we invite each other over for meals, we don't keep accounts. It would be rude for me to keep track of the number of meals I've fed my friends and expect us all to settle accounts

26. Graeber, *Debt*, 94–102.

27. Smith and Davidson, *The Paradox of Generosity*, 78–79.

28. Smith and Davidson, *The Paradox of Generosity*, 78–79.

at some point. We're generous towards each other with a general expectation that we will continue to be generous towards each other.[29]

Things are different when we don't want the relationship to continue. The Thai restaurant I go to doesn't want me to owe them one or for me to invite the chef over to my house for dinner. They may appreciate relationships with repeat customers, but their business model is based on serving anyone—preferably lots of people—and not having to maintain relationships over the long-term. So I pay at the end of the meal and our relationship is over. We might start a new relationship if I come back for another meal, but each experience is a new relationship that begins when I order and ends when I pay. Community members, where there is social trust and where there are social bonds, share; strangers, where there is no social trust and social bonds are tentative and often temporary, pay. By keeping relationships open, generosity builds communities.[30]

I started this section with a story about how our idea of community has changed over the last few centuries. We used to imagine ourselves as part of a community. Just as importantly, we used to find it much harder to imagine ourselves apart from a community. Now, we imagine ourselves as individuals. We are buffered from the no-longer-enchanted world and from each other. It can be hard for us to understand this—the premodern world is alien to us—but it means that we know fewer friends and neighbors and more strangers. And, even in modern terms, we are less and less engaged with those strangers.

And that's too bad. Being part of a community is good for us in a variety of ways. People who are engaged with their modern communities are more likely to be happy, healthy, safe, and well educated. And while we can't make the same claims about premodern communities—and there are plenty of things about those communities that we wouldn't want to reclaim—there are reasons to believe that the sense of interconnectedness that people in those communities had was beneficial to them. At the very least, we would be better off if we understood that our well-being depends on the well-being of our neighbors, and that the choices we make now have impacts on generations that aren't here yet.

It's no surprise that generosity is one powerful way to build communities. It increases social trust and bonding, making generous people more likely to believe that it's safe to engage in relationships with their neighbors. It helps us see the world as a place of abundance and blessing, where we

29. Graeber, *Debt*, 100–2.

30. Graeber, *Debt*, 100–2.

are free to share with our neighbors. It gives us a sense of agency, helping generous people believe that their generosity matters. Together, these mechanisms form a virtuous cycle: each gift makes us more likely to see the benefits of giving again. And, as a result of these and other mechanisms, generous people are more likely to be engaged with their communities, have more social connections, and have stronger bonds with other people in their social networks. Generosity is the cornerstone of strong communities, and strong communities benefit us all. And, of course, that means that charity—one form of generosity—confers these benefits as well.

Charity Skepticism and Community

Before I close this chapter, I need to return to Corbett and Fikkert's Christmas story one more time. In this story, the people of Creekside Community Church come to see the people who they were excited to help as people who are fundamentally irresponsible and untrustworthy. The people living in the nearby housing project go from being the victims of unemployment, domestic violence, and other social problems to being "unwed mothers who just keep having babies in order to collect bigger and bigger welfare checks." The residents didn't change, and Corbett and Fikkert are quick to point out that there are a variety of reasons that these families have trouble escaping poverty (and according to Corbett and Fikkert, of course, one of those reasons is the very project that the members of Creekside had taken on). But the change in church members' attitudes is important: as they saw the residents fail to improve their situation, they grew to disdain the residents. Corbett and Fikkert, taking on some of that attitude themselves, chalk it up to compassion fatigue.[31]

Of course, one of the core arguments of charity skepticism is that charity does more harm than good. And behind that argument is the idea that people who are living in poverty either already are irresponsible or are made irresponsible through receiving charity. Think of Lupton's claim that mission trips and service projects weaken the people being served, foster dishonest relationships, erode the work ethic of the recipients, and deepen dependency. Or Payne's quiz about whether you could survive in poverty, which includes things like knowing how to get a gun (even with a police record), how to get someone out of jail, and how to fight. Charity skepticism repeatedly presents people living in poverty as though they cannot use

31. Corbett and Fikkert, *When Helping Hurts*, 62–63.

charitable gifts responsibly, either because they are hurt by charity itself or because of some kind of culture of poverty.[32]

Another core argument of charity skepticism—and one that I'll look at in more detail in the next chapter—is that the right way to help people living in poverty is a sort of compassionate capitalism. According to the skeptics, we shouldn't give people money. Instead, we should provide loans, encourage employment and entrepreneurship, and teach people to adopt middle-class cultural values. In other words, we should teach people to be self-sufficient. For example, one reason that Lupton is against charity is that he believes that it puts the person who gives above the person who receives. But Lupton also provides an example of parity (in which both parties are equal): a thrift store. According to Lupton, a thrift store "relies on attracting paying customers to purchase as many clothes as they are able." In other words, equality appears where people stop sharing and start paying.[33]

In the last section, I mentioned the question that motivated Taylor's work in *A Secular Age*: how did we go from a society where it was almost impossible to not believe God to one where it wasn't only possible, but easy and increasingly common? I also mentioned that I have a similar question: how did we go from a world where charity was the privileged way of helping people who live in poverty to one were charity skepticism is not only possible in our wider society, but popular even in Christian churches? Fortunately, at least one part of the answer to these questions might be the same. As we began to imagine ourselves as buffered individuals whose fates were not dependent on anyone else, we could also imagine ourselves as self-sufficient. And we could demand self-sufficiency from others. That included imagining that people living in poverty were responsible for their own condition: they could choose either to remain poor or to do the work to escape poverty. The same centuries-long shift from premodern social imaginaries to modern ones made charity skepticism possible.

Similarly, one result of the decades-long decline in social capital has been a similar decline in social trust. When people are embedded in communities, we tend to trust each other more. As we have become less embedded—more isolated and individualistic—that trust has evaporated. That includes both the thick trust we have for close acquaintances and the thin trust that we have for strangers. And it certainly includes whatever trust we had for people who live in poverty. Put together, these trends— along with the research showing that giving people money works and that

32. Lupton, *Toxic Charity*, 16; Payne et al., *Bridges Out of Poverty*, Kindle locations 564–88.

33. Lupton, *Toxic Charity*, 37.

stronger communities are good for us—suggest that charity skepticism isn't the result of a hard-nosed look at the realities of charitable giving. Instead, they suggest that charity skepticism is the result of growing individualism and isolation. Charity skepticism may very well be one more thing that is hurting all of us. And that's true both because charity skepticism is driving us away from community-building generosity and because it is driving us towards community-damaging exchange.

The Generosity Dividend

The evidence that charitable giving is good for the people who receive it is clear. As I showed in the last chapter, many studies have shown that people who receive charitable gifts—especially when those gifts are large—benefit from it. The evidence that charitable giving helps the giver isn't as clear, but it is compelling. On the one hand, there is strong evidence that generous people are happier, healthier, have greater senses of purpose, avoid depression, and have a greater interest in personal growth. On the other hand, there is good evidence that community is good for us and that generosity contributes to building strong communities. The case for giving being good for givers might not be as strong as the case that it is good for receivers. But it is strong enough to give us good reasons to be generous.

Of course, there are some caveats to that claim. First, the research shows that generosity in general is good for us. That includes financial giving, but it also includes things like neighborly and relational generosity. It's possible that helping my middle-class neighbor move is just as good for me as—maybe even better for me than—donating $100 to a farmer in Kenya or giving $5 to the homeless man hanging out near the gas station. But it's also true that if generosity in general is good for us, charitable giving almost certainly is, as well.

Second, none of this means that we can't be generous and have a superiority complex. Corbett and Fikkert are right that human pride can distort the good impulse to help others and change that impulse into a God complex. Of course, that sense of pride doesn't only show up when we give money or participate in a mission trip. Pride can be just as much of a problem when we help someone find a job, provide a loan, or open a thrift store. The kind of help doesn't cause or prevent pride. What can prevent pride is the early Christian belief that the person who is receiving charity is in a position of privilege. The giver might be providing for the material comfort of the receiver, but it is the receiver who is contributing to the giver's eternal well-being.

Even with those caveats, the case for generosity being good for the people who are giving is strong. If we want to live better lives—if we want to be happier and healthier individuals, if we want safer and more educated communities, among other things—one excellent way to do that is to develop habits of generosity. That may include things like comforting family members, watching over our friends' houses, and volunteering. It definitely includes giving to people experiencing poverty. Generosity pays a very real dividend. Once again, charity works.

7

A Charitable Community

In 1850, a fifteen-year-old Scottish immigrant worked as a messenger for a telegraph office in Pittsburgh. The work was hard, and the hours were long, but it wasn't nearly as bad as his previous work in a cotton factory and a bobbin factory. He took his job seriously. He memorized the layout of the Pittsburgh streets and learned the names and faces of the businessmen he delivered to. He could even deliver the right message to the right person if he happened to see them on the street. He was friendly with his coworkers, met powerful men, and received gifts—like fruit and pastries—from his customers. He didn't have much free time—he was often in the telegraph office until eleven at night—and his family didn't have money for books. But Colonel James Anderson opened his personal library of almost 400 books to the working boys of Pittsburgh. Every Saturday, the boy and his friends took books out of that library to read during the week. It was something that he would never forget.

Time passed. The boy grew up. He worked in the railroad and steel industries. He made smart investments in things like oil and sleeping cars for trains. When he retired in 1901, the one-time messenger boy was the richest man in the world (worth more than $300 billion in today's dollars). He was also remarkably generous. Besides giving to countless organizations, he founded Carnegie-Mellon University, the Carnegie United Kingdom Trust, Carnegie Hall, the Carnegie Hero Fund, and, in a nod to his humble beginnings and the kindness of Col. Anderson, 3,000 public libraries. Andrew Carnegie was one of the first of a new breed of millionaire philanthropists.

He also represented a deep tension of our modern age. On the one hand, he accumulated wealth with an efficiency bordering on ruthlessness (if not well over the line): social historian Oliver Zunz describes some of Carnegie's views as "unalloyed Social Darwinism." On the other hand, Carnegie wanted to use his fortune—and his managerial skill—to make society better. When he was thirty-three years old, he wrote himself a memo in which he resolved to retire at thirty-five and live on an income of $50,000 per year, giving the rest to good causes. On one side, modern people live in a disenchanted world, lead buffered lives, and are interested in well-being in the here and now. We understand the world as something that can be exploited and controlled, and the accumulation of wealth as a good thing. On the other side, we are heirs to the Christian tradition—whether we're Christian or not—and that tradition demands charity.[1]

Dan Pallotta talks about this tension in his TED Talk, "The Way We Think About Charity is Dead Wrong." First, he characterizes the Puritans as aggressive capitalists who were interested in making a lot of money and as Calvinists who were taught to hate themselves for their selfish impulses. Second, he describes charity as a sort of release valve for capitalism: The Puritans—and, later, we—could endanger their souls by making a lot of money and then save them by giving a small amount to charity. Finally, he calls for his own reformation of the nonprofit sector. In order to be effective, he says, the charitable sector needs to pay executives more, invest in marketing, spend more on overhead, and generate profit for investors. In other words, the way to resolve the tension between charity and capitalism is to ditch charity altogether.[2]

The tension between capitalism and charity is a tension between modern social imaginaries and pre-modern ones. In the last chapter, I started looking at some parts of modern social imaginaries. In this chapter, I'm going to continue doing so by looking at the solution to the tension between capitalism and charity that charity skeptics propose: a kind of compassionate capitalism that uses the same tools that have created unimaginable wealth in the modern age to solve big social problems. I'm also going to look at a way of imagining the world that predates that tension and was fundamental to the early church: a community based in charity. Finally, I'll start looking at the thing that will be the subject of the final chapter: whether we can reclaim that charitable community in the modern world.

1. Zunz, *Philanthropy in America*, 18.
2. Pallotta, "The Way We Think About Charity is Dead Wrong."

Compassionate Capitalism

Charity skeptics aren't just arguing against charity. They're also arguing for a particular way of imagining the world and human society. Part of this is that they tend to favor a kind of white American middle-class culture. For example, Ruby Payne regularly refers to poverty culture and differentiates it from middle-class and wealthy culture. According to Payne, people living in generational poverty have their own culture and belief systems, including a matriarchal family structure, an oral tradition, specific gender roles, and a belief in fate. Similarly, people in the middle class have a patriarchal family structure, a more formal language, and are focused on work and achievement. In his book *The Non Nonprofit*, Steve Rothschild cites Payne approvingly and provides a similar picture of the cultures of poverty and the middle class.[3]

Another part of this—which is deeply related to that preference for white American middle-class culture—is that they favor capitalism as a way of solving problems. On the one hand, this means helping people living in poverty enter a middle-class life centered on being part of the modern economy. When Payne lists the hidden rules of the different classes, people living in poverty know where to look for discarded but edible food, how to live without a checking account, and where to find free medical care. People in the middle class, though, know how to use a credit card and checking account, how to get a good interest rate on a car loan, and how to handle a mortgage. Building bridges out of poverty is intimately connected with economic integration, including consumption and debt.[4]

On the other hand, favoring capitalism means preferring business solutions to social problems. Charity skeptics tend to believe that traditional for-profit businesses will improve most people's lives, including the lives of people experiencing poverty. Where those businesses are unable to help, social businesses can step in to help many others. These businesses are built to solve social problems, accept money from investors, and (if successful) pay those investors back the amount that they invested. However, the investors don't receive any profits from their investments; instead, profits are reinvested in the business itself. Finally, where not even social businesses can help, the nonprofit sector will step in. But, as we'll see, that nonprofit sector will be very different from the one we're used to: it won't really be a nonprofit sector at all.

3. Payne et al., *Bridges Out of Poverty*, Kindle locations 754–91, 645; Rothschild, *The Non Nonprofit*, 105–7.

4. Payne et al., *Bridges Out of Poverty*, Kindle locations 565–609.

In this section, I'm going to look at this way of imagining the world. I'll start by looking at what capitalism is, both as an economic system and as a way of imagining the world. One key part of that will be the role of markets in making moral judgements. Then, I'll move on to look at capitalism in its compassionate and not-so-compassionate forms. Finally, I'll argue that one effect of compassionate capitalism is to crowd out the very values that allow capitalism to be compassionate. That presents a very real threat to Christian morality, and, especially, a morality that is based in the theology of charity that I sketched out in chapter four.

Most of us don't usually think about what capitalism is. Since the collapse of the Soviet Union and the liberalization of most of the world's economies, capitalism can feel just as natural and inevitable as a disenchanted world, buffered senses of self, and a focus on well-being here and now. With no real alternative on the table, capitalism is just the way things are. But if we want to understand the ideas that charity skeptics promote, we need to have a clear idea of what makes capitalism . . . well, capitalism. At its most basic, capitalism is an economic system: it's a way of organizing certain human activities and relationships. But capitalism is also part of our modern social imaginaries. It both expresses and reinforces the way that we imagine ourselves and the world around us, including the idea that the world is a disenchanted place that can be used and exploited, that we are individuals with no real connection to each other, and that we should strive to have our best lives now.

As an economic system, capitalism is an arrangement where private parties—individuals or, more often, corporations—own the things that we use to produce and distribute goods and services, and operate those things to make a profit for those owners. All of those things that we use are the means of production. And the means of production include natural resources like forests and oil fields, industrial resources like factories and mines, and distribution networks like highways and the internet. In our modern information economy, they can even include the personal data— like lists of friends, advertising preferences, and websites visited—owned by services like Facebook and Google. In practice, some of the means of production might be owned by the public or regulated by the government. But, in general, they are owned by private parties who are trying to make money off of them.

As part of our social imaginaries, capitalism encourages us to think of the world as a market. In economic terms, a market is just a space where people can exchange things. These places can be physical (like a brick and mortar store) or virtual (like Amazon or eBay). Things there are for sale, and their value is determined by assigning a price. Market thinking applies those same rules to things that haven't traditionally been a part of markets. Or, to put it another way, market thinking expands the idea of the market to cover more parts of our lives. For example, things for sale now include access to the carpool lane while driving alone, the chance to kill an endangered animal, the right to pollute air and water, and the advertising space on people's bodies. And a key feature of market spaces is that they don't make moral judgements. More accurately, they make moral judgements on very different terms than the ones we're used to. Market spaces measure value in terms of money. Something is worth what someone will pay for it, whether that something is someone's noblest cause or basest appetite.[5]

Today, capitalism and market thinking are global phenomena in two ways. First, they're geographically global. Almost every country in the world participates in capitalism in some way, even if their own economies are strictly regulated. And societies that don't participate in capitalism are still affected by it. Individuals, corporations, and governments buy, own, use, and sell the resources that those societies rely on whether or not those societies are capitalist ones. No one is untouched. Second, capitalism and market thinking are increasingly socially global. The idea that everything is for sale, and that determining a price is the same as assigning a value, are becoming integral parts of our social imaginaries.

This is just a sketch of capitalism as an economic system and market thinking as an aspect of our modern social imaginaries. But this sketch will help us understand charity skeptics' proposals and their potential consequences. And there are two very important potential consequences. First, market thinking undermines the idea of a moral obligation to help people living in poverty. Second, capitalism tends to concentrate wealth and power in the hands of people who already have them, and that expansions of market thinking only exacerbate that problem.

"A lot of people say now that business will lift up the developing economies," says Dan Pallotta in his TED Talk, "and social business will take care of the rest." With one caveat, Pallotta believes that, too. There is no shortage of people who believe that traditional businesses—or newer models like social business and triple bottom line businesses—can create solutions to big social problems like poverty, long-term care for people with disabilities, and environmental destruction. While charity skepticism is opposed to charity in most cases, charity skeptics are also eager to propose solutions to social problems that rely on capitalism and reinforce market thinking. This is what

5. Sandel, *What Money Can't Buy*, 3–5, 14.

I mean by the term *compassionate capitalism*: the belief that capitalism can care about and serve the people who have traditionally been served through charity.[6]

There are at least two sides to compassionate capitalism. The first side is focused on bringing people who live in poverty into the market. For example, Robert Lupton suggests that instead of giving things to people experiencing poverty, we should encourage them to take out loans, start their own businesses, find jobs (even for low wages), and buy what they need. Similarly, and as we saw earlier in this chapter, Ruby Payne writes that people experiencing generational poverty need to learn the hidden rules of the middle class. When she describes what middle-class people know, many of the items on her list concern taking on and handling debt. And her list of what the wealthy know has several items that are about paying other people to do things. To charity skeptics, being self-sufficient means being fully integrated into the modern economy.[7]

The second side of compassionate capitalism is focused on the organizations that want to help those people (as well as any other organization that wants to solve a large social problem). For example, Dan Pallotta and Steve Rothschild both argue that nonprofit organizations need to act more like for-profit businesses if they are going to have the kinds of impacts that they want to have. This includes everything from paying their executive staff more, to spending more money on marketing, to understanding who their customers really are. While Pallotta and Rothschild have a lot of suggestions, one of them stands out as an example of compassionate capitalism: the idea that nonprofit organizations need to be able to generate profits that they can share with investors. Or, to put that more bluntly, the idea that nonprofit organizations need to become for-profit enterprises.

By definition, nonprofit organizations use the revenues they make to address social problems, reinvesting any surplus revenues—they are nonprofits, after all—in realizing their mission instead of distributing those profits to their owners. The best-known examples are 501(c)(3) organizations. These organizations are operated for specific purposes, like charity, religion, or education; and they cannot operate for the benefit of private interests like owners or shareholders. They are, in a sense, almost the opposite of for-profit businesses. And they are often funded mostly by donations and grants.

---

6. Pallotta, "The Way We Think About Charity is Dead Wrong," 0:59.

7. Lupton, *Toxic Charity*, 113–25, 152–54, 37–39, 51–57; Payne et al., *Bridges Out of Poverty*, Kindle locations 589–629.

One of the biggest challenges that nonprofit organizations face is getting enough money to have the kinds of impacts that they want to have. According to Pallotta and Rothschild, part of this problem is that nonprofit organizations don't have the same access to capital markets that for-profit businesses do. For example, when a business needs a large amount of money, it can sell shares. To keep the math simple, imagine that a business needs $100,000 to invest in growth. It can sell 1,000 shares to investors for $100 each. The business gets its money, and an investor who buys 100 shares (and invests $10,000) owns 10 percent of the company. If the company then makes $1,000,000 and chooses to share that profit with its investors, the person who owns those shares would make $100,000. The company gets access to cash and a smart investor can make a lot of money. And, of course, there are other tools that businesses—and investors—can use to make money.[8]

Pallotta and Rothschild believe that nonprofits should use similar tools to get access to capital. One example that Rothschild provides is the model used by Lumni—a for-profit company that provides money to low-income students in Colombia, Peru, Chile, and the United States. Instead of providing loans to students, Lumni uses income sharing agreements. Lumni pays a student's educational expenses, and, after graduation, that student pays a percentage of their income to Lumni for a set period of time. Investors make money by investing in the impact funds that provide money to—and are paid back by—students. Think of it as investing in a group of students. If that group, on average, gets jobs that pay well, then the fund is profitable, and those profits can be paid out to investors. The students get an education that might otherwise not be available to them. The investors get to make a social impact that they believe in . . . and make a profit.[9]

The two sides of compassionate capitalism share a common faith that capitalism can power positive social impacts like creating meaningful jobs that pay a living wage, empowering people who live in poverty, and making education available to low-income students. More than that, charity skeptics argue that capitalism should be our preferred method for helping people in poverty and solving other big problems. And while they're right that enterprises that make profits for their owners can power positive social change, we'll see that there's no reason that they have to. Markets might be a useful tool for making money, but they simply don't care whether people's preferences are moral or not. And subjecting charitable work to the vagaries of the

8. Pallotta, "The Way We Think About Charity is Dead Wrong," 8:50; Rothschild, *The Non Nonprofit*, 153.

9. Rothschild, *The Non Nonprofit*, 156–58; Lumni, "How it Works"; Lumni, "Investors."

markets is at least as likely to divert their attention away from positive social impact as it is to help people living in poverty.

As an economic system, capitalism has had an unparalleled ability to create wealth. Wealth is only one part of a standard of living, and it is almost impossible to compare standards of living between premodern and modern people. But it's fair to say that people living in relative poverty in developed nations today enjoy wealth that their premodern—and pre-capitalism—ancestors would find unbelievable. A lot of the amenities that people living in capitalist societies enjoy exist because someone somewhere could make money producing those goods and services. Even the fact that you're reading this book is evidence that several people thought it would be profitable to produce and sell it. Capitalism's ability to harness human self-interest and put it to work is widely acknowledged, and it shouldn't be overlooked.

But, as I've already said, markets don't care whether they are put to work for some higher good, and capitalism has also been a force for destruction. For example, while it's true that Andrew Carnegie invested his wealth in many things that he believed made the world a better place, it's also true that when workers organized a union at the Homestead Steel Mill in 1892, Carnegie and his colleague Henry Clay Frick crushed it ruthlessly. Carnegie avoided direct responsibility by setting sail for Scotland. Frick, however, offered a contract that called for a 22 percent reduction in wages, causing the union to go on strike. Frick called in the Pinkerton Agency—a private detective agency that "investigated" labor unions and broke strikes—who had an actual gunfight with the striking workers. The Pinkertons were defeated, but the state militia was called in and the town was placed under martial law. After four months, the workers gave in and the strike collapsed. There was no union at the Homestead Mill for the next forty years. While this may seem astonishing to us, events like this were not uncommon in the late nineteenth and early twentieth centuries.[10]

Today, workers in developed nations don't have gunfights with private detective agencies that work to undermine unions. But that doesn't mean that wages, working conditions, or other parts of the job are fair. And in other parts of the world, things are worse. In the first chapter, I told the story of the Rana Plaza textile factory in Savar, Bangladesh. When employees reported cracks in the building, they were told to return to work or lose a month's pay. The building collapsed the next day, killing more than 1,000 workers and injuring another 2,500. While there are building and safety codes in Bangladesh, the government didn't enforce those codes against the

10. Loomis, *Out of Sight*, 31–32; Wikipedia, "Homestead strike."

powerful textile industry. And, like Carnegie on his ship to Scotland, the apparel companies who contracted with the textile companies at Rana Plaza kept an arm's length between themselves and the factory workers. Complex supply chains ensured that the companies at the consumer end of those chains were insulated from seeing the damage.[11]

The damage that unbridled capitalism can do isn't limited to workers. In Nigeria, oil companies operate with impunity, and they've done immense damage to the Niger River Delta. Between the mid-1970s and the early twenty-first century, there were the equivalent of multiple oil spills every other day. Mangrove forests and the ecosystems they support have died, fish have been poisoned, crops have been destroyed, and people lack access to clean water. The ecological disaster of the Niger River Delta has major effects on the environment and on the people who live in the area. It's still going on today. And, of course, the Niger River Delta isn't the only environmental disaster area in the world.[12]

These three disasters—each revealing part of the dark side of capitalism—are the result of the relentless logic of market thinking. Remember that the people who own the means of production are using them to make a profit for themselves. There's a delicate balance to that effort. On one side, they want to sell their goods and services to as many people as possible for as much as those people are willing to pay. On the other side, they want to produce those goods and services for as little as possible. The second side of the balance means keeping wages low and avoiding regulation. That means that there is a real financial interest in making sure that some people need work badly enough that they won't complain about low pay or poor working conditions, as well as ignoring safety and environmental protections. Capitalism may have the power to create immense wealth, but it has no impulse to make sure that the wealth it creates is equitably shared.

When Pallotta talks about compensation in the nonprofit sector, he tells us that someone with an MBA from an elite university and ten years of experience could choose between making $400,000 a year in the for-profit sector or $84,000 a year as the executive director of a nonprofit focused on hunger. Pallotta, adopting the worldview of the market, argues that the MBA has $400,000 worth of talent and that he would be smart to take the for-profit job. After all, he could donate a substantial amount to that nonprofit, take a tax deduction, sit on the board, and even supervise the person

11. Loomis, *Out of Sight*, 9–10.

12. Loomis, *Out of Sight*, 140–41; Wikipedia, "Environmental issues in the Niger Delta."

who only has $84,000 worth of talent. From a purely economic sense, it just doesn't make sense for that person to sacrifice more than $300,000 of earning potential every year. Pallotta argues that this is why nonprofits need to pay their executives more.[13]

Pallotta's example shows us the increasing power of market thinking. When Pallotta talks about the MBA, he imagines that this person has $400,000 worth of talent and that "the poor SOB who decided to become the CEO of the hunger charity" does not. And from the market's point of view, he's right. On the one hand, the market's way of ascribing value is tautological: someone who makes $400,000 a year is worth that precisely because that's what someone is paying her, and the act of paying her $400,000 a year makes her worth that. On the other hand, it's reductive: the person directing the nonprofit for $84,000 is worth $84,000; he isn't worth $84,000 and his sense of purpose, or $84,000 and his noble actions. He has no value beyond what someone is willing to pay him.[14]

That way of thinking can lead to a dangerous conclusion. Markets make financial judgements, not moral ones. And market thinking dictates that the person with the elite MBA should take the for-profit job. In fact, she should strive to make as much money as possible, whether that means helping people living in poverty or creating a complex supply chain that uses sweatshops to make her products. At the same time, she should spend the money she makes on whatever makes her happy. Again, whether that's giving to a charity that helps people who are hungry or hunting endangered animals for sport. The market doesn't even care why she gives to the nonprofit. She can do that because of a genuine desire to help or because she wants to lord it over some poor sap who is worth less than she is. According to market thinking and the logic of capitalism, as long as she is willing to pay for her happiness—and someone is willing to be paid to make her happy—everything is fine.

Pallotta and Rothschild believe that the rules that keep nonprofit organizations nonprofit also hurt them. And they believe that allowing those organizations to play by the rules of the for-profit sector would help them and allow them to help others more effectively. And it is true that this is possible. But it is also true that, under the rules of market thinking, it is only possible as long as it is more profitable than doing something else. And that forces non-nonprofits to make choices that we might rather they not make. For example, it may be profitable to fund the education of someone who will make a lot of money managing a factory that ignores safety standards;

13. Pallotta, "The Way We Think About Charity is Dead Wrong," 3:40.
14. Pallotta, "The Way We Think About Charity is Dead Wrong," 3:40.

and it may be unprofitable to fund the education of someone else who will make very little money rooting out the corruption in their local government that allows that factory to ignore safety standards. To put it simply, adding a profit motive to a nonprofit organization changes its mission; and the more tightly that value is connected to money, the less it is connected to morality.

Charity skeptics argue that, one way or another, markets can help us solve big social problems. And they're right. There are many social businesses that are making money and doing good in the world. And ordinary citizens are able to use market pressures to force businesses that aren't as socially minded to do the right thing. For example, the basic idea of a boycott is to make it less profitable to do something that people disapprove of. And this brings me to my final point in this section: markets are not independent of the people in them. When we say that the market rewards this or disapproves of that, we are simply saying that we—the people who are giving money to companies—are rewarding this or disapproving of that.

But the reverse is also true: we are not independent of the markets that we participate in. And those markets are constantly asking us to think in terms of the market: to choose jobs based on lifetime earning potential, to buy products based on price for performance, to invest in portfolios with high returns, and to do all of these things without thinking too much about the non-economic impacts of those actions. We are caught in the tension that Pallotta accused the Puritans of being caught in. On the one hand, we have a social imaginary that is increasingly focused on money as the sole indicator of value. On the other hand, we have other values that are independent of the market and that we want to honor. The nonprofit sector creates a social space where honoring those other values—independent of the economic concerns of the marketplace—is possible.

In this section, I've focused on one side of the compassionate capitalism that charity skeptics present: the idea that nonprofit organizations need to become more like for-profit businesses in order to be successful. But across the board, charity skeptics suggest that capitalism—and only capitalism—can solve big problems like poverty. Work requirements for assistance, a preference for loans over gifts, and a desire to see more low-income entrepreneurs (who often have had to take loans in order to start their businesses) all suggest that more involvement in markets and market thinking holds the answer to poverty. Charity skepticism is certainly in favor of increasing the power that capitalism has as part of our social imaginaries. Given the prevalence of market-based solutions in charity skepticism, one might even suspect that charity skeptics are skeptical because the two ideas—charity and capitalism—aren't entirely compatible.

And that matters. By suggesting that nonprofit organizations become more like their for-profit counterparts, charity skeptics are suggesting that we weaken one of the few major alternatives to market thinking in our culture. Once the non-profit sector becomes nothing more than a compassionate version of the for-profit sector, it's a short step to seeing market thinking take over a social space that has prioritized other values. And that means that it's a short step to imagining that the only problems worth solving are the problems that it is profitable to solve. Worse, it's possible to create a capitalistically virtuous cycles: investing both in the corporations that make a profit by causing problems like poverty and the ones that claim to solve those problems. If that sounds ridiculous—and absurdly dystopian—it is only because we have other values that override market thinking. And the long-term effects of increasing the power of market thinking in our social imaginaries is to replace those other values with the one value that markets care about: money.

Christian Community

In chapter one, and again in chapter three, I told the story of Julian the Apostate. Remember that Julian was the last pagan emperor of Rome and that one of his pet projects was revitalizing the Roman pagan religion. As part of that, he tried to introduce charity to Roman temples. He allocated supplies to the province of Galatia and ordered the high priest to use them for strangers and beggars. The project failed. Roman pagan social imaginaries didn't have a place for charity.

About 150 years before Julian took the throne, the North African theologian Tertullian wrote his "Apology." We're used to using the word *apology* to mean something like saying, "I'm sorry." But Tertullian used it in a different sense: an argument made in defense of something. Tertullian spends most of his "Apology" defending Christians against charges that pagans were making against them in the late second century. These were charges like accusing Christians of murdering and eating babies. But Tertullian also describes the Christian community of his time. In one particularly important passage, he writes that there was no buying and selling of the things of God. The church wasn't asking people to buy their membership or position of power in the church. When the church did ask for money, it was for a voluntary donation to a community chest. The funds in that chest were used to do things like support people living in poverty, provide for orphans and elders, and care for prisoners. As Tertullian puts it, when someone puts their faith in Christ and joins the church, they become "nurslings of their confession," and can rely on the other members of the Christian community to care for them.[15]

About a generation before Tertullian used charity to defend Christians, the Greek satirist Lucian used it to mock them. In a work called "The Passing of Peregrinus," a philosopher named Peregrinus takes advantage of Christian communities. When he is arrested for his scam, the Christians visit him, stay with him, bring him elaborate meals, and give him money. Lucian writes that the "poor wretches . . . despise all things indiscriminately and consider them common property." He continues by saying that any charlatan can take advantage of the generosity of these "simple folk" to become wealthy.[16]

Julian's failure to launch charity in a pagan context, Tertullian's miniature welfare state, and Lucian's mocking story about Peregrinus taking advantage of Christians show us two things. First, that sharing was a common practice among early Christians; it was a practice that was so normal for Christians that any pagan could observe it for themselves. Second, that charity set Christians apart from the rest of Roman society. And, as I argued in chapter four, charity wasn't just a practice that Christians had. It was a fundamental part of the Christian worldview. Moreover, while modern society is obviously very different from ancient Roman society, that worldview—that way of imagining human society and the cosmic order—still sets Christians apart.

In this section, I'm going to explore Christian charity and the sharing economy that it creates as an alternative to modern capitalism. First, I'll look at sharing among the early and tight-knit group of believers that we see in the book of Acts. Second, I'll look at how that sharing economy grew and expanded—including how it supported a massive welfare system—as Christianity spread. Third, I'll examine what Paul's admonition that those who do not work should not eat tells us about early Christian sharing. Finally, I'll ground the Christian sharing economy in the practice and theology of charity.

The book of Acts gives us two summaries of life among the early believers, and both of them highlight the economic life of that community. In the second chapter, Acts tells us that all who believed were together and held all things in common. They ate together with glad and generous hearts. And if there was anyone among them who was in need, they sold what they had

15. Tertullian, "The Apology," chapter 39.

16. Lucian, "The Passing of Peregrinus," 12–13; Montero, *All Things in Common,* Kindle locations 1771–1801.

and distributed the proceeds. Similarly, in the fourth chapter, Acts tells us that the believers didn't claim private ownership of their possessions. And, again, that there was no one among them in need because anyone who had land or a house would sell it and give the proceeds to the apostles, who would distribute it to anyone in need.[17]

To some, the early Christian economy looks like communism. We need to be careful, though. The Christian economy isn't the coercive economy of the Soviet Union or North Korea, and the early church didn't force anyone to give their wealth to the community. Instead, it was the natural outgrowth of the theology we saw in chapter four. In that chapter, I argued that Christians believe in a generous God who creates and sustains a fundamentally generous world; that the world is broken by sin, which stems from a disoriented faith; that material wealth is a major cause of disoriented faith as we put the trust and loyalty that we should put in God in that wealth; and that charity is a way of demonstrating a living faith in God as it shows that we aren't putting our faith in money and as it forces us to rely on God for our well-being. In a community where everyone is willing to give their wealth away to care for people living in poverty, we should expect to see some sort of sharing economy.[18]

Roman Montero provides an illustration of the early Christian sharing economy by using the Spanish phrase *mi casa es su casa* (my house is your house). The idea behind the saying is that a host's guest can use the host's house as though it's their own. As Montero tells us, no one uses this phrase literally. No host signs over the deed to the house. No guest starts repainting rooms. But the early church seems to have taken sharing to something like that extreme. Some believers sold their property and handed the proceeds from the sale over to the apostles to be distributed to people living in poverty. Others probably simply shared what they had, opening their homes, kitchens, and other property to other believers in the spirit of a literal *mi casa es su casa*. The Christian economy was a sharing economy. And the Christian community was a sharing community.[19]

The Christian sharing economy sounds a lot like the sharing economy we learned about in the last chapter. In pre-monetary societies, people shared what they had. For example, if your neighbor asked you for an egg, you would simply give them an egg, knowing that the favor would be

17. Acts 2:43–47; Acts 4:32–37.

18. Miranda, *Communism in the Bible*; Montero, *All Things in Common*; Acts 5:1–11.

19. Montero, *All Things in Common*, Kindle locations 1215–22; Acts 4:36–37, 5:1–11.

returned if you were ever in need. Similarly, in our daily lives, we tend to act according to a principle like "from each according to their ability, to each according to their need." As long as the request and the cost are reasonable, we're happy to help. And that's true whether it's a guest asking for a glass of water or a refugee asking for a place where they can escape the threats of their homeland. The early Christians built an economy out of that kind of sharing.

It might be tempting to write that kind of sharing economy off as something that might work in a small community but that isn't tenable on a large scale. Three things should keep us from doing that. First, the early church inherited a substantial sharing economy from Judaism in the form of a welfare system. We've already seen a couple of examples of this. In chapter one, we learned about the requirement that the Israelites keep the first fruits of certain harvests in their own towns to give to marginalized groups. In chapter three, we looked at the tradition of leaving the edges of fields unharvested so that people who needed to could take that food for themselves. Jewish law is full of examples like this. And, again as we saw in chapter three, caring for people living in poverty was the highest of all the commandments.

Second, the number of early Christians suggests that this was more than an occasional practice among a single tight-knit community. In "The Passing of Peregrinus," Lucian establishes that Christians were known for their seemingly foolish generosity. He wouldn't have used that generosity in his story if his readers wouldn't have recognized it. Similarly, in his "Apology," Tertullian uses the example of Christian generosity as though it's something that anyone could go and see for themselves. Both authors write as though Christian sharing is both extravagant and widespread. What's important here is that sociologist Rodney Stark estimates the number of Christians around the time that these authors wrote in the late second century at (probably) somewhere between 100,000 and 200,000. Just as importantly, these Christians lived throughout and beyond the Roman Empire, and included people of every class, ethnicity, language, and dozens of other demographic categories. Sharing wasn't an isolated practice, it was part of a widespread Christian culture.[20]

Third, the early Christians built on this sharing economy to create a massive welfare system within the borders of the Roman Empire. I've already mentioned Tertullian's "Apology" a couple of times. Tertullian spends most of this work defending Christians against the chargers that pagans

20. Stark, *The Triumph of Christianity*, 156–57; Montero, *All Things in Common*, Kindle locations 1731–38.

were making against them. But he also spends some time describing the Christian community. He talks about worship and the fact that people couldn't buy positions in the church (a practice that was common in Roman religion). Most importantly for my purposes, he also writes about the church's welfare system. Every month, churches took up a voluntary collection that was used to care for people living in poverty, bury the dead, provide for orphans and the elderly, help people in prison, and so on. And Tertullian adds that Christians think of themselves as one body, with one soul, holding all things in common (with the exception of their wives; he goes on to note that his pagan neighbors have the opposite arrangement).[21]

Tertullian is describing two things here. On the one hand, when he writes about the monthly collection, he's writing about a welfare system. In chapter three, I mentioned that Roman society didn't have many of the things we think of as charitable. There weren't soup kitchens, homeless shelters, or free clinics. The Roman Empire also didn't have social services. There were no food stamps or housing vouchers. Nevertheless, the Christian church built an impressive welfare system that provided help to people in need: in the mid-third century—about fifty years after Tertullian wrote—Christians in Rome were supporting about 1,500 widows and other people! While it might seem normal to us to have a robust welfare system—and while charity skeptics lament the number of people who use that system—it was a fairly new idea in the Roman world.[22]

On the other hand, when he writes about holding all things in common, he's writing about an economy. Early Christians might have supported their welfare system through monthly offerings, but, as Montero points out, no one would confuse that kind of sharing with the kind of sharing that includes sharing wives. Instead, Tertullian must be describing the same kind of sharing economy that existed among the early believers in the book of Acts. Even at the end of the second century, Christians were living in a sharing economy. And that tells us that it wasn't a small and temporary experiment. Instead, writes Montero, it was—and was meant to be—a new economic reality: "long-term, institutional, widespread, and organized," "firmly based on a moral framework of mutual obligations," and "something that a non-Christian could witness with his own eyes and distinguish as a unique feature of the Christian community." Sharing is the foundation of Christian economics.[23]

21. Tertullian, "The Apology," chapter 39.

22. Stark, *The Triumph of Christianity*, 113.

23. Montero, *All Things in Common*, Kindle locations 1244–52, 1388.

The word *foundation* is doing some important work there. The early Christian community quickly came up against a basic problem with sharing economies in cultures where that isn't the only option. Imagine that you live in a village where everyone owns a sheep and where there's a common area where people can let their sheep graze. The common area needs regular upkeep, and the village has a custom that makes sure everyone does their part. For example, the village might be divided into family groups, and tradition since time immemorial dictates that family group A will tend to the field during one month, while family group B will care for it during the next month, and so on. As long as everyone does their part, everything works. Now imagine that one member of the village has found a way to shirk his duty. He lets his sheep graze in the common area, but never contributes to its care. He's a free rider; he gets something for free when others have to pay for it through their labor. Many people imagine that something similar would inevitably happen in any community where things were shared too readily: someone would find a way to get more out of that system than they gave.

In his second letter to the Thessalonians, Paul points to something like this. He knows that when he visited that community, he and his companions had a right to share the community's food. After all, they had come to share the gospel. But instead of relying on the church's hospitality, they worked, and paid for their food. Paul also knows that there are people among the Thessalonians who are not doing any work—sharing the gospel or otherwise—but who are taking advantage of the church's hospitality. In order to curb the problem, he gives the Thessalonians this commandment: "Anyone unwilling to work should not eat."[24]

This passage is often used by people who want to add work requirements to our already meager welfare system, since it sounds like Paul is suggesting that people should have to find work and pay for the things they need. But that would put Paul at odds with everything else we've learned about the early Christian community. So it's important to recognize two things. First, that people can only take advantage of the Thessalonians' generosity because the Thessalonians are generous. They are living out the Christian ideal that no one claim any private possessions, but share things in common. That is why some people were able to use the things that they held in common without contributing to them. Paul's concerns only make sense if sharing is the foundation of the Thessalonians' economic relationships.

Second, in order for Paul to suggest that anyone who is unwilling to work should not eat, he must also mean that anyone who is willing to work

24. 2 Thess 3:6–15.

will be able to find work to do. It's simply unbelievable that he would tell a Christian community that people must find a job that will pay the bills or face a life of poverty, hunger, or homelessness. And the system where Paul's admonishment makes the most sense is one where anyone who wants to contribute to the community can do so, and where the act of contributing to the community gives the person access to a sharing economy that will support them. This might mean that the community itself bears some responsibility for finding a way for a person to contribute. For example, the church might need to be the employer of last resort, or decide that there can be a willingness to contribute but no need to actually do so. And in either case, someone's contribution might not be proportional to what they receive from the sharing economy. The smallest contribution gets access to the whole sharing economy, just like the largest does. Regardless of the specific mechanism used, this is the only way that Paul's command and the sharing economy that we see elsewhere—including long after Paul wrote—can coexist.

This is what I mean when I say that sharing was the foundation of early Christian economics. The Christian worldview assumes that sharing—holding all things in common—is the basic economic relationship between people in the generous world that God has created. In a broken world, however, where it seems like resources are limited, other structures can be built on top of that. And that includes things like a requirement that people contribute to the sharing economy of the community if they want to be included in it. Christians expect that the world will be repaired eventually, and attempt to build something as close as possible to the utopia that will exist then in the here and now. And what matters—what makes an economy authentically Christian—is that it is rooted in sharing, and that any other aspects of that economy keep sharing at its foundation.

Charity is the heart of Christianity. First, it's at the core of the Christian understanding of God and the world. In the theology that I sketched out in chapter four, I argued that Christians understand God and the world that God creates as fundamentally generous, sin as the condition of having a disoriented faith, and salvation as a reorientation of faith towards God. I also argued that charity is God's preferred way of reorienting faith. Early Christians recognized that wealth was a major source of disoriented faith. Therefore, while people living in poverty had no choice but to put their faith in God, relatively wealthy people could reorient their faith towards God by giving up their material wealth and participating in the divine economy of abundance. As Jesus says in the Gospel of Luke, "Do not be afraid, little flock, for it is your Father's good pleasure to give you the kingdom. Sell your possessions, and give alms."[25]

Second, charity is how Christians are called to show love for the world. The divine command to provide for people living in poverty by sharing our wealth with them appears again and again throughout the Bible. God commands the Israelites to leave crops at the edges of their fields and grapes in their vineyards specifically for people living in poverty. Jesus offers a parable where eternal judgement is based on whether people fed people who were hungry, welcomed strangers, and visited people who were in prison. And Jesus makes it clear that doing (or not doing) those things for people in need is the same as doing (or not doing) them for the one who will judge the nations. Through the act of giving to God, charitable giving reenacts God's charity towards the world.[26]

The Christian sharing economy embodies both of these sides of charity. On the one hand, it frees the believer from the dangers of material wealth. By refusing to claim private ownership of anything and sharing what she has with others—by living out a fairly literal version of *mi casa es su casa*—she lives as though she has nothing. And she cannot put her faith in the wealth that she doesn't have. On the other hand, a sharing economy is a strikingly efficient way to provide for people living in poverty. When everyone shares what they have with anyone who needs it, then, as long as the community as a whole has enough resources for everyone, no one has to live in poverty.

One clause in that last sentence might be cause for concern. It's obviously true that, as long as the community as a whole has enough resources, no one needs to live in poverty. But part of our modern social imaginary is the idea that there isn't enough to go around. This is an especially important part of capitalism. As Montero notes, modern economics is the study of capitalism. And as Sendhil Mullainathan and Eldar Shafir tell us, when they told a colleague about their research into scarcity, that colleague replied by saying, "There is already a science of scarcity. You might have heard of it. It's called economics." A big part of the reason that this clause is concerning is that we are primed to assume that the community as a whole will never really have enough and certainly will never have a guarantee that there will be enough.[27]

But that assumption is not a Christian one. Christians believe that, while the world we live in may be broken by sin, it and the God who creates

25. Luke 12:32–33.

26. Deut 24:19–20; Lev 19:9–10; 23:22; Matt 25:31–46.

27. Montero, *All Things in Common*, Kindle locations 1254–57; Mullainathan and Shafir, *Scarcity*, 10–11.

and sustains it are fundamentally generous. It is a matter of faith that God will provide enough—more than enough—for a world that is faithful towards God. And there are good reasons to believe that this is true. The descriptions in Acts make it clear that there was no one in the Christian community who was living in poverty and Tertullian makes it sound like the churches he knew had more than enough to support their welfare system. Even Julian the Apostate's famous quote—"the impious Galileans [Christians], in addition to their own, support ours [the Pagans]"—suggests that Christians had more than enough for themselves. Even if it seems strange to our modern ears, it is at least possible that a large-scale sharing economy—one where everyone is given the opportunity to participate both as contributor and beneficiary—can work for everyone.

A Charitable Community

I began this chapter with the idea that we live in a deep tension. On the one hand, the modern social imaginaries that we explored in the last chapter support the idea that the resources our world provides can and should be exploited for private gain. On the other hand, we are the heirs of a long tradition of caring for people who live in poverty. As charity skeptic Dan Pallotta tells us, this tension can give us a nicely contained system with a carefully calibrated release valve. Like Andrew Carnegie, we can ruthlessly pursue profits with little regard for other values and then use charitable giving as a sort of ethical Band-Aid. In cooking, an ounce of sauce covers a multitude of sins. In the rest of our lives, a few dollars to the right nonprofit can do the same thing.

In this chapter, I've looked at two different ways of imagining our economy that could resolve that tension. On one side, there's the compassionate capitalism that charity skeptics champion. This includes ideas that we've seen in previous chapters, like giving loans to budding entrepreneurs, teaching people job skills, and helping people envision themselves as middle-class. It also includes reforming the nonprofit sector so that nonprofit organizations can use investments to solve social problems while also producing returns for investors. Effectively, that means reforming the sector in a way that all but eliminates it. On the other side, there's the sharing economy envisioned by the early Christian community. That community imagined a world where everyone would have the opportunity to contribute to the community and to take what they needed from a common source.

But, while I do think that charity skeptics are largely intent on resolving that tension—maybe keeping enough charity around to assuage our guilt when we see someone who really cannot help themselves—I don't think that we really need to do so. As a Christian, I recognize that we live in a broken world. That brokenness includes a self-interested drive, and capitalism is a good way to harness that self-interest and generate wealth. As we'll see in the next chapter, I also believe that the world will one day be healed, and we'll be able to set that self-interest aside in a way that we can't imagine now. In the meantime, the Christian vision of a sharing economy—and a nonprofit sector that isn't interested in creating returns for investors—can be a counterbalance to unfettered capitalism. It can prompt us all to ask whether capitalism reflects our values and it can provide the boundaries that we desperately need.

As I've written before, many of the books, seminars, and other media produced by charity skeptics are aimed specifically at churches. And many churches and church-related nonprofits have adopted many of the ideas that charity skeptics promote. But the church is not called to mirror the broken world that we live in. It is called to be an outpost—maybe even an embassy—of the kingdom of God. As part of that mission, it is called to be a community that embodies the nature of the God we worship. It is called to have a sharing economy. It is called to be a charitable community.

8

The Kingdom of God

I opened this book with two stories. One of them was the story that charity skeptics tell, a story that taps into something deep in the American psyche and a story that only seems to be growing more popular. It imagines poverty as something bigger than not having enough money. For people living in situational poverty, it might mean lacking a variety of resources, including financial, emotional, and mental resources. For people living in generational poverty, it also means being part of a culture that encourages a sense of victimization, powerlessness, and entitlement. And because charity skepticism imagines that poverty is about more than money, it imagines that giving money to people experiencing poverty will range from being useless to being dangerous.

At best, according to charity skeptics, giving money might help someone who is embedded in a culture of poverty move from financial poverty to the financial middle class. But, without knowing how to navigate middle-class culture, they will squander what they were given and slide back into poverty. At worst, giving money will lead the recipient to believe that they have a right to that money. This will encourage their sense of entitlement, deepen their dependency, and erode their work ethic. In the first case, addressing a financial situation without addressing a cultural one fails to help. In the second case, it hurts.

Skeptics tell us that, instead of giving people money or goods, we should adopt a kind of compassionate capitalism. For people living in poverty, this means learning the skills they need to find jobs, start their own businesses, buy what they need, take out loans, and manage money. For nonprofit organizations, it means adopting new ways of raising the money they need to address big social problems, including ways that generate profits that can be shared with their investors. And, for people who want to help people who are experiencing poverty, it means abandoning charity in all but the most desperate cases—such as cases where someone from the middle class has fallen into poverty—and, instead, focusing on supporting employment, entrepreneurship, and consumerism.

The other story was the story of charity: a particular way of giving that is rooted in a connection to the divine, directed specifically towards people living in poverty, and emphatically not about changing the recipient of its gifts. This story imagines that poverty is about not having enough money, even as it can be expanded to be about not having access to enough food, water, hospitality, and all of the other things that we need to participate fully in our communities. While it recognizes that people experiencing poverty may come to have a certain mind-set, it also understands that it is poverty that causes the mind-set and not the other way around. This means that giving someone money—and, especially, giving someone enough money to lift them out of poverty—should also change their mind-set and help them develop the tools that they need to stay out of poverty.

The story of charity also imagines that charity does more than help the person who receives the gift; it helps the person who gives that gift. Rooted in Judaism and Christianity, charity is based on four beliefs about the nature of the world we live in. First, the world and the God who creates and sustains it are fundamentally generous. Second, the world is broken by our disoriented faith and that material wealth is a leading cause of that disorientation. Third, God has a special relationship with—a preferential option for—people who are living in poverty. Fourth, all of this comes together in the belief that the best way to move through life—to flow with the natural currents of the cosmic order—is to imitate divine generosity towards the universe by sharing freely with people living in poverty. According to the story of charity, charitable giving not only helps the person experiencing poverty by giving them what they need to survive, it also helps the person who gives that gift by reorienting their faith. And it helps a broken world by doing some of the work of healing it.

Over the course of this book, I hope that I've shown two things. First, that the story of charity is at the heart of the Christian faith in two ways: it is at the center of the Christian understanding of the world and it is the way that Christians are called to care for the world. For those of us who are Christian—and that includes a lot of the people who charity skeptics are talking to and writing for—charity is an important part of our identity and our religious practice. Second, that even outside of the religious dimensions of charity, real-world research supports the effectiveness of generosity. In chapter five, I showed that current research strongly suggests that giving money to people living in poverty tends to help those people: people experiencing poverty tend to make good choices with the financial resources that they have, and they tend to invest additional resources in things that will help them over the long term. Similarly, in chapter six, I showed that research supports the idea that giving is good for the people who give: people who develop a habit of generosity are happier, healthier, and have a greater sense of purpose than people who do not. In the same chapter, I showed that there are good reasons to believe that generosity strengthens communities. Charity appears to be an excellent way to improve the lives of the people who receive it and the people who give it.

Early in *Toxic Charity*, Robert Lupton unveils his Oath of Compassionate Service, telling the reader to avoid doing for others what they could do for themselves, limit one-way giving to emergencies, and empower people through employment and lending. Later in the book, he goes into detail about these points, telling us that giving establishes dependency and implies that the recipient has nothing of value to give in return, that lending builds mutual trust and respect, and that we need to carefully listen for what people living in poverty are not telling us. Overall, it is an oath of charity skepticism and compassionate capitalism, a fact captured in its statement that while giving might be bad, investing—"making money *with* the poor"—is "the ultimate method of sharing resources," bringing communities experiencing poverty into our modern economy.[1]

As I wrote in chapter one, after reading *Toxic Charity*, I came across this oath while filling out an application for a grant from a church. That church had taken Lupton's lessons to heart, and they weren't the only ones. Churches and Christian nonprofits across the United States have been adopting Lupton's Oath. Others have been implementing Ruby Payne's curricula. Still others have been imagining how they can become more business-like. In other words, they've been accepting charity skepticism. And while I think that many of these churches, like the skeptics themselves, have been doing this because of their compassion—I believe that charity skeptics really do want to help people living in poverty—I also think that adopting charity skepticism is dangerous. Not only does it deny a core part of the Christian faith and a distinctive practice of the historical Christian community, it cuts off a highly effective way of helping people living in poverty.

1. Lupton, *Toxic Charity*, 8–9, 128–32.

In the book of Acts, when the Holy Spirit comes to the community of believers at Pentecost, it causes them to speak in other languages. As a crowd gathers around them, some of the people in that crowd are amazed and perplexed, wondering what this miracle could mean. In this chapter, I'm going to end this book by proposing that those of us who are Christian should embrace our charitable heritage. More than that, I'm going to propose that by embracing that heritage, we can set ourselves apart as embassies of the kingdom of God and take on the work of co-creating the world that God has envisioned since the beginning: a world of abundance and generosity, a world of justice and mercy. Of course, in that same story from the book of Acts, some people in that crowd sneer and say that the believers are drunk. You can't please everybody.

Embassies of the Kingdom

One of the biggest challenges that we face when it comes to helping people living in poverty is that we tend to imagine that any form of help—from public assistance programs like the Supplemental Nutrition Assistance Program to private charities like food pantries and housing rehabilitation projects—are safety nets. It's as though we think of life as a kind of high wire act. In a normal act, the acrobat walks safely across the wire from one platform to another. If he follows his training, does what he's supposed to do, and nothing unexpected happens, he will succeed. If something goes wrong, there's a safety net below him. That net will catch him if he falls, keeping him from hitting the ground far below. But it is only there in case of an emergency; in normal circumstances, it isn't meant to be used at all. And, of course, we can distinguish between people who are generally self-sufficient and people who are ill-equipped or reckless. One of those kinds of people rarely uses the safety net, if they use it at all. The other kind seems to be in it constantly.

The problem with imagining things this way is that life isn't like a high wire act. We are not carefully walking across a tightrope with only our skills and wits to guide us. There's no such thing as self-sufficiency. Instead, we are all embedded in complex webs of social support. Some of those webs are effective and others are not. Some of us are enrolled in high quality educational programs from a young age, some of us are not. Some of us live in neighborhoods that are quiet and safe, some of us do not. Some of us are connected to jobs that are secure and well-paying as soon as we graduate, some of us are not. All of us are reliant on the communities that surround us, and, for a variety of reasons, those communities are incredibly diverse.

Life is much more like a blanket toss than a high wire act. In this activity, a crowd holds a strong blanket at about waist height. Another person stands in the middle of the blanket and, as the crowd pulls and slackens the blanket, is bounced higher and higher until they are thrown into the air. The person at the center of the blanket participates in their jumps—they can add or withhold their own power from the power of the crowd—but they are also at the mercy of the people holding that blanket. When she can rely on those people, she knows that she won't hit the ground. The foundation that she is resting on is also the thing propelling her into the air and the safety net that catches her as she falls back down.

The differences between these two ways of imagining life—as a high wire act and as a blanket toss—are important. When we imagine life as a high wire act and the programs that help people living in poverty as safety nets, it follows that anyone who is using those programs is using them because they messed up and fell from their high wire. And it becomes important to make the distinction between people who fell because of things they couldn't control (emergencies like hurricanes and house fires) and people who fell because they are irresponsible or reckless (people who live in chronic poverty because of their poverty culture).

But when we imagine life—and the programs that help people living in poverty—as blanket tosses, our understanding of responsibility changes. When someone is experiencing short-term poverty, the blanket is there to catch them, and we can pull together to get them back on their feet and into the air. When someone is experiencing long-term poverty, it is almost certainly true that the community is failing to do its part in pulling and slackening the blanket. And that's true whether we're talking about individuals or groups. The reason that First Nations people, black people in the United States, and people in developing nations have high poverty rates is in large part because the larger community—and, especially, colonial powers—didn't fulfill its responsibility in the blanket toss. In many cases, that larger community pulled the blanket right out from under the people experiencing poverty. In addition, when we use the image of the blanket toss, we can recognize that up and down—being in the air and resting safely on the platform that will propel the person back into the air—is a natural cycle. While we still have agency and responsibility for how high we go and what we do while we're up there, we are also at the mercy of forces we can't control.

Our modern world imagines life as a high wire act. The early church imagined it as a blanket toss. As we saw in the last chapter, it even developed a sort of blanket toss economy where anyone who was part of the community could rely on their friends and neighbors to support them by sharing with them. And the church has traditionally imagined the kingdom of God as a blanket toss reality where everyone will have enough, where God will continuously provide for the world, and where we will all know that we can rely on God's generosity to see us through.

In this section, I'm going to explore that idea of the kingdom of God by returning to the images of the garden of Eden and the New Jerusalem that I looked at in chapter four. I'll use these images to illustrate that the kingdom of God is defined in part by its abundance. Then I'll turn to a few parables from the Gospel of Matthew and Jesus' insistence that the kingdom of God is part of our present reality. This will echo what I've already written about generosity being part of the fundamental nature of the universe that God creates and sustains, but it will also point to the idea that the kingdom of God is something that we can inhabit in the here and now. Finally, I'll look at a passage in Paul's letter to the Corinthians to argue that the church has a special relationship with the kingdom of God and that the institutional church—even as an imperfect reflection of that kingdom—is called to be an embassy of it.

Near the end of the book of Revelation, John of Patmos offers a vision of a new heaven and a new earth. First, he sees a new Jerusalem come out of the heavens. He hears a voice tell him that God will now live among mortals, wiping away every tear. Death, mourning, and crying will no longer exist. God will give the gift of water from the spring of life to the thirsty. Then, John describes the new Jerusalem. Much of that description is about the ornate beauty of the city, with a jasper wall, clay foundations, gold streets, and every kind of jewel. But two other parts of that description stand out. First, as I mentioned in chapter four, there is no temple. God is the temple of the new Jerusalem. Second, while nothing unclean will enter the city, the gates are always open. In a stunning display of hospitality, people are free to come to and go from the new Jerusalem.[2]

Finally, in an image that echoes the garden of Eden, John sees the river of the water of life, flowing from the throne of God down the middle of the street, with the tree of life spanning it. The water of life is crystal clear, the tree always produces fruit, and the leaves of the tree are for the healing of the nations. In Genesis, in the garden of Eden, we also saw the tree of life and a great river that fed what the author of that story took to be four important rivers in the Near East. In both stories, we're presented with the lush imagery

---

2. Rev 21:9–27.

of gardens, trees, and rivers. In the beginning, and at the end of time, the world is characterized by natural—maybe even supernatural—abundance.[3]

Both of these images point to the fundamental nature of the universe. While we know that there was never a real garden in Eden, and we might think that John's vision is more of a mystical experience than a concrete description of the renewal of the world, these aren't simply stories about times that were or that are to be. They're stories about what is; they're stories about the world that we live in now. While that world might look like a place where resources are limited—and our broken world is certainly a place where resources are distributed inequitably—the biblical claim is that the universe is a place of abundance. The resources that we need are in fact present. Even if we don't yet have the faith to share them.

In the Gospel of Matthew, Jesus shares two sets of parables that tell us that the kingdom of God—a kingdom characterized by the same abundance that we see in Genesis and Revelation—already exists in the world around us. In the first set, Jesus compares the kingdom of God to a mustard seed and to yeast. In one parable, a man plants a small mustard seed that grows into a large mustard shrub, and birds nest in its branches. In the other parable, a woman adds yeast to a large amount of flour and all of that flour is leavened. Both of these parables point to the idea that the kingdom is small in size and currently hidden, but they also tell us that the kingdom is present in the world and growing.[4]

In the second set of parables, Jesus compares the kingdom of God to a hidden treasure and a valuable pearl. In the first parable of this set, a man finds a treasure hidden in someone else's field. He hides the treasure again, sells everything that he has, and buys the field (and the treasure that is hidden in it). In the second parable, a merchant is searching for pearls to trade and finds a particularly valuable one. Like the man in the first parable, he sells all of his possessions and buys the pearl. These parables aren't focused on the small size of the kingdom of God or—despite the buried treasure in the field—on the idea that it is hidden. Instead, they point to the idea that the kingdom is so valuable that people would give up everything they own in order to have it. But they also tell us that the kingdom is something that we can find in the here and now.[5]

The first set of parables tells us that the kingdom of God is ubiquitous. Like a mustard seed or a small amount of yeast, it might be hard for us to

3. Rev 22:1–7; Gen 2:9–14.

4. Matt 13:31–33.

5. Matt 13:44–45.

see. But it is spreading through the world like a mustard plant in a field or leaven being stirred into flour. The second set of parables tells us that the kingdom of God is accessible. It isn't something that exists only in the distant past or the (possibly) distant future. It isn't even something that is buried and unreachable in the depths of the cosmic order. Instead, like a treasure hidden in a field or a pearl of great price, it is something that we can find and take hold of in our present lives. And that means that we can live in a world characterized by the same abundance and generosity that are part of that kingdom.

In his epistle to the Corinthians, Paul tells his readers—members of the church in Corinth, of course, but also the whole church—that they are the body of Christ. He begins the passage by writing about spiritual gifts like wisdom, knowledge, faith, healing, and performing miracles. Different people have different gifts, which all come from the same Holy Spirit. And he compares this to the body having different parts. A body is made up of many parts that are all members of the same body. My hands are part of my body, just like my eyes and my ears. And no part of my body is any more or less important than any other part. Finally, he tells his readers that they are the body of Christ, and that they are each individuals members of the body of Christ. Not everyone has the same gift, but everyone is equally part of the body. "If one member suffers, all suffer together with it," he writes, "if one member is honored, all rejoice together with it."[6]

There are two important points here. First, as I just said, the church is the body of Christ. While different members of that body—different denominations, different organizations, different congregations, different individuals—bring different things to the table, they are all united in Christ. And because the church is the body of Christ, it makes sense that the church should embody Christ's kingdom. As a human institution, the church might fail to live up to that lofty ideal. But as a community animated by the Holy Spirit, it also has the responsibility and the ability to strive for that ideal. When the church is really, truly, fully the church, it is also the visible presence of the kingdom of God in the world.

Second, Paul continues his letter by pointing to spiritual gifts that are greater than the ones he has listed so far. And the spiritual gift that he tells us is the greatest, is love. In this passage, Paul tells us that if he speaks in tongues, has prophetic powers, understands mysteries, can move mountains with his faith, or even gives away his possessions and his own life, but does not have love, then all of those other gifts are nothing. He then goes on

6. 1 Cor 12:1–31.

to describe love in what is probably the most popular wedding Scripture in the world, worth quoting (almost) in full:

> Love is patient; love is kind; love is not envious or boastful or ar-rogant or rude. It does not insist on its own way; it is not irritable or resentful; it does not rejoice in wrongdoing, but rejoices in the truth. It bears all things, believes all things, hopes all things, endures all things. Love never ends . . . And now faith, hope, and love abide, these three; and the greatest of these is love.[7]

It's important not to leave this Scripture at weddings. In chapter three, I wrote that our English word *charity* comes from the Latin word *caritas*, which is one of the two Latin words that was used to translate the Greek word *agape*, a word that Christians have used to denote divine love. That is what is happening here: Paul is drawing a link between the spiritual gift of love and God's love. And while etymology isn't an argument, the Society of Biblical Literature's Greek text uses *agape* here, and the Latin Vulgate uses *caritas*. All of these clues tell us that the love Paul is describing is intimately linked to God's generous love. And, as I wrote in chapter four, God's love is a charitable love: God gives most generously towards those who cannot reciprocate and without any apparent concern for the worthi-ness of those recipients.

The church is a complicated thing. On the one hand, it is the visible presence of the kingdom of God in this world. It embodies a human reflec-tion of divine love for world. And that divine love is a charitable love. On the other hand, it's a huge set of imperfect human institutions made up of a variety of imperfect humans. It includes congregations ranging from stately cathedrals to little storefront churches, mission organizations engaged in countless ministries, institutions of higher education, and countless other expressions. It includes saints and sinners. All of these are part of the body of Christ, and we all struggle to live up to the claim that Christ has placed on our lives.

The distance between the church as divine community and church as human institution can be captured in the idea of the church as an embassy of the kingdom of God. We often think of an embassy as a building that houses a group of diplomats, but it is the group of diplomats that is really the embassy. We—the people of the church—are the embassy of the kingdom of God. And just like any other diplomatic mission, we are charged with representing that kingdom in a place where we are far from home and often living under different laws and customs. Members of a diplomatic mission

---

7. 1 Cor 13:4–8, 13.

are in a country, but not part of that country. Similarly, the church is in the world, as the saying goes, but not of it.

And that means that the church has a special responsibility to live out the values of its home country—the kingdom of God—even though we are far from home. And more than that, we have a responsibility to transform the world that we live in by living out those values. We are empowered by the Holy Spirit to live lives characterized by the abundance of the kingdom of God, to share the abundance that we have been given, and to invite others into the kingdom. And the way that we do that is by sharing what we have freely with anyone who needs it; by embodying the sort of blanket toss community where everyone knows that they can rely on their friend and neighbor to support them when they fall and return them to the air. We might do that imperfectly—we are, after all, far from home—but we strive to do that all the same.

Charity and Justice

Anyone who has worked in the nonprofit sector for a long enough time—especially in the part of the sector that helps people living in poverty or that works on broader justice issues—has heard the story. Once upon a time, there was a small village that sat just downstream of a bend in a wide river. One day, one of the villagers saw someone floating down the river, obviously unconscious and in grave danger. The villager dove into the river, swam out to the person who was floating, and brought them back to shore. The villager revived the person, and the whole village helped them recover. And no sooner had they recovered, than another person was floating down the river, and another, and another.

Over the next few weeks and months, the villagers became experts at rescuing people from the river. They built towers to monitor the river, piers that reached out into it, and ways for one to signal the other. Networks of ropes crisscrossed the river so that rescuers had something to grab on to. Teams watched from the towers and waited on the piers twenty-four hours a day, seven days a week, in case another person came floating their way; and there was always another person floating their way. The entire town was dedicated to rescuing them. And even once a person was rescued from the river there was work to be done. If they were alive, there was a network of caregivers to help them on the road to recovery. If they weren't . . . well, there was another network to take care of them.

Eventually, an intrepid young woman noticed what the village had become and realized that this wasn't sustainable. The village was putting more and more resources towards rescuing people from the river, and yet more and more people kept floating down the river. Villagers were being pulled away from their normal work to tend to the river and the people being rescued from it. Eventually, the village would be putting so much into its rescue operation that there would be nothing left for the rescuers! And the problem still wouldn't be solved. So the young woman went to the village council and proposed an idea: instead of spending their time only rescuing people from the river, she would lead an expedition upriver to find the source of the people who were floating down it, and stop them from ending up in the river to start with. Instead of treating a symptom, as it were, they would cure the disease.

The point of this story is to illustrate the difference between charity and justice. The people who tell it would tell you that the villagers are being charitable when they pull the people from the river. They are addressing the immediate needs of people who are in real danger. And, in this case, that's important work. The people floating down the river are experiencing a real emergency, and even charity skeptics will tell you that an emergency is the right time—maybe even the only right time—for charity. But they aren't doing the deeper work of justice: addressing the cause of the problem and ensuring that no one had to experience floating down the river into the unknown. And for those who tell the story, the emphasis tends to be on how we should be doing more justice work. Once justice is done, the thinking goes, there won't be any need for mere charity.

In this section, I'm going to push back against that idea. In fact, I'm going to suggest the exact opposite: that it is only when we are charitable— charitable in the sense I've been using it as care rooted in the divine, directed towards people experiencing poverty, and unconcerned with reforming the recipient—that we can realize justice. I'll do that by looking at the relationship between justice and righteousness through the translation of a Greek word that straddles the two ideas. Then, I'll turn to a similar relationship between charity and justice, suggesting that charity is a starting point for justice. Finally, I'll make a bolder claim: that charity and justice are not two different things, but the same thing on two different scales. Charity, I'll argue, is justice.

"Blessed are those who hunger and thirst for *dikaiosunen*," says Jesus in the fifth chapter of Matthew's ospel, "for they will be filled." A few verses later, he tells his listeners that they are blessed when they're persecuted for the sake of *dikaiosunes*, because the kingdom of heaven—Matthew's term for the kingdom of God—belongs to people who are persecuted in that way. I've left those two Greek words untranslated on purpose. They're

both based on the Greek root *dik-*. And the precise meaning of that stem
is a little bit contested. On the one hand, as philosopher and theologian
Nicholas Wolterstorff writes, when people are translating Plato, *dik*-stem
words tend to become English words related to justice. On the other hand,
when people are translating the Bible, they tend to become words related to
righteousness.[8]

It would be easy to think that there's a conspiracy here. Wolterstorff
writes that he has encountered two English translations that use justice-oriented words for *dik*-stem words, both of which were Catholic translations
created in the early 1970s. In the years since these translations first appeared,
they have replaced those justice-oriented worlds with righteousness-orient-
ed ones. He theorizes that this change might be in response to liberation
theology, which emphasized justice and which many English-speaking
theologians looked down on. Similarly, a lot of current theologians, pastors,
and others who are nervous about justice-oriented conversations in religious communities might prefer it if *dik*-stem words are about righteousness instead of justice.[9]

And in modern English, those two words—righteousness and justice—have two very different meanings. We don't use the word *righteous*
very often anymore. When we do use it, we tend to be describing "a person
intensely preoccupied with his own moral character who has few 'sins' to
his debit." On the one hand, we use it to describe the interior state of a person, and we usually mean that they're not just righteous, but self-righteous.
Meanwhile, we still use justice in quite a few ways: distributive justice concerns the fair allotment of resources, rectifying justice tries to repair things
when there's a breakdown in distributive justice, and so on. Regardless of
the specifics, justice is about interpersonal relations. Justice is present when
people are in relationship in a certain way, and it doesn't exist when people
are not in relationship that way. Righteousness is about what a person is like;
justice is about how people relate to each other.[10]

Wolterstorff writes that it's not a simple matter of deciding on the correct translation, the right choice between two very different words. He suggests that context has to tell us whether it's best to translate *dik*-stem words
with righteous-oriented words, justice-oriented words, or something else
entirely. I'm going to push that even further. There are two reasons that I've
spent the last few paragraphs with this weird Greek stem. First, it's incredibly common in the New Testament (and a similar idea is common in the

8. Wolterstorff, *Justice*, 110–13.

9. Wolterstorff, *Justice*, 111.

10. Wolterstorff, *Justice*, 69, ix, 111–12.

Old Testament, although there it helpfully involves two different Hebrew words). Early Christianity was all but obsessed with this idea. Second, this discussion of *dik*-stem words illustrates an important idea: that divine justice—even in the sense of right relationships between people—is inseparable from righteousness. How we are as people-in-relationship has something to do with how we are as people-as-individuals.[11]

This dovetails nicely with something I mentioned in chapter three. Remember French philosopher Blaise Pascal's idea that if someone who doesn't believe wants to be a believer, it would be good for them to imitate the believer. He tells them to go through the motions of faith, and faith will come to them. And even if faith never comes, going through the motions will make them honest, humble, generous, and so on. Fake it till you make it, and even if you never make it, you'll be better off for the effort. I used this idea to suggest that part of what charity does is build the character of the person who gives it. By giving freely to people who are experiencing poverty, we imitate the generosity that God has towards the world. And by doing that, we become more like the people who God wants us to be. Ideally, this creates a virtuous loop: by giving, we become more generous; and in becoming more generous, we are more likely to give.

Think about that as charity (the act of giving) and charity (the personal quality) being intimately related. Each of these sides feeds the other one. The same thing is true about righteousness and justice. By doing justice, we become more righteous; and when we become more righteous, we tend to do more justice. Or, to capture the ambiguity of those *dik*-stem words a little bit better: when we do the right thing, we make ourselves into people who are more likely to do the right thing; and as we become the kind of people who are more likely to do the right thing . . . well, we find it easier to do the right thing. Who we are as people and how we are in the world are tied together in an endless circle.

Justice is a slippery idea, and scholars in ethics, political philosophy, and other fields are actively debating what justice is and what a just society might look like. Some people frame justice in terms of individual rights; in those terms, justice means something like not violating a person's rights. Other people think about justice in terms of fairness; things are just as long as people are treated fairly (whatever that might mean). Still other people see justice as being about equality; justice means something like treating

11. Wolterstorff, *Justice*, 113. The Hebrew words in question are *mishpat* and *tsedeqa*, which are usually translated as "justice" and "righteousness," respectively. Importantly, these words are frequently paired together. Something in the Jewish and Christian imagination links these two ideas together.

people equally. There are other ideas, too, and many of them overlap and wrap around each other. It would take more space than I have here to do justice to any of them. So, I'm not going to try to define justice here.

But, from a Christian perspective, justice must be related to living how God wants us to live. On the one hand, this means being who God calls us to be as individuals. On the other hand, it means relating to each other in the ways that God wants us to relate to each other. As we saw above, these aren't distinct ideas. We are who God calls us to be when we relate to each other in the way that God wants us to relate to each other. And we relate to each other in the way that God wants us to when we are who God calls us to be. Each of those ideas is part of the other. And when we achieve one of those goals, we also achieve the other one.

This is where we can start to see a deep connection between justice and charity. If justice is related to living how God wants us to live—both as individuals and as a society—then it must be part of having a correctly oriented faith. Charity is the practice that reorients our faith. It takes our faith away from earthly things like material wealth and puts it in God. And it does that specifically by asking us to give our material wealth to people who need it and to rely on God's generosity alone. People who cultivate charity in themselves are also reorienting their faith towards God, and we should expect that charitable people will also be more just (or righteous).

And that brings me to a bold claim: we should expect people who practice charity to also practice justice. It's important that I am clear here. When I write that we should expect people who practice charity to also practice justice, I mean charity in the sense that I defined it earlier. Charity is a form of giving that is rooted in a connection to the divine; directed specifically towards people living in poverty or, perhaps, other forms of deprivation that are connected to poverty; and emphatically not concerned with reforming the recipient, but with transforming the giver. Charity is an opening towards justice precisely because it develops right relationships both with God and with people who are experiencing poverty. To put that in terms of the story that started this section, the villagers were only able—in a very literal sense—to go on an expedition upriver because they had done the work of being charitable towards the people who were floating down it.

Let me make that claim even bolder: charity is justice. In chapter three, I briefly mentioned a sermon by the fourth century Greek bishop Basil of Caesarea. In this sermon, Basil makes a passionate case for sharing our excess with people living in poverty, entreating his listeners to "distribute their wealth lavishly." During his sermon, he takes a moment to speak to his listeners who are asking, "Whom do I treat unjustly by keeping what is my own?" And he answers that question—which involves one of those trouble-some *dik*-stem words—by linking charity and justice together in a way that strongly suggests that giving charity is not something different from doing justice . . . it is doing justice.[12]

Basil's argument takes place in a few steps. First, he points out that all of us come into, and leave, the world with nothing. This means that everything that we have must have been entrusted to us by God. Second, he asks why it is that God has distributed things to people unequally; why it is that some people are rich while other people live in poverty. He dismisses the idea that God might be unjust, and instead proposes that God is giving different opportunities to the rich and the poor. The former are rewarded for their benevolence and stewardship, and the latter are honored for their patient endurance and struggles. Finally, he makes an explicit connection between justice and charity. People who have wealth and do not share it, he says, are stealing from the people who need it. The excess of the wealthy rightfully belongs to people who are living in poverty. "You are thus guilty," he writes, "of injustice toward as many as you might have aided and did not."[13]

Poverty is the result of injustice. That means a couple of different things. On the one hand, it is the result of the unjust human systems of distributing goods. It is unjust that the textile worker in Bangladesh has to face unsafe working conditions, it is unjust that the service industry worker in the United States doesn't make enough to afford a decent apartment or health insurance, it is unjust that people of color are systematically excluded from wealth and power, and so on. On the other hand, poverty is the result of people who have wealth holding onto the wealth that they have and re-fusing to give it—maybe even to return it—to those to whom it rightfully belongs. And again, like justice and righteousness, these are two sides of the same coin. Unjust systems exist precisely to propagate an unjust distribution of wealth; and the unjust distribution of wealth gives the wealthy the power to create systems that perpetuate it. Addressing one problem addresses the other.

When we give to charity—whether that's an organization that pro-vides support for people who live in poverty, or to a panhandler we meet downtown—we aren't giving what is rightfully ours to someone else. We are giving someone what is rightfully theirs. And in a Christian understand-ing where Christ is present in the person who is experiencing poverty, we are returning to God what rightfully belongs to God. When we do that, we aren't doing something that is different from justice. We are doing justice.

12. St. Basil, *On Social Justice*, Kindle locations 1074, 1161–78.
13. St. Basil, *On Social Justice*, Kindle locations 1161–78.

Some of us might even be doing the only justice that we can do. Most of us have very little control over how much money we make or how much we have at any given time. What we can control—to some extent, at least—is what we do with that money. By giving it to someone who needs it more, we are working to restore justice.

The story that I told at the beginning of this section doesn't really have an ending. It always concludes with people leaving the village to go upstream and stop whoever is throwing people in the river. And it might be the kind of story that really doesn't have an ending. But I like to imagine that it continues with the troupe from the village finding a town, where they see townspeople carrying other people from huge mills to the river. The villagers confront the townspeople and tell them to stop putting bodies in the river. But the townspeople look at the clothes the villagers are wearing and tell them the story of their town.

"This town produces all of the cloth for the entire region," they say. "You probably buy yours from the town in the hills to the east, but it's made here. Once, we were prosperous. The mills were safe, and we had doctors who could care for the injured. But people keep demanding more cloth for cheaper prices. And we know that if we charge what we must to protect our people, another town will start making cloth and undercut us. Then the mills will close and there will be no work and we all will starve. So we reduced our safety standards and stopped paying the doctors. Now the work is dangerous, there are no doctors to care for the sick or injured, and the graveyards are full. So now when someone dies or is too injured to work, we put them in the river. It's all we can do."

After hours of going back and forth, the villagers realize two things. First, they realize that the townspeople really do want to make a better life for themselves, but they don't see any way to make the changes that they need to make. The town is simply too poor to make those changes by themselves. If it's going to improve safety standards, hire doctors and other caretakers, and diversify its economy, it will need help from outside sources. Second, they realize that injustice wasn't just something that was happening upstream. The villagers were just as much a part of the web of injustice as the townspeople. Maybe they were an even bigger part of that web. After all, they had the resources that this town so desperately needed and they didn't even know it existed. Then, maybe, the villagers realize that the charity they had discovered in themselves could be expanded to care for and develop this town.

Charity and justice aren't two different things that we can choose between. They are two sides of the same coin. When we commit acts of charity, we are giving people the things that they are entitled to and that have been kept from them. And justice on any scale will require us to do the same thing, whether it's creating a system that ensures that people in our town who are hungry have access to food or making restitution for resources stolen from a formerly colonized people. Charity is just our name for justice on an interpersonal level; justice is just our name for charity on a systemic scale. Charity is justice.

Where We Go from Here

I worked as a fundraising professional in the nonprofit sector for twelve years. I raised millions of dollars; developed annual, major giving, and planned giving programs, and capital campaigns; made numerous presentations to individual and organizational donors; crafted direct mail pieces, e-newsletters, and websites geared towards generating revenue; and became a Certified Fund Raising Executive. I worked for a seminary, a medical school, and a community organization that helped people who were living in poverty. I gave workshops and consulted with churches and other nonprofit organizations. If I do say so myself, I was very good at my job. But, like every other fundraiser I've met—and like many other nonprofit professionals—I faced a basic problem: there was never enough money to do what we wanted to do.

In 2018, I left my development career to become the pastor of a church in rural Iowa. Unlike many other congregations, the one that I serve is more or less financially stable and secure. As the pastor, I have a discretionary fund of a few thousand dollars. In principle, I can use that fund for anything that I think is appropriate. Historically, it's been used in two ways. First, to pay bills for church members who are struggling. Second, to pay bills for people sent to us by the local Referral Center. This is an organization that, among other things, screens people who come to it for cash assistance before referring them to a local congregation. Whether it's used for church members or other community members, it has not been used for direct cash assistance. Instead, a person can bring a bill, and we'll write a check to the company. In practice, though, it's a few thousand dollars that sits in an account and does nothing. Very few church members come to the church for financial help. The Referral Center rarely sends anyone to my office.

I'm telling you this because it's a new situation for me. My wife and I have a line in our household budget for giving, and we tend to use it pretty liberally. It gets built up. It gets spent down. And we give to organizations that we trust, to friends who are struggling, and to strangers we meet on the street. But now I have another resource that exists to help people who need help. It's not my resource. It's a resource I've been entrusted with. And with that power comes responsibility. How do I use this money to help people who need help? How do I do that responsibly?

That's a question that a lot of us face. If you're reading this book, you probably want to help people who are experiencing poverty. And you probably want to do that in a way that is effective and responsible. You might even be part of a church or another nonprofit organization that wants to do the same things. Charity skeptics have provided one set of answers: (almost) never give, make loans, change cultures of poverty, and so on. In this book, I've provided a different set of answers centered around a simple idea: charity. In this section, I'm going to take that idea and offer some preliminary thoughts on how we can apply it in the real world. I will not offer detailed prescriptions. Every church, and every person, is different, and must approach the question of how we live charitable lives from within their own contexts. Instead, these are starting points for thinking about how to do just that.

The first principle I want to offer is that there is room for every kind of service when it is offered in love. It's true that the theories and frameworks that charity skeptics use—ideas like poverty culture, or that giving money to someone contributes to their dependency—are deeply problematic. It's also true that the programs and projects that people like Robert Lupton propose can be good. There is room for thrift stores, food co-ops, and even microloans to entrepreneurs. There is also room for financial literacy classes, job training programs, and cultural competency classes (both for people encountering workplaces for the first time and for the managers of those workplaces). And, of course, there is room for food pantries, free clothing shelves, almsgiving, and other traditional services. The fact is that if we want to have a significant impact on poverty—and, especially, if we want to eliminate it entirely—we're going to need every tool that we can get our hands on.

But there are two things that we should keep in mind regardless of the specific programs that we use. First, those of us who have wealth cannot dictate the ways that we serve on the basis of some deficiency that we imagine that the people who use them have. So, for example, we are in no position to say that we must serve in one way because we believe that another way will foster a sense of entitlement among people who are experiencing poverty. To put that another way, we have no right to try to reform people living in poverty. And attempting to do so is not only unethical, it is uncharitable.

Second, when we make programs like the ones proposed by charity skeptics the only option, we do real harm both to the people we are serving and to ourselves. As we saw in chapter five, charity works. It isn't just an effective way of helping people living in poverty, it may be one of the most effective ways to do that. Taking it out of the picture means withholding real help from people who need it. Just as importantly, as we saw in chapter six, charity is good for the people who give it. People who are generous— and, specifically, people who develop habits of generosity—are happier and healthier. We owe it to ourselves to cultivate a charitable spirit. So, even though all options need to be on the table, there are good reasons to favor charitable ones.

For both churches and Christian individuals, the most important piece of all of this is that we must offer any service in Christian love. And that means that charity must be at the root of our service to people experiencing poverty. That service must be rooted in our relationship with God, meaning that we should reflect—seriously, thoughtfully, and prayerfully— on what Jesus would do. It must be focused on people experiencing poverty. That doesn't mean that we can't consider other forms of deprivation. It does mean that we should treat every person we serve as though they were Christ himself. Finally, it must be about our own transformation and redemption. We are not called to reform other people, but to serve them. And when we serve in Christian love, we move the world a little closer to the kingdom of God.

The second principle is that we need to be open to building positive relationships with the people who we serve. We may only see someone who uses a food pantry, or someone to whom we give a few dollars when we see them on the street, once. That's fine. No one owes us a relationship, and a relationship certainly isn't a requirement that we can tack onto the services that we offer. I can't tell someone who is hungry that they need to join a food co-op and make friends. I can't tell someone who is asking for spare change that they need to join me for a cup of coffee. Attempting to force a relationship is unethical and unchristian; especially when there is the kind of difference in power that exists when one person has something another person needs.

But it is also the case that some people who we serve will be with us for a long time. There are people who will come to a food pantry month after month. There are folks who we will see on the street day after day. And while we cannot require relationships, we must be open to them for two reasons. First, those relationships provide opportunities to serve outside the confines of a single volunteer experience or one transaction. When we can see someone who we are serving as a genuine friend, we can offer help out of genuine love. And when we can build a foundation of real trust, we can offer up hard truths. Second, and inversely, those relationships can transform us. We can think about and change larger systems that affect our friends. And we can listen to the hard truths that people experiencing poverty no doubt have to share with people who have wealth.

The critical thing here is to understand each other as human beings. One of the biggest challenges of charity skepticism is that it understands people living in poverty as a set of problems to be solved: they are entitled, they are dependent, they live in a culture of poverty, and so on. When we form real relationships with people experiencing poverty, we can't help but understand them as people—people both much like us and very different from us in all of the wild diversity of the human race—who are made in the image of the divine, the precious children of a loving God. We wouldn't hesitate to help our friends when they are in need. And, as with many of the other things we've looked at so far, imitating friendship can lead to true friendship. By serving, we build the kingdom of God.

Finally, the third principle is that we should always strive for greater generosity. For Christians, our generosity is tied to divine generosity. First, God created a world out of generosity, and by giving freely we imitate that divine generosity. Second, generosity is part of the fabric of the world that God creates and sustains. When we are generous, we ride the currents of the cosmic order. Generosity is a good way to go through life. Third, God is found in and among people who are experiencing poverty. When we are generous towards people living in poverty, we are generous towards God. All of these aspects of generosity are interwoven. When we are charitable, we imitate God, riding the currents of God's creation, by giving to God. We are connected to the divine in every way. Charity is a mystical experience.

Even in secular terms, though, more generosity appears to be a good thing. Small gifts make a difference. Helping a hungry person now, even if she will be hungry again later, is important. Giving someone a place to sleep tonight, even if he will need to find somewhere else to sleep tomorrow, matters. But large gifts can make a bigger difference. In chapter two, we learned that poverty affects how people think and make decisions. When our gifts take some of the pressure of poverty off of a person's shoulders—when they provide some slack and free up mental bandwidth—they can have effects long after we give them. For example, not having to pay rent for a month or two may provide the space that a family needs to get ahead of the curve. Similarly, having access to low-cost or free healthcare would make a real difference in almost anyone's life.

One of the deepest challenges of many ways of helping people who are living in poverty is that we keep looking for ways to be stingy. Refusing to engage in one-way giving, adding work requirements and time limits to as-sistance, demanding returns on investments, and so on, are all ways to avoid being generous. And that only becomes worse when we trick ourselves into believing that refusing to give is the true generosity. Christianity demands something else: that we look for ways to be even more generous, that we look for new and more charitable ways to support each other, and that we work together so that everyone can have the best possible life. Earlier in this chapter, I used the metaphor of a blanket toss to describe that kind of vision. And the world characterized by that love for one another is the kingdom of God.

The Kingdom of God

Part of the appeal of charity skepticism is that it asks us to imagine that we are each walking on our own high wire. I have to admit that there is something nice about imagining that I have made it as far as I have in my life because I am smart, skilled, and diligent. And the idea that my success is mine alone, and that other people's hardships are theirs alone, is a pleasant one. But it just isn't true. I have benefitted immensely from a network of support that spans generations. I was raised by parents who took an interest in my education and made sure that I went to quality schools, and through those schools I was connected to networks that helped me get good jobs, and so on. And beyond that, I benefit from legacies of racism, colonialism, and patriarchy. The fact is that I am not the master of my fate. I have simply been part of a very effective blanket toss.

It's easy to see why charity skepticism appeals to so many Americans. We are a culture that believes that people can pull themselves up by their own bootstraps, that celebrates rags-to-riches stories, and that champions the high wire attitude. It's even easy to see why charity skepticism is ap-pealing to so many Christians. Our churches and Christian nonprofits have adapted to a modern faith in our individual ability to make of our lives what we want to make of them. Work hard, play by the rules, be successful. But that attitude is neither Christian nor true. We are not here because of our own work; we are not saved by our own merits. We are here because God created us. We are saved because God took pity on us. We are the products of God's charity.

The church is many things. It is a place where we can come together to worship the God who loves us and be in fellowship with our friends and neighbors. It is a community that reaches out in love and serves others. At its best, it is a little piece of the kingdom of God here in a broken world; a place and a community where people can see what the world could be like. That sets it apart from everything else. That makes it different. And that gives the church an amazing opportunity to be more than a reflection of the world as it is. It gives the church the chance to be, however imperfectly, the world as God wants it to be. And that world is one that is full of *agape*, of *caritas*, of love, of charity.

Bibliography

Anderson, Gary A. *Charity: The Place of the Poor in the Biblical Tradition.* Kindle ed. New Haven, CT: Yale University Press, 2013.

————. *Sin: A History.* Kindle ed. New Haven, CT: Yale University, 2009.

Badger, Emily. "The Double-Standard of Making the Poor Prove They're Worthy of Government Benefits." *The Washington Post,* April 7, 2015. https://www.washingtonpost.com/news/wonk/wp/2015/04/07/the-double-standard-of-making-poor-people-prove-theyre-worthy-of-government-benefits/?utm_term=.5ddc265fad52.

Banerjee, Abhijit, et al. "Six Randomized Evaluations of Microcredit: Introduction and Further Steps." American Economic Journal: Applied Economics, 2015, 7(1) 1–21. http://pubs.aeaweb.org/doi/pdfplus/10.1257/app.20140287.

Banerjee, Abhijit V., and Esther Duflo. *Poor Economics: A Radical Rethinking of the Way to Fight Global Poverty.* New York: PublicAffairs, 2011.

Basil the Great. *On Social Justice.* Popular Patristics Series Book 38. Kindle ed. Translated by C. Paul Schroeder. Yonkers, NY: St. Vladimir's Seminary Press, 2009.

Beaumont, Hilary. "Three Years After a Factory Collapse Killed 1,130 Workers, This Brand is Still Making Clothes in Bangladesh." *Vice,* April 22, 2016. https://news.vice.com/article/three-years-after-a-factory-collapse-killed-1130-workers-this-brand-is-still-making-clothes-in-bangladesh.

Benhassine, Najy, et al. "Turning a Shove into a Nudge? A 'Labeled Cash Transfer' for Education." American Economic Journal: Economic Policy 2015, 7(3) 86–125, 117. https://www.poverty-action.org/sites/default/files/publications/104040-JRN-PUBLIC-Turning-a-Shove-into-a-Nudge_0.pdf.

Blattman, Christopher, et al. "The Economic and Social Returns to Cash Transfers: Evidence from a Ugandan Aid Program." http://cega.berkeley.edu/assets/cega_events/53/WGAPE_Sp2013_Blattman.pdf.

Bowling Alone. "Research." http://bowlingalone.com/?page_id=7.

Center for Poverty Research at the University of California, Davis. "What Are the Poverty Thresholds Today?" https://poverty.ucdavis.edu/faq/what-are-poverty-thresholds-today.

————. "What Is the Current Poverty Rate in the United States?" https://poverty.ucdavis.edu/faq/what-current-poverty-rate-united-states.

Clement of Alexandria. "Who is the Rich Man That Shall Be Saved?" *New Advent.* http://www.newadvent.org/fathers/0207.htm

Collins, Daryl, et al. *Portfolios of the Poor: How the World's Poor Live on $2 a Day.* Kindle ed. Princeton, NJ: Princeton University Press, 2009.

Corbett, Steve, and Brian Fikkert. *When Helping Hurts: How to Alleviate Poverty Without Hurting the Poor . . . and Yourself.* Expanded ed. Chicago: Moody, 2012.

Davis, Katy, and Nicki Cohen. "Three Myths about the Underbanked, Part Two: 'I Can Tell You Exactly Where My Paycheck Is Going.'" *ideas42 blog.* http://www.ideas42.org/blog/three-myths-underbanked-part-two-can-tell-exactly-paycheck-going/.

Desmond, Matthew. *Evicted: Poverty and Profit in the American City.* Kindle ed. New York: Penguin Random House, 2016.

Eagleton, Terry. *Reason, Faith, and Revolution: Reflections on the God Debate.* New Haven, CT: Yale University Press, 2009.

Edin, Kathryn J., and Luke H. Shaefer. *$2.00 a Day: Living on Almost Nothing in America.* Kindle ed. New York: Houghton Mifflin Harcourt, 2015.

Ehrenfreund, Max. "Kansas Has Found the Ultimate Way to Punish the Poor." *The Washington Post,* May 21, 2015. https://www.washingtonpost.com/news/wonk/wp/2015/05/21/kansas-has-found-the-ultimate-way-to-punish-the-poor/?utm_term=.c8f70b3b23fb.

Ehrman, Bart. *Did Jesus Exist?: The Historical Argument for Jesus of Nazareth.* New York: HarperCollins, 2012.

Garfield, Bob, and Brooke Gladstone. "'Busted' #5: Breaking News Consumer's Handbook: Poverty in America Edition." *On the Media.* New York Public Radio, New York, NY, WNYC, October 28, 2016. http://www.wnyc.org/story/breaking-news-consumers-handbook-poverty-america-edition/.

GiveDirectly. "Hellen's Profile." *GiveDirectly.org.* https://live.givedirectly.org/newsfeed/806b7c24–32dd–4466–b63b–060cbe4e0bf9/172574?context=newsfeed#payment_3.

———. "Jane's Profile." *GiveDirectly.org.* https://live.givedirectly.org/recipients/a529cb12–20d2–4d22–bac9–9950cb00e90e.

———. "Operating Model Overview." *GiveDirectly.org.* https://www.givedirectly.org/operating-model.

———. "Research on Cash Transfers." *GiveDirectly.org.* https://www.givedirectly.org/research-on-cash-transfers.

Goldberg, Michelle. "A Crowd-Sourced Escape from Poverty?" *The Nation.* November 25, 2013. https://www.thenation.com/article/crowd-sourced-escape-poverty/.

Graeber, David. *Debt: The First 5,000 Years.* Brooklyn, NY: Melville House, 2011.

Gross, Robert A. "Giving in America: From Charity to Philanthropy." In *Charity, Philanthropy, and Civility in American History,* edited by Lawrence J. Friedman and Mark D. McGarvie, 29–48. New York: Cambridge University Press, 2002.

Hardoon, Deborah. "An Economy for the 99%." *Oxfam International.* January, 2017. https://www.oxfam.org/sites/www.oxfam.org/files/file_attachments/bp-economy-for-99-percent-160117-en.pdf.

Haushofer, Johannes, and Jeremy Shapiro. "Household Response to Income Changes: Evidence from an Unconditional Cash Transfer Program in Kenya." *Poverty Action Lab.* https://www.povertyactionlab.org/sites/default/files/publications/974%20Give%20Directly.pdf.

Innovations for Poverty Action. "Conditional Cash Transfers for Education in Morocco." *Poverty-Action.org.* https://www.poverty-action.org/study/conditional-cash-transfers-education-morocco.

————. "The Impact of Unconditional Cash Transfers in Kenya." *Poverty-Action.org.* https://www.poverty-action.org/study/impact-unconditional-cash-transfers-kenya.

Internal Revenue Service. "Exempt Purposes—Internal Revenue Code Section 501(c)(3)." *Irs.gov.* https://www.irs.gov/charities-non-profits/charitable-organizations/exempt-purposes-internal-revenue-code-section-501c3.

Kaye, Leon. "U.S. Court Dismisses Rana Plaza Lawsuit." *Triple Pundit.* http://www.triplepundit.com/2016/05/u-s-court-dismisses-rana-plaza-lawsuit/.

Kersley, Richard, and Antonios Koutsoukis. "The Global Wealth Report 2016." *Credit Suisse.* https://www.credit-suisse.com/us/en/about-us/research/research-institute/news-and-videos/articles/news-and-expertise/2016/11/en/the-global-wealth-report-2016.html.

Kottasova, Ivana. "These 8 Men Are Richer Than 3.6 Billion People Combined" *CNN Money.* http://money.cnn.com/2017/01/15/news/economy/oxfam-income-inequality-men/index.html.

Kuhn, David Paul. "The Gospel According to Jim Wallis." *The Washington Post,* November 26, 2006. http://www.washingtonpost.com/wp-dyn/content/article/2006/11/21/AR2006112101801.html.

Lewis, Oscar. "The Culture of Poverty." *Scientific American,* October 1966.

Ley, Samantha. "Salary for a Professor of Economics." *Chron.* http://work.chron.com/salary-professor-economics-6401.html.

Loomis, Erik. *Out of Sight: The Long and Disturbing Story of Corporations Outsourcing Catastrophe.* New York: The New Press, 2015.

Lucian of Samosata. "The Passing of Peregrinus." *Tertullian.org.* http://www.tertullian.org/rpearse/lucian/peregrinus.htm.

Lumni. "How it Works." *Lumni, Inc.* http://lumni.net/en/about.

————. "Investors." *Lumni, Inc.* http://lumni.net/partners-2.

Lupton, Robert. *Toxic Charity: How Churches and Charities Hurt Those They Help (and How to Reverse It).* New York: HarperOne, 2011.

Miller, Talea. "She's 22, from Rural Zimbabwe, and a Mogul in the Making." *Medium,* March 3, 2016. https://medium.com/@Kiva/she-s-22-from-rural-zimbabwe-and-a-mogul-in-the-making-d14ec5c88724.

Miranda, José P. *Communism in the Bible.* Maryknoll, NY: Orbis, 1982.

Montero, Roman. *All Things in Common: The Economic Practices of Early Christians.* Kindle ed. Eugene, OR: Resource, 2017.

Morduch, Jonathan, and Rachel Schneider. *The Financial Diaries: How American Families Cope in a World of Uncertainly.* Kindle ed. Princeton, NJ: Princeton University Press, 2017.

Mullainathan, Sendhil, and Elder Shafir. *Scarcity: Why Having Too Little Means So Much.* New York: Henry Holt, 2013.

Ng, Jennifer C., and John L. Rury. "Poverty and Education: A Critical Analysis of the Ruby Payne Phenomenon." *Teachers College Record,* July 18, 2006. http://www.tcrecord.org/Content.asp?ContentID=12596.

Pallotta, Dan. "The Way We Think About Charity is Dead Wrong." Filmed March 2013 in Long Beach, California. TED Video. https://www.ted.com/talks/dan_pallotta_the_way_we_think_about_charity_is_dead_wrong/transcript?language=en.

Pascal, Blaise. *Pensées (Thoughts).* Kindle ed. Translated by W. F. Trotter. Overland Park, KS: Digireads, 2009.

Payne, Ruby. *A Framework for Understanding Poverty: A Cognitive Approach*. 5th rev. ed., Kindle ed. Highlands: aha! Process, 2013.

Payne, Ruby K., et al. *Bridges Out of Poverty: Strategies for Professionals and Communities*. Kindle ed. Highlands, TX: aha! Process, 2009.

Philanthropy Roundtable. "Statistics on U.S. Generosity." https://www.philanthropyroundtable.org/almanac/statistics/u.s.-generosity.

Prosperity Now. "Asset Poverty Rate." http://scorecard.prosperitynow.org/data-by-issue#finance/outcome/asset-poverty-rate.

———. "Extreme Asset Poverty Rate." http://scorecard.prosperitynow.org/2016/measure/extreme-asset-poverty-rate.

———. "Income Poverty Rate." http://scorecard.prosperitynow.org/data-by-issue#finance/outcome/income-poverty-rate.

———. "Liquid Asset Poverty Rate." http://scorecard.prosperitynow.org/data-by-issue#finance/outcome/liquid-asset-poverty-rate.

Putnam, Robert D. *Bowling Alone: The Collapse and Revival of American Community*. New York: Simon & Schuster, 2000.

Rashi. "Rashi on Leviticus 23:22." *Sefaria.org*. https://www.sefaria.org/Rashi_on_Leviticus.23.22?lang=bi.

Rhee, Helen. *Loving the Poor, Saving the Rich: Wealth, Poverty, and Early Christian Formation*. Kindle ed. Grand Rapids: Baker Academic, 2012.

Reagan, Ronald. "Address Before a Joint Session of Congress on the State of the Union." Speech, Washington, DC, February 4, 1986. *The American Presidency Project*. http://www.presidency.ucsb.edu/ws/index.php?pid=36646.

Rothschild, Steve. *The Non Nonprofit: For-Profit Thinking for Nonprofit Success*. Kindle ed. San Francisco: Jossey-Bass, 2012.

Sandel, Michael J. *What Money Can't Buy: The Moral Limits of Markets*. New York: Farrar, Straus and Giroux, 2012.

Sealander, Judith. "Curing Evils at Their Source: The Arrival of Scientific Giving." In *Charity, Philanthropy, and Civility in American History*, edited by Lawrence J. Friedman and Mark D. McGarvie, 217–39. New York: Cambridge University Press, 2002.

Sefaria.org. "Mishnah Peah." *Sefaria.org*. https://www.sefaria.org/Mishnah_Peah?lang=bi.

Severus, Sulpitius. "On the Life of St. Martin." In *A Select Library of Nicene and Post-Nicene Fathers of the Christian Church*. Second Series, Volume 11. New York: T & T Clark, 1894. http://www.tertullian.org/fathers2/NPNF2-11/Npnf2-11-05.htm#P156_9980.

Shaw, Hollie. "Judge Rejects Joe Fresh Class Action Related to Bangladesh Factory Disaster." *Financial Post*, July 17, 2017. https://business.financialpost.com/news/retail-marketing/judge-rejects-joe-fresh-class-action-related-to-bangladesh-factory-disaster.

Smith, Christian, and Hilary Davidson. *The Paradox of Generosity: Giving we Receive, Grasping we Lose*. Kindle ed. New York: Oxford University Press, 2014.

Smith, Christian. "Does Naturalism Warrant a Moral Belief in Universal Benevolence and Human Rights?" In *The Believing Primate: Scientific, Philosophical, and Theological Reflections on the Origin of Religion*, edited by Jeffrey Schloss and Michael J. Murray, 292–317. Kindle ed. New York: Oxford University Press, 2009.

Smith, James K. A. *How (Not) to Be Secular: Reading Charles Taylor*. Kindle ed. Grand Rapids: Eerdmans, 2014.

Spicker, Paul. "Poverty as Wicked Problem." *CROP Poverty Brief*, November 2016.

Stark, Rodney. *The Triumph of Christianity: How the Jesus Movement Became the World's Largest Religion*. Kindle ed. New York: HarperCollins, 2011.

Taylor, Charles. *A Secular Age*. Cambridge, MA: The Belknap Press of Harvard University Press, 2007.

Tertullian. "The Apology." *New Advent*. http://www.newadvent.org/fathers/0301.htm.

Thompson, Derek. "7 Facts About Government Benefits and Who Gets Them." *The Atlantic*, December 18, 2012. https://www.theatlantic.com/business/archive/2012/12/7-facts-about-government-benefits-and-who-gets-them/266428/.

Walton, John H. *The Lost World of Genesis One: Ancient Cosmology and the Origins Debate*. Downers Grove, IL: InterVarsity, 2009.

Wikipedia. "Environmental issues in the Niger Delta." *Wikipedia, The Free Encyclopedia*. https://en.wikipedia.org/w/index.php?title=Environmental_issues_in_the_Niger_Delta&oldid=830693364.

———. "Homestead strike." *Wikipedia, The Free Encyclopedia*. https://en.wikipedia.org/w/index.php?title=Homestead_strike&oldid=845716707.

Wolterstorff, Nicholas. *Justice: Rights and Wrongs*. Princeton, NJ: Princeton University Press, 2008.

World Bank Group. "Kenya." https://data.worldbank.org/country/kenya.

———. *Poverty and Shared Prosperity 2016: Taking on Inequality*. Washington: The World Bank, 2016. https://openknowledge.worldbank.org/bitstream/handle/10986/25078/9781464809583.pdf.

Yglesias, Matthew. "The Best and Simplest Way to Fight Global Poverty." *Slate*, May 29, 2013. http://www.slate.com/articles/business/moneybox/2013/05/unconditional_cash_transfers_giving_money_to_the_poor_may_be_the_best_tool.html.

Zunz, Olivier. *Philanthropy in America: A History*. Princeton, NJ: Princeton University Press, 2012.

Index of Subjects

Index of Scripture